A Cultural Study of Drinking and Sobriety

ALCOHOL and the JEWS

CHARLES R. SNYDER

Southern Illinois University Press
CARBONDALE AND EDWARDSVILLE

Feffer & Simons, Inc.
LONDON AND AMSTERDAM

Library of Congress Cataloging in Publication Data

Snyder, Charles R
Alcohol and the Jews.

(Arcturus books; AB 140)
Reprint of the ed. published by Free Press, Glencoe, Ill., which was issued as no. 1 of Monographs of the Yale Center of Alcohol Studies.

Bibliography: p.
Includes index.
1. Alcohol and the Jews. I. Title. II. Series: Yale University. Center of Alcohol Studies. Monograph; no. 1.

[HV5185.s6 1978] 362.8'4 77-24885
ISBN 0-8093-0846-0

ARCTURUS BOOKS ®

Reprinted by arrangement with Charles R. Snyder
Arcturus Books Edition February 1978
This edition printed by offset lithography in
The United States of America

CONTENTS

PREFACE TO THIS EDITION

EVENTS since the first publication of this study have at the very least lent support to the broad outlines of my argument regarding changes in Jewish drinking patterns. We read in the *New York Times*, for example, about the rise of alcoholism and increasing recognition of alcohol problems among Jews in that great city, all of which is attributed, in an oversimplified though not altogether incorrect formula, to growing acculturation, or the absorption of Jews into the mainstream of American life. Against this background, it seems appropriate to make available once again to the reading public the results of an investigation that sought to detect changes in Jewish drinking patterns, to illuminate the conditions associated with change, and to identify the sociocultural factors with which the traditional sobriety of the Jews was most closely linked.

The reception given my research by critics from various fields was, by and large, encouraging. Of course reviewers raised a number of questions that merit response but cannot be addressed, much less fully answered, in the compass of these brief remarks. I do want to take this occasion, however, to draw the reader's attention to a few important problems and promising lines of inquiry that have emerged since the time of initial publication.

One of the knottier problems emanating from my work has been a tendency on the part of some readers to construe the ritualization of drinking and its supposed consequences in a far too mechanical and abstract manner. They thereby divorce ritual usage from its actual historical context while imputing to it virtually magical properties as a prophylaxis for alcoholsim. This kind of thinking, to which I may have unwittingly contributed, has led at times to naïve programmatic suggestions symbolized by the query of a non-Jewish, professional woman and mother who asked: "Doesn't your study imply that if we all drank more regularly in the home and introduced the children early to alcohol we could get rid of alcoholism?" And it has unfortunately led a handful of serious scholars to formulate the most abstract and disembodied hypothesis predicting an absence of phenomena like inebriety and alcoholism in any and all societies where some kind of use of alcohol in so-called "religious ritual" is found. When the results of such indiscriminate attempts to generalize prove disappointing, the impression is left that the ritualization of drinking has had nothing whatsoever to do with the traditional sobriety of the Jews, notwithstanding their widespread use of beverage alcohol. Both of these abortive lines of thought, however, not only fail to consider other factors that I suggested are intimately connected with Jewish sobriety, but neglect entirely the fact that the extensive ritual drinking of Orthodox Jews is an expression or manifestation, as well as reinforcement, of a wider and more fundamental network of norms, ideas and sentiments integrated in a moral community. Apart from such a context, ritual drinking loses its force and meaning.

Although drinking patterns in general, rather than alcoholism *per se*, are the focus of my work, the question of alcoholism enters into the definition of the problem and surfaces in a variety of ways throughout. In this regard, two Canadian investigators, Wolfgang Schmidt and Robert Popham, have recently reopened the study of Jewish alcoholics in an article properly titled, "Impressions of Jewish Alcoholics" (*J. Stud. Alc.* 37:931–39, 1976). Curiously, these researchers ignore the fact that over the years other scientists have paid attention to Jewish alcoholics, admittedly in investigations of modest scale, as studies pertaining to the subject cited in the present volume testify. (Even as far back as the first decade of this century, L. Cheinisse, writing in Paris, was already summarizing observations on the religious and cultural backgrounds of Jewish alcoholics.) Consequently, they fail to locate their own work in the accumulating though still small body of research on this important question. Moreover, while rightly affirming their reluctance to draw any conclusions from clinical records of 29 cases, Schmidt and Popham in the end throw caution to the winds. They suggest, in reference to an argument they have earlier (p. 932) equated with my own, that "remoteness from Jewish culture" is not "a sufficient explanation for the drinking problems" (p. 938) of the supposed alcoholics whose records they studied. Yet in view of the complex of factors—normative orientations, dynamic factors, and functional alternates—which my own work, following that of Robert F. Bales, posited as involved in alcoholism, remoteness from Jewish culture could hardly be "a sufficient explanation" for the emergence of alcoholism among nominal Jews. Correctly understood however, it should be seen as a condition for such a development. Furthermore, as Schmidt and Popham themselves recognize (p. 932), it is not distance from an undefined Jewish culture but from traditional religious Orthodoxy and the associated culture most clearly in evidence historically among Eastern European Jews that is important from my vantage point. And in this connection they find only four of the 29 patients whose records they studied exhibiting what they call an "orthodox orientation" (p. 933) at the time of treatment, none of whom, apparently, showed the pattern of alcoholic behavior common to North America or reported episodes of gross intoxication (p. 936). Most critically, Schmidt and Popham's category of "orthodox orientation" turns out to be by definition (p. 933) so broad as to include persons who would not be considered Orthodox by the criteria employed in my research, and it simply remains unclear whether any of their four cases were fully Orthodox in the sense relevant to my thesis. Indeed, upon close examination, their definitions and data are so ambiguous with regard to *Orthodox religious observance*, as well as with regard to alcoholism, that the findings may be interpreted readily, though still inconclusively, as being quite in accord with my own research, as previous studies of Jewish alcoholics have been. Yet assuming these limitations can be overcome, the kind of study Schmidt and Popham have undertaken needs to be extended and repeated in the future. And I join them in exhorting other researchers to undertake such inquiry wherever circumstances permit.

A second line of research that I believe to be of fundamental importance is well exemplified by Mark Keller's stimulating essay on "The Great Jewish Drink Mystery" (*Br. J. Addict.* 64:287–96, 1970). Proceeding from the findings and conclusions of my own study, among others, Keller has begun seriously to explore the fascinating historical question of when, in their essentials, the drinking patterns described, and especially sobriety, become institutionalized. On the strength of compelling evidence from the Biblical record, he argues that Jews in ancient times were far from the notably sober people that contemporary social science has depicted, at least for recent generations. When, then, in the logical historical experience of the Jewish people, and under what circumstances, did change begin to take place and the prototypes of the drinking patterns of recent history appear? Was the Babylonian Exile over 2,500 years ago the pivotal historical moment? Or was the change a painfully slow, gradual accretion from the later experiences of Jews in the Diaspora? Or what? Keller himself, while acknowledging the possible impact of the Babylonian Exile, sees evidence of crucial events signaling the shift to sobriety and its identification as a Jewish trait in the period beginning with the Restoration under Ezra and Nehemiah. As he puts it: "It is in this time span, not more than 200 years, between the establishment of the Second Temple and the reappearance of the Jews on the scene of world history . . . that the basis of Jewish sobriety was firmly laid" (p.292). And this was a time not only of intense rejection of pagan gods, whose worship included orgiastic drinking, but also of the acceptance of the centrality of the Torah in the life of the people, of the institution of the local synagogue for much worship and popular education, and, significantly for our purposes, of "the positive integration of drinking in religiously oriented ceremonials in the home and synagogue, including meals and rites of passage" (p. 294). Thus Keller concludes: "The integration of moderate drinking with most religious actions, and most important activities with religion, may have gone hand in hand with the displacement of the pagan gods and their ways, including the interest in orgiastic drinking." Still, while I am myself inclined to set great store by his conclusion and the soundness of his scholarship, Keller's tentativeness regarding his findings clearly calls for further research along the lines suggested by his splendid first effort.

So we need, in my judgement, more studies of Jewish alcoholics and more historical work on the appearance and institution of now traditional drinking patterns, including, of course, the sobriety for which Jews were to become noted. And to these I would add at least one more line of inquiry which stems from the limitations of my own research. Conducted as it was at time when most social science investigations tended to be male-centered, my study failed to explore adequately the cultural attitudes and practices of Jewish women regarding beverage alcohol and its usage, both in respect to possible changes which may be taking place and to the contributions which women, directly and indirectly, may have made in sustaining the traditional patterns of drinking and sobriety of the Jewish people. I hope this blind spot in research of the past may be overcome in the future.

Charles R. Snyder

Carbondale, Illinois
August, 1977

PREFACE TO FIRST EDITION

The research on which this monograph is a report was planned and initiated in cooperation with Ruth H. Landman, to whom the author is particularly indebted. At later stages, help and suggestions were received from Philip Grossman, Walter Johnson, John T. Liell, William P. Mangin, William Phillips, Patricia H. Snyder, Norman Zide, and Maurice Zigmond. Mark Keller and Fred L. Strodtbeck offered valuable suggestions at many points in the preparation of this report. The writer is especially grateful to Selden D. Bacon and Robert Straus for making available the questionnaire materials on Jewish students which were gathered in their College Drinking Survey, and for their advice, encouragement and constructive criticism. To the many New Haven Jewish men and to the Jewish college students whose cooperation made this study possible, the writer expresses his thanks. He is grateful, too, to Georgina Whitney and Alice Gibson who typed the manuscript.

Special thanks are due to I. Rogosin who generously supported the carrying out of this research.

Finally, the author wishes to acknowledge a special debt in the realm of ideas to Selden D. Bacon and Robert F. Bales, and to his first teacher in sociology, the late Raymond Kennedy.

Alcohol and the Jews

Chapter 1

PROBLEM AND APPROACH

The Challenge to Sociological Study

DURING the past hundred years a sizable body of statistical data has been accumulated which indicates that various ethnic groups in Western society exhibit strikingly different rates of drinking pathologies.[1] Data collected by ethnographers during the same century point likewise to a wide range of variation in drinking practices and in the pathological manifestations of drinking among "primitive" peoples (16, 43). At the present time there is no doubt that great differences in drinking patterns and pathologies exist between certain groups in our own society and among different societies throughout the world.

These elementary facts raise a basic question for students of alcohol problems: Why are drinking pathologies widespread in some groups and virtually absent in others? Posing this question leads to further questions: What constitutes culturally normal drinking in a particular group? What are the various uses and functions of beverage alcohol in different social settings? Why do some groups abstain? How do individuals learn to drink normally? How effective are the social controls upon drinking in different groups? How are diverse ways of drinking related to the incidence of drinking pathologies? In what manner are ways of drinking linked with other aspects of a group's culture? At the present time there are only the beginnings of scientific answers to these and related questions. Indeed, little is known of the role of drinking in our own society or in those of its subgroups whose rates of drinking pathologies differ from one another widely. There has been considerable theorizing about certain differences in group rates which are well established in fact. But this has been largely speculation resting on tenuous assumptions about the cultures of the groups involved and their patterns of drinking.

[1] "Drinking pathologies" is used here in a very broad sense to designate classifications of inebriety dealt with by police, courts, welfare and other social agencies, as well as the more extreme medical classifications such as alcoholism, alcohol addiction, chronic alcoholism, alcoholic psychoses, and so forth. Rates of drinking pathologies refer to data compiled over the years by hospitals, police, physicians and others on the incidence of these various alcohol-related phenomena in specific groups.

A few years ago the Yale Center of Alcohol Studies began an extensive social science research program with the aim of expanding the knowledge concerning drinking in the United States. Particular ethnic and status groups were chosen for study which were deemed strategically significant for furthering the understanding of normal as well as abnormal drinking. The present research on the Jewish group comprises one part of this broader research program. The specific purposes of this introductory chapter are to detail the rationale for the special study of the Jewish group; to discuss briefly the speculative and systematic work of others on this group which has influenced the formulation of the present study; and to outline our own research approach.

Since a basic concern in this study is the problem of group differences in rates of drinking pathologies, it must be stated at the outset that a social science or cultural approach to this problem assumes that genetic or purely physiological factors cannot wholly account for known differences. Cultural investigation by no means precludes the possibility that such factors may be involved in certain kinds of drinking pathologies, such as alcoholism. But, even if non-cultural causes should be found essential, manifestations of genetic or physiological tendencies are certainly conditioned by culture. And should it be established that constitutional factors play a negligible role in the etiology of drinking pathologies, psychological, psychiatric and cultural research would seem to be the principal avenues for reaching an understanding of these phenomena.

With regard to psychic tensions, which are generally thought to play an important role in drinking pathologies, it is assumed in this research that these enter into the combination of factors which determine a given case of alcohol addiction or other pathology. Acute psychic tensions may be decisive in determining why, in the same cultural setting, one person becomes addicted to beverage alcohol while another does not. However, it is also assumed that differences in the incidence of the kinds of psychic tensions which enter into drinking pathologies cannot fully account for differences in the rates of drinking pathologies between groups. While acute psychic tensions may be present in each instance, the rates of drinking pathologies in different groups are not simple functions of their incidence.

This latter assumption has some empirical foundation. Bales (7), for instance, has presented an impressive body of statistical data indicating that neuroses and psychoses are about equally common in the Irish- and Jewish-American groups. These are groups, however, whose rates of drinking pathologies differ extremely. Thus, insofar as the rates of neuroses and psychoses reflect the extent of acute psychic tensions in both groups, high rates of drinking pathologies among the Irish and low rates among the Jews cannot be imputed to an excess of psychic tensions in the former group and their scarcity in the latter. On the contrary, the data suggest the operation of other factors and it is our view that these are cultural in nature. Their specification is a task for subsequent chapters.

The Jewish group was chosen as particularly relevant for study on the basis of certain well-established facts. A brief presentation of the facts which determined the selection of this group will help to clarify its strategic significance.

All the evidence from both European and American sources indicates that in the Jewish group drinking pathologies are rare. Whether a comparison is made with groups in Western society in general or with other ethnic groups in the United States, the rates of drinking pathologies among the Jews are consistently low. This generalization is not confined to any particular category of drinking pathologies: it applies to the more extreme forms as well as to simple public inebriety. This point is illustrated in a comparison of the rates of first admissions with alcoholic psychoses per 100,000 of various foreign-born national groups to the New York State Hospital System.[2] In 1929–1931, the rates of six groups were as follows: Irish, 25.6; Scandinavian, 7.8; Italian, 4.8; English, 4.3; German, 3.8; Jewish, 0.5.

Data documenting the difference between Jews and non-Jews come from a variety of sources.[3] The definitions of basic classificatory terms such as "Jews" and "alcoholic psychosis" are not the same in all cases, and they are seldom stated explicitly. Methods of sampling and the limitations of the sample populations are often not clear. The times and places in which these studies were made vary greatly. Hence, statements about the absolute rates among Jews cannot be made. Nevertheless, the relative position of the Jews always stays about the same; as a group, they rank consistently low with respect to drinking pathologies.

[2] From the tabulation of Haggard and Jellinek (38), after Benjamin Malzberg (Psychiat. Quart. **9:** 538, 1935).

[3] The most exhaustive compilation of data showing low rates of drinking pathologies among Jews in the United States is contained in Bales (7). References to several studies indicating a similar situation in Europe may be found in Glad (31).

If the Jews were a group who seldom or never drank alcoholic beverages, these statistics might not be remarkable. It is when the rates of drinking pathologies are seen in relation to the facts on the incidence of drinking among the Jews that they assume their full significance.

The widespread drinking of alcoholic beverages among the Jews for more than 2,000 years is a matter of historical record; abstinence has never gained currency as a value in Jewish culture.[4] On the contemporary scene, the high incidence of drinking among Jews is documented by the findings of Riley and Marden (78). Comparing the number of abstainers, occasional drinkers, and regular drinkers (i.e., those who drink three or more times a week) in three religious categories, these investigators found that the Jews have the smallest number of abstainers (13 per cent) compared to Catholics (21 per cent) and Protestants (41 per cent). Among the regular drinkers, the Jews (23 per cent) ranked between the Catholics (27 per cent) and the Protestants (13 per cent). In the category of occasional drinkers, the Jewish group ranked highest (64 per cent), the Catholics next (52 per cent) and the Protestants lowest (46 per cent). The obvious conclusion from these data, which will be further supported in Chapter 2, is that the incidence of drinking in the Jewish group is high, both in an absolute and in a relative sense. Stated in terms of the individual, it is very likely that an American Jew has had alcoholic beverages to drink in the course of his life, and in more than an isolated instance. As Riley and Marden point out, their data on Jewish drinking, together with the low rates of drinking pathologies, contradict the view that a high incidence of drinking is necessarily associated with high rates of drinking pathologies. It is important to note, also, that high-proof liquors have been known to the Jews and used by them for a long time. Wine has traditionally been preferred for certain religious uses, but distilled beverages have been widely consumed. More exact data on preference and use of types of beverages will be presented later on; it is safe to assert here, however, that exclusive use of mild beverages is not the explanation for the low rates of drinking pathologies among the Jews.

The existence of a group numbering many millions who drink a

[4] Historical Judaism encouraged drinking as a part of religious practice, although it condemned excessive drinking. Ascetic sects have arisen now and then in the course of Jewish history and some of them, like the Rechabites of the Biblical era, were abstainers. But none of these sects had a large following and the abstinence principle was never taken over by the larger group. See Bainton (5) on this point.

variety of alcoholic beverages extensively with few pathological consequences is a challenge to the student of alcohol problems. The challenge is enhanced by the fact that absence of neuroses and psychoses cannot be invoked to explain the low rates of drinking pathologies. How the Jews as a group manage to drink extensively but in a pattern of moderation with few pathological consequences is the basic problem we are investigating.

Lines of Exploration in the Present Research

Around a very small nucleus of data on Jewish drinking practices many theories have been developed to account for the low rates of alcohol pathology. Bales (7) and others have critically reviewed the writings in this field.[5] In the ensuing discussion only those ideas which have influenced the formulation of the present study will be considered. The aims of this preliminary discussion are to make as explicit as possible those hunches and hypotheses regarding Jewish drinking which seem on *a priori* grounds to offer fruitful lines of investigation, and to show the areas in which factual research is most needed.

1. Early Rationalistic Theories

One group of theories which try to explain the low rates of drinking pathologies among Jews may be classed as rationalistic. The views of Immanuel Kant (48), as usually interpreted, and of Fishberg (11, 27) among others, belong in this category. Although the explanations of these writers no longer appeal to many students in the field, the implications of their views merit discussion. Kant suggested that Jews, and members of other minorities, drink only in moderation because they fear censure from the larger society for uncontrolled behavior. Fishberg thought that each Jew is aware, as a result of a long historical tradition, that it is wise to be sober. In addition to fearing censure, each Jew knows that his advancement in the world depends upon his being more virtuous than the Gentile, as by this means the disadvantages of birth into a minority group may be offset. As a result the Jew, although he drinks, drinks moderately.

While these writers made an important contribution in calling attention to the general sobriety of the Jews, their explanations

[5] The present discussion relies heavily at several points on Bales' earlier review. For another suggestive critique of the literature, see Glad (31). For a popular review stimulated by the present research, see Glazer (32).

seem a bit vague and one-sided. One may detect, behind theories of this kind, the tacit assumption that in some unspecified way each Jewish individual avoids excessive drinking because he knows, by rationally assessing the consequences which may ensue, that excessive drinking "doesn't pay" or may be dangerous. Yet it is known that excessive drinking in the form of alcohol addiction or alcoholism is particularly impervious to ordinary rational controls. The incipient addict usually knows that, in general, excessive drinking "doesn't pay" and may be dangerous, and still is unable to control his drinking behavior. Moreover, such theories suggest the priority of the individual's relation to the outgroup, rather than to fellow Jews, in influencing him to drink moderately. In the light of what is known in the social sciences about social control generally and about controls on drinking behavior in particular, it seems far more likely that the effective normative controls on drinking are located within Jewish culture itself and are activated primarily by Jews themselves. That Kant and Fishberg have hit upon Jewish cultural aspects and values which are relevant to Jewish drinking behavior is probable; more will be said on this subject later on, especially in Chapter 5. However, the role of the Jewish group and of its cultural values in shaping the individual's drinking behavior and attitude is not made clear in their explanations.

Actually, Myerson (70, 71) advanced beyond Kant and Fishberg when he emphasized the negative sanctions applied by Jews themselves to the inebriate. But as Bales (7) has correctly pointed out, Myerson fell into the "extreme rationalist fallacy" when he emphasized the more remote negative sanctions (loss of friends or job, the possibility of being refused for marriage, and even complete social ostracism) as crucial to the low rates of drinking pathologies. If the Jews are as temperate as the known facts would suggest, it seems likely that sanctions of this kind would be exceedingly rare and far removed from the experience of the average individual. Even granting that some groups other than the Jews take a less antagonistic attitude toward the inebriate, many groups with higher rates of drinking pathologies apparently apply strong negative sanctions to persistent inebriates. It is understandable, of course, that rationalistic explanations should have been offered to account for the low rates of drinking pathologies among Jews. Familiarity with certain aspects of Jewish culture can easily lead to uncritical acceptance of such a point of view. Much has been made of the Jew's need to be ever on the alert in the face of anti-Semitism; and the emphasis on learning in Jewish culture places great value on clear reasoning. But it is one thing to value rational behavior and quite another for the conscious mind to control pathological cravings.

The criticism of these rationalistic interpretations implies that to account for Jewish moderation it is not enough to assert that each person, when confronted with certain alternatives with respect to drinking, reasons what is wisest and best. Long before the individual Jew reaches such a decisive moment, he must have deeply internalized ways of behavior that render persistent inebriety well nigh impossible. And these ways must concern the act of drinking rather than remote consequences, even if they depend upon other aspects of the group's culture which at first glance seem unrelated to drinking. Therefore, in the present study, factors relating to moderation have been sought which are of immediate relevance to the drinking situation. These factors must be of sufficient intensity to be effective for the potential Jewish alcohol addict as well as for the average Jew, and of sufficient generality to encompass a substantial portion of the entire Jewish group.

2. *Early Sociological Thought on Drinking and Social Solidarity*

From among the many speculative theories which have been advanced to explain the low rates of drinking pathologies among the Jews, that of Cheinisse (18) meets several of the objections which have been raised against extreme rationalist views. Cheinisse was probably the first to think of differences in the rates of drinking pathologies between groups as a function of general sociological variables. In 1908 he took note of Durkheim's (24) explanation of the rarity of suicide among Jews in terms of social cohesion–anomie theory, and proposed that the low Jewish rates of suicide, crimes of violence and drinking pathologies might all be related to their social solidarity. Cheinisse cited Durkheim on the Jews as follows:

> "The persecution which Christianity has visited on them for so long has produced unusually strong feelings of solidarity among the Jews. The necessity of fighting against a general hostility, the impossibility of even freely communicating with the rest of the population, forced them to hold close to one another. Consequently, each community became a small, compact and cohesive society, which had a very vital feeling of itself and its unity. Here everyone thought and lived alike; individual differences were rendered almost impossible because of community living and the tight and constant surveillance by everybody of each individual."[6]

[6] Translation mine.

In this view, the characteristic sobriety of the Jews is related to general traits of the Jewish community and does not depend solely on the "wisdom" of the individual. Of course, Cheinisse and Durkheim were referring to the involuntary ghetto community which is a thing of the past, although for a majority of American Jews, who have recently come from eastern Europe, it is only a few generations behind. Nevertheless, many features of the close life of the ghetto seem to be still discernible in America.[7] Hence, broadly speaking, the kind of community of value and sentiment, and the intensification of social interaction and sanction, to which Cheinisse and Durkheim referred, may well be of significance for Jewish drinking today.

This formulation seems, however, to contain a basic deficiency: it fails to show how specific norms are elaborated with respect to drinking in Jewish culture. In this respect Cheinisse makes an error of omission analogous to that of rationalists who focused attention on remote consequences of excessive drinking. Social solidarity may be important in sustaining normative orientation in general, and in providing conditions for the effective transmission and sanction of drinking ways; and these hypotheses will be explored in the present research. But social solidarity does not describe the drinking ways in Jewish culture nor explain how they counter the development of drinking pathologies. Therefore, the kinds of factors to which Durkheim and Cheinisse allude are here taken as necessary but not sufficient conditions in explaining the low rates of drinking pathologies among the Jews.

A consideration of this defect in Cheinisse's theory, as well as its

[7] By contrast with the ghettos of Europe, the American community is large, dispersed, heterogeneous and secularized. Nevertheless, the pattern of urban concentration persists in large measure, as does the disproportionate representation of Jews in the trading and shopkeeping occupations. Distinctive Jewish neighborhoods are evident in many American cities, ethnic institutions such as Hebrew schools and Synagogues flourish, while the charitable functions of the ghetto are reproduced on a larger scale. Although there is considerable interurban mobility, this does not seem to disrupt primary-group ties; the mobile person is likely to move from one Jewish neighborhood to another where new Jewish social relationships are quickly established through friends and relatives. Familial ties appear strong and the highly endogamous nature of the group ramifies kinship endlessly; indeed, with all its diversity, the Jewish group has traits of an extended family. From within, pressure to keep the group intact makes it difficult for individuals to dissociate themselves. From without, occasional flourishes of anti-Semitism at home and conflicts abroad heighten minority group consciousness in a society whose values tolerate cultural pluralism. For some documentation of the characteristics mentioned here, see the following: Wirth (108) on community pattern; Koenig (56) on occupational distribution; Brav (14) and Kennedy (54) on family solidarity and endogamy. A description of the emergence of a new Jewish community indicative of social and geographic mobility may be found in Gans (28).

positive suggestions, underlines again the need for factual investigation to determine what the ways of drinking of the Jews actually are. In the present report, this is understood to mean more than the collection of essential behavioral data on the incidence and frequency of drinking, kinds and amounts of beverages consumed, and the like. Data must also be included on the culturally approved and disapproved modes of drinking; the social contexts in which drinking typically is learned and practiced; the beliefs, purposes and sentiments associated with drinking; and the interrelationship of these elements with other aspects of Jewish culture.

3. Food and Drink and Eating Pathology

In 1923 Feldman (25) commented that Jews ordinarily take a drink after having eaten something, while English Gentiles generally drink without having had anything to eat. In view of the well-known effect of food in reducing the "effects" of beverage alcohol, a possible customary synchronization of eating and drinking warrants consideration. Our own investigations do indicate that eating just before, during or just after drinking in order to offset the effects of alcohol is a common practice among Jews and that a close association of food and drink is customary in many situations. However, there is not the extreme integration of eating and drinking which apparently typifies groups such as the South Italians (60), and Feldman's idea that drinking among Jews occurs only after eating is patently contradicted by the facts on ritual drinking, which often occurs before eating.

There is, nonetheless, a further sense in which the role of food in Jewish culture may bear an important relation to Jewish drinking pathologies. This is the possibility that among the Jews "excessive" and "compulsive" eating may represent what Bales (7) has appropriately called an "alternate means of adjustment"—alternative, that is, to addictive drinking as found in certain other cultures. Stated more precisely, this hypothesis asserts that Jewish cultural norms orient the individual toward drinking and eating, respectively, so that "compulsive" eating is more likely to be selected as a means of alleviating psychic tensions (whatever their source may be) which in other groups are more frequently reduced by addictive drinking.[8]

[8] Whether or not the cultures of other groups with comparable valuations of food and drink predispose toward addictive eating is a question for future research. It is interesting that the eating patterns of South Italians (60), who also exhibit low rates of drinking pathologies, show at least surface similarities to the Jewish ones. At the other end of the scale of inebriety,

And if the food complex takes priority as a focus for many neurotic problems (priority in the sense of "choice of symptoms") which might otherwise be expressed or "resolved" through excessive drinking, it would have the net effect of keeping the rate of drinking pathologies low.

That food is in fact the focus of extreme emotional problems in the modern Jewish community is strongly indicated by studies of food pathologies. Hall's (39) comparative research shows that "the Jewish child remains an infant, so far as taking food is concerned, much later than other children." Hall notes the great anxiety of Jewish mothers lest their children fail to eat enough, even though the children were eating quite satisfactorily in the opinion of pediatricians. More recently, Brim has shown a significant tendency on the part of Jewish mothers to have recourse to forced feeding when confronted with persistent refusals to eat on the part of their children.[9] Bales (7) reports that his own limited observations are consistent with Hall's findings and adds that a pattern of compulsive eating, analogous to addictive drinking, may be common in the American Jewish group. In Bruch and Touraine's (15) study of obese children, slightly over 50 per cent of the obesity cases were of Jewish origin. Even though this sample was not representative, it suggests the prevalence of obesity among American Jews. Significantly, the "family frame" of these obese individuals was likened to the family constellation described by Chassel (17) in his paper on the etiology of "essential alcoholism."

In view of these considerations, some preliminary data were gathered in our research on tendencies to forced feeding, compulsive eating and obesity among Jews, in addition to data on the use of food in social situations, attitudes toward food, and relations between eating and drinking. No attempt will be made to present and analyze these data within the body of the present report. At this

---

Horton's (43) cross-cultural findings of a high correlation between inebriety and food scarcity is consistent with the hypothesis that such a tendency exists. Note should also be taken of Bales' (7) observation of the apparent devaluation of food in Irish culture, and the aversion to food as well as the irregularity of diet common to alcohol addicts as reported by Haggard and Jellinek (38). Wexberg (106) has recently called attention to the total substitution of addictive eating for addictive drinking by some alcoholics. The fact that this substitution may occur in the individual alcoholic lends plausibility to the notion that an entire cultural group may, in effect, substitute the one type of addiction for the other. Further research on the eating histories of alcoholics and the drinking histories of compulsive eaters would seem to be called for.

[9] O. G. Brim, personal communication.

juncture it is desired only to sharpen awareness of the factor "alternate means of adjustment" as possibly affecting group rates of drinking pathologies—a subject to which we shall return in Chapter 6—and to emphasize the need for additional research in this area.[10]

4. *Recent Sociological Work on Drinking and Religion*

Considering all the speculation on the low rates of drinking pathologies among the Jews, it is a surprising fact that until the early 1940's no one took the trouble to investigate just how Jews drink. Bales (6, 7) was the first seriously to undertake this task, and his results and interpretations are illuminating. There are intrinsic limitations in Bales' heavy reliance on documentary sources, raising questions concerning the accuracy and inclusiveness of his descriptive material. Partial clarification of these apparent limitations will be gained from additional data gathered in the course of the present research. It will be useful here, however, briefly to summarize Bales' point of view and to indicate the kinds of data required to check the validity of his findings and conclusions on Jewish drinking.

According to Bales the Orthodox Jew, from the eighth day of his life on, is surrounded by religious ceremonies that include the act of blessing and drinking wine. He is introduced to ceremonial drinking early in life, and the experience recurs frequently at weekly Sabbath rites, at holy days throughout the annual religious cycle, and in *rites de passage*. On all these occasions the amount of alcohol consumed is small, and the more extreme effects of drinking are neither sought nor experienced.

The function of the act of drinking is, in Bales' view, symbolic and communicative. It expresses the relationship of each participant to the Jewish group as a whole and to the most sacred symbols of the group. The success of drinking and its meaning for the participants is judged by conformity to prescribed usage—not by the effects of alcohol on the organism. The religious ceremonies at which the cup of wine plays a part dramatize the individual's relationship and subordination to the family, the community and God. Drinking thus occurs in the presence of the most powerful sanctions in Orthodox Jewish life.

[10] The attention given to eating pathologies may seem to imply that no other possible alternatives to excessive drinking exist for the potential alcoholic. No such conclusion is intended. In his original suggestion of a substitution of compulsive eating for addictive drinking Bales warned that there are undoubtedly other alternatives. However, data from physiology, psychology and sociology appear to justify assigning priority to an exploration of the relations between eating and drinking in future studies of drinking behavior.

The devout Jew who learns to drink in such a context develops what Bales has called a "ritual attitude" toward drinking. The act of drinking becomes psychologically dissociated from the "effects" of alcohol on the individual. Drinking in a ritual manner becomes so much confounded with his personal and Jewish identity that drinking for the "effects" of alcohol would be alien and profane to the Orthodox Jew.

Whether or not Bales' theory is correct is a challenging question to the student of alcohol problems. On the basis of his analysis but rather scanty evidence, Bales suggested that the decline of religious Orthodoxy among Jews in America is associated with changes in their attitude toward drinking, an increase in inebriety, and convergence of the rates of drinking pathologies with general American norms. The changing conditions of the modern community provide an excellent laboratory for testing this hypothesis; and this has been done in the present research. Before turning to our findings, however, it must be observed that Glad's work (31) challenges Bales' conclusion concerning the role of Orthodox religious practice in Jewish moderation.

5. *Drinking and General Cultural Values*

In a social–psychological investigation of Jewish drinking, which is the only systematic study besides that of Bales, Glad (31) concentrated on the attitudes of a small sample of American Jewish adolescents, comparing them with two other groups, and his data may be indicative of changes in drinking patterns among Jews. Glad's findings show clearly that the younger generation drinks in "social" situations which are not of a religious character, as well as in certain religious contexts. Glad believes nevertheless that there is a distinctive attitude toward the act of drinking among Jews. He agrees with Bales that Jews do not drink for affective purposes, but he has characterized the Jewish drinking attitude as "instrumental" rather than ritual in character. Jews drink in situations where other than affective ends are paramount, but drinking is required by custom as appropriate in achieving these ends. The quest for broader social ends, rather than the "effects" of alcohol, imposes restraints on the individual in the drinking situation.[11]

The possible fruitfulness of this line of reasoning lies in a delinea-

[11] Glad has not implied that individuals and groups other than the Jews do not drink in this manner, rather that the incidence of this type of drinking is high in the Jewish group.

tion of the kinds of ends which are typically sought by Jews (and means by which they seek these ends) in those situations in which they drink. On these points Glad is uncertain, but he does offer the following suggestion:

> "It seems possible that the attitudes toward drinking . . . are merely auxiliary attitudes related to more central values in the cultures considered; that is, the affectivity purposes of drinking among the Irish may be an expression of a general cultural valuation of proximate goals . . . as more important than the ultimate goals of understanding, recognition and achievement [which are more important to Jews]. From this frame of reference it seems possible that these general cultural values may be responsible for the evaluations of drinking that have been discovered in this study, and that the general values as well as the evaluations of drinking are effectively related to the alcoholism rates. There is hardly adequate basis in the present data to justify such a conclusion, but note should be taken of its possibility."[12]

There are, nonetheless, certain parallels in Bales' and Glad's views of the orientation toward drinking in Jewish culture which must not be obscured by the choice of the different terms "ritual" and "instrumental." Both have stressed that the act of drinking is not performed in Jewish culture for the purpose of inducing those changes in emotional state and behavior which are associated with intoxication. The Jew does not drink with the aim or idea of getting "tight" or "drunk," to "feel gay," or the like. Alcohol is not sought primarily for its psychophysical effects on the human organism. On the contrary, according to these investigators, the purposes of drinking are of a different kind. They agree that drinking is essentially social in character and that conformity to the proprieties of the situation is the valued aspect of the entire complex of drinking customs.[13] But Glad has emphasized that Jews drink extensively as a means to the achievement of practical social ends, as well as for the religious communion which Bales has described.

The basic point at issue between Bales and Glad is the role of traditional religious practice in defining and sanctioning Jewish ways of drinking conducive to sobriety. From statistics on the rates of drinking pathologies, Glad reasoned that the low rates of drinking

[12] The recent work of Zborowski (109), Bienenstock (12) and others of the Columbia research project, appears to confirm emphasis on such values in the "Shtetl"—a type of East European Jewish community—from which the majority of American Jews have come.

[13] Obviously neither Bales nor Glad has implied that Jewish drinking is primarily social in a purely "convivial" sense.

pathologies apply to the Jewish group as a whole, regardless of Orthodoxy. However, on the basis of the statistics at the disposal of Bales and Glad, there does not seem to be any justification for making a final conclusion on the significance of Jewish religious practice for drinking behavior. As previously noted, the statistics on drinking pathologies are too crude to provide knowledge of absolute rates, and in none of the populations on which these statistics are based is the dimension of Orthodoxy, as it is relevant to Bales' theory, specified. Further research of a different order is called for. To determine which of these views is sound, the contemporary Jewish community must be studied to discover the extent of relevant religious practice and its impact on different generations. This variable can then be related to actual drinking ways and attitudes, and the level of inebriety and drinking pathologies may then be evaluated in relation to actual religious practice. Data bearing on these points have been gathered in the present research and will be dealt with especially in Chapters 3, 4 and 6.

The Present Approach

In the foregoing sections some of the hypotheses which seem to offer the most promising leads for research on Jewish drinking have been outlined. Throughout, the need for a delineation of actual drinking ways among the Jews has been emphasized. An important aim of the present research is therefore to provide a sociological description of Jewish drinking behavior. This material may then be used to test the theoretical notions which have been presented.

The possibility of testing several of these notions in the present investigation rests upon the fact of cultural changes in the Jewish group which coexist with certain features of traditional Jewish life. The study of drinking patterns within the Jewish group in relation to other elements of Jewish culture which exhibit different degrees and phases of change in various parts of the community may be expected to shed light on the kinds of cultural factors involved in the traditionally low rates of drinking pathologies. When possible, of course, comparisons will be made with other groups, and a body of facts will be developed which should facilitate future comparative studies. Emphasis in the present research is being placed, however, on cultural persistence and change within the Jewish group itself in relation to persistence and change in drinking ways and their pathological manifestations.

Definition of the Group, Sampling Procedures and Techniques of Investigation

All this points to the necessity of defining the Jewish group broadly in our research in order to encompass the widest possible range of drinking behavior, explore related sociocultural variables, and test different theories of Jewish sobriety. Thus the defining convention suggested by Herskovits (40) and used successfully in field studies of ethnic groups (104, 105) has been adopted here. By this convention, a Jew is defined as any person who so identifies himself and is recognized as such by others.[14] This definition, while broad, is still not the broadest possible. It does not include persons who might recognize or be found to have had some former affiliation with the Jewish group but who have since renounced or lost their Jewish identity. Analysis of the drinking patterns of such persons would be theoretically pertinent to the present study, but in practice these persons are exceedingly difficult to locate for study. Thus little would be gained by extending our definition to include them. That the definition adopted is both workable and broad enough to fulfill the aims of this research may be judged by the results presented in the present and later chapters.

The basic materials for this study were obtained from two sources: first, from interviews with a random sample of 73 New Haven Jewish men; second, from questionnaires administered to a sample of 644 male Jewish college students as part of the College Drinking Survey.[15] The rationale for sampling procedures and the techniques used in obtaining data from these two sources warrant further consideration.

To insure representation of a wide range of sociocultural characteristics, an approximately random sample of New Haven Jewish men was developed, using the 1951 Greater New Haven Directory (112) as the basic reference.[16] To develop this sample, a list of names was compiled by recording the top and middle names appearing in each column of each page in the alphabetic section of the Directory. Obvious Italian and Irish names were eliminated from this first list of more than 4,000 persons, and since the Italians and the Irish are the two largest ethnic groups in New Haven, the original list was enormously reduced by this step. The remaining names were then taken to a

[14] Problems of definition, and the merits of this and alternative definitions, are briefly discussed in Snyder (90). See also Herskovits, "Who are the Jews?" in Finkelstein (26), vol. 2.

[15] Questionnaires were administered under the direction of R. Straus and S. D. Bacon as part of a nationwide survey of college drinking patterns. Many findings of this survey have been reported in Straus and Bacon (96).

[16] The working definition of the New Haven area is given in Snyder (90), where details on the conventions used in establishing the New Haven sample are also to be found. In the same work the question of the Directory's inconclusiveness is considered. In general, the Directory is the most comprehensive available listing of adults in New Haven, but it fails to include much of the city's vagrant population among whom "problem drinkers" are often found. However, the available evidence suggests that there are few Jews in this stratum (97). Although sample bias would tend to exclude the rare homeless Jewish man (possibly with a drinking problem), this is not of serious consequence to the present study which is primarily focused on typical drinking patterns. Auxiliary sampling procedures would be required for a study of the Jewish Skid Row type. Also, only men are considered in the present study.

local Jewish welfare agency with extensive files on members of the New Haven Jewish community and a vested interest in knowing the names of all Jews residing in the city. By comparing with the agency's files, certain men on the list were immediately identified as Jewish. Agency staff members were able to identify a substantial proportion of men on the list as definitely not Jewish. But since the agency's files were incomplete, some names could not be identified as either Jewish or non-Jewish. The residual list of persons whose ethnic identity was in doubt was pared down through further inquiries among agency staff members. In the few remaining doubtful cases, ethnic identity was determined by directly questioning other community members or the men involved. The result of this procedure was a sample of 164 men of presumed Jewish identity. Because of time and budget limitations, only 73 of these 164 were interviewed. There is no reason, however, for assuming that this sample of 73 is less random than the original sample of 164 since no special criteria were used in its selection.

The cooperation of the Jewish men chosen for interviewing in this manner was quite satisfactory. Only 11 of the men contacted finally refused to be interviewed. This represents a 13 per cent rejection rate when computed on the basis of the number of men with whom final commitments had been made at the time interviewing was terminated. When computed on the basis of the number of men initially contacted, the rejection rate is 11 per cent. It is probable that the rejection rate would have been below 10 per cent had the interview required less time.

In contacting men for interviews, the interviewer presented a letter of introduction and briefly explained the most general aims of the Yale Center's sociological research program. Care was taken not to refer to special features of the Jewish situation lest fears of anti-Semitism put respondents on the defensive. The interviewer also emphasized the investigation of similarities and differences in "normal drinking behavior" to avoid arousing the anxieties and suspicions of possible "problem drinkers." At the same time anonymity was assured prospective respondents.

The times and places for interviews were arranged to suit the convenience of respondents. This often necessitated more than one interview session. Interviews usually took place in the respondent's home but occasionally at his place of work or at the Yale Center of Alcohol Studies. The minimum time for an interview was 90 minutes, the maximum, 7 hours. Ordinarily, interviews lasted between 2 and 3 hours.

The interview combined questionnaire and schedule techniques and involved the use of both "structured" and "open ended" questions. The contents of these questions together with responses from an actual interview as well as a note on procedures are included in the Appendix and do not require extended discussion. We may note, however, that the interview divided naturally into three general sections. The first section consisted of rather matter-of-fact questions on characteristics such as age, sex and marital status, which were read by the respondent and answered in writing. The second section consisted for the most part of questions on drinking behavior and attitude. These were administered in a conversational manner by the interviewer. The third section, requiring both written and conversational techniques, consisted of questions on a variety of topics some of which, as anticipated, were quite disturbing to the respondents—e.g., questions touching on the minority situation. Within and between these three sections the organization of questions tended to progress from neutral to more guarded topics. The interviewer therefore had opportunity to assess and reassess the situation and gain the confidence of the respondent before introducing a topic which might have disrupted the interview.

Supplementing the information on the New Haven Jewish men are data from questionnaires administered to the 644 male Jewish college students included in the College Drinking Survey. These questionnaires were designed to elicit the most general information on the drinking customs of American college students and, consequently, cannot be expected to yield detailed information on the sociocultural characteristics and drinking patterns of particular groups, such as the Jews.[17] In further contrast to the New Haven study, the impersonal questionnaire technique was used in the College Drinking Survey, and the questionnaires were administered to groups of students in the classroom rather than individually. Each of these techniques for gathering data—interview and questionnaire—has well-known advantages and disadvantages. Depending on the situation, either technique may be more revealing than the other. But where similar findings emerge from the use of these different techniques, as in the present research, confidence in the validity of the results is enhanced.

The general sampling procedures used in the College Drinking Survey have been outlined elsewhere (96) and need not be dealt with here. Attention must be called, however, to the fact that Jewish students in the Survey were not drawn from any single locale or college setting. The sample of Jewish students represents an aggregate of Jewish youth scattered in 18 different colleges in various parts of the United States. Moreover, some selection was introduced in the sampling procedures of the College Drinking Survey. Of outstanding importance to this study was the inclusion of Orthodox Jewish students in greater proportion than their probable proportion in the American Jewish population would warrant.[18] Because of these sampling procedures and the intrinsic limits of the universe under study, findings from the Jewish student sample cannot be thought of as direct measures of the incidence of sociocultural traits in the American Jewish population. Nor are findings from this sample directly indicative of characteristics of particular communities, as are the findings from our New Haven sample. Even generalizations about drinking and other characteristics of Jewish college students based on this sample must be asserted cautiously.

Despite these qualifications, the sample of Jewish students is of decided value in studying relations among sociocultural phenomena pertinent to this research. For example, if intoxication varies inversely with religious participation among Jews, this should be evident in data from both the

[17] An outline of topics covered in the College Drinking Survey questionnaire is appended in Straus and Bacon (96).

[18] This was done to insure representation of Orthodox Jews in sufficient numbers for statistical processing.

New Haven and the student samples. Our basic interest is precisely in relations of this kind and their interpretation, rather than in traits of particular Jewish communities, college students, or the American Jewish population as such. Thus, it does not matter that there are disproportionate numbers of Orthodox or frequent religious participants among the Jewish students sampled. For our special purpose, the student sample constitutes an invaluable supplement to the sample of New Haven Jewish men. Then, too, the discovery of relations among drinking patterns and other sociocultural phenomena which transcend the apparent diversity of these two samples may be taken as a measure of the importance of cultural factors and of the validity of a cultural approach in the study of drinking behavior.

Chapter 2

JEWISH DRINKING PATTERNS

THE STUDY of Jewish drinking patterns is best begun by describing the traditional religious rituals and ceremonies in which alcoholic beverages are used. At least two reasons dictate this review before reporting the results of field research. The first has to do with the fact that the vast majority of American Jews are of eastern European origin, having been in this country for only one or two generations. Most of the Jewish men interviewed in New Haven were of eastern European background, as were a majority of the Jewish student respondents in the College Drinking Survey. The countries, such as Poland and Russia, from which these Jews or their recent forebears emigrated were distinguished from the countries of the "emancipated" West (e.g., Germany) as strongholds of Jewish traditionalism and religious orthodoxy. The drinking patterns embodied in the Orthodox religious culture therefore provide an appropriate base line against which to view variations in patterns among American Jews in different degrees and phases of acculturation. The second reason is that the extensive integration of drinking in the rituals of Orthodox Judaism has been seen as the source of normative attitudes thwarting the development of drinking pathologies among Jews (6, 7). Note was taken of these ideas in Chapter 1; to develop their nuances and work out and examine their implications critically is the burden of much of the discussion in the present and later chapters. Before this can be done, content must be given to the traditional drinking patterns themselves, with some reference to the broader religious and cultural context of which they are a part.

The most fruitful way of describing and suggesting the behavioral effects of traditional Jewish drinking patterns is to consider the ways in which culturally defined drinking situations impinge on the Orthodox Jew in the course of life, from the time of birth until death. A threefold classification of drinking occasions into (*a*) *rites de passage*, (*b*) weekly Sabbath observances, and (*c*) annual holy days and festivals will aid the organization of the materials, although departure from this scheme will sometimes be necessary in following the course of the life cycle. Since the labor of piecing together the occasions for drinking and the norms, ideas and sentiments associated with drinking among recent generations of Orthodox Jews was begun by Bales (7), his work is used as our major reference.[1] There are, however, some noteworthy gaps and misplacements of emphasis in Bales' description. Of special importance is his stress on the use of wine for religious and ceremonial purposes to the virtual exclusion of other alcoholic beverages, although Jewish tradition and practice incorporates their use in many instances. Hence, in summarizing traditional Jewish drinking Bales' work is supplemented at a number of points, particularly by reference to the *Shulchan Aruch* (29). This is the last great codification of Jewish law and custom and is authoritative among Orthodox Jews today.[2]

The Traditional Patterns

1. Early Rites de Passage

The first rite de passage and the first drinking occasion in the life of the Jewish boy is his circumcision, which takes place on the eighth day after birth. The day of the circumcision is marked as a semifestival. The guests at the ceremony wear their best clothes, and the room where the operation is performed is decorated for the occasion. Tradition requires the presence of at least 10 adult males, including the operator (*mohel*) and the child's godfather. The minimum of 10 (a *minyan*) represents the quorum required for acts of public worship among Orthodox Jews. During the circumcision ceremony the child is placed on a special chair, called the "Seat of Elijah." The godfather holds the child on his lap for the operation proper. The mohel recites a benediction over a cup of wine, at the same time giving the child its name.[3] The godfather drinks of the wine and a few drops are customarily given to the child (29). A lunch or banquet follows the ceremony.

[1] Unless otherwise indicated, our reference throughout this section is to the original, unpublished work of Bales (7). A brief summary of traditional Jewish drinking was published by Bales (6) in another connection. Neither Bales' nor the present description of traditional Jewish drinking can claim to be exhaustive insofar as historical and regional variations are concerned. The description probably applies in a general way to the bulk of Jews from eastern Europe who emigrated to America in the 1880's and 1890's as well as to American Jews who are nominally Orthodox and religiously observant today.

[2] The *Shulchan Aruch* (The Prepared Table) was compiled by Rabbi Joseph Karo of Safed (1488–1575). We refer, throughout this section, to Ganzfried's (29) popular condensed version of the original.

[3] In commenting on the uses of wine at circumcision Bales notes the mohel's former practice of taking a mouthful of wine and applying oral suction to the wound. He suggests that this practice was medical rather than religious in nature, since it has been replaced by modern methods of cleansing the wound.

The rite of circumcision marks the entry of the child into the moral community of Orthodox Judaism, making the child a party to the covenant with Jehovah and binding him to Jehovah's Commandments. The ceremony concretely dramatizes the child's entrance into and membership in the traditional moral community. Commenting on the significance of the wine on this occasion, Bales observes:

> "The cup of wine [at circumcision] may be considered a visible symbol and seal of the completed act of union, and in its significance as 'The word of God,' 'the commandment of the Lord,' may be conceived as representing His part in the covenant. On this symbolic level there appears to be at least a partial identification of the moral community and its norms with Jehovah and His Commandments, with the wine serving as the concrete symbol of both . . ."

If the Jewish child is the first son, the second important rite in his life is the redemption of the first-born son, which ordinarily takes place 30 days after birth. In this ceremony the father presents the child before the *cohen* who pronounces a benediction and then formally inquires whether the father prefers to give the child up or redeem him for value.[4] The father pays redemption money and the child is declared redeemed, in accord with ritualized procedure. This part of the rite is followed by a banquet at the father's house, but first a blessing is recited by the cohen over a cup of wine, as Bales describes the ritual following Glover (33). However, the *Shulchan Aruch* specifies, in addition, that after blessing the child, the cohen "says the benediction over a goblet of wine; and if there be no wine obtainable he says the blessing over some other beverage which is used there [in the locale]."

At the rites of his own circumcision and redemption, the child is unable to understand and appreciate the ideas and sentiments involved. Nonetheless, as he grows older, he will see these ceremonies performed for other children and know that he was once the central participant. In later life, he will probably participate in these ceremonies as a member of the minyan and insure their reenactment for his own sons.

2. Sabbath Drinking: Kiddush and Habdalah, and the Cup of Benediction

It is otherwise with the drinking rituals of the Sabbath, of which the principle ones are *Kiddush* and *Habdalah*. The *Shulchan Aruch*

[4] The cohen is a priest, by virtue of descent from the Aaronic family. In Orthodox practice a rabbi (unless he happens to be a cohen) cannot substitute in this ceremony.

prescribes that the father instruct his son in these rituals as soon as he is old enough to understand what Sabbath means: "The time for training a child for the performance of the positive commandments depends upon the ability and understanding of each child. Thus, if he knows what Sabbath signifies, it becomes his duty to hear Kiddush and Habdalah, and the like." The Sabbath being a weekly occurrence, the ideas and sentiments associated with it have an inescapable recurrent impact on the Jewish child brought up in a religious home.

Among Orthodox Jews, Sabbath observance includes three essential rituals in which drinking is of central significance. The first of these is the Kiddush (literally "sanctification") which marks the transition from the secular part of the week to the day set apart as sacred. The Kiddush ritual may be thought of as an instance of the broader principle of sanctification and the embracing idea of holiness which Kohler brings out as basic to Orthodox Judaism in this passage:

> "The Jewish religion, having for its fundamental ethical principle the law of holiness: 'Ye shall be holy: for I the Lord your God am holy' (Lev. XIX, 2) accentuates the perfectability of the whole man, while demanding the sanctification of all that pertains to human existence. 'The Lord did not create the world for desolation; he formed it for human habitation' (Isa. XLV, 18) is the principle emphasized by the rabbis (Pesachim, 88b). In the ideal state of things nothing should be profane. 'In that day there shall be (inscribed) upon the bells of the horses: Holiness unto the Lord! And the pots in the Lord's house shall be like bowls before the altar'."[5]

The Kiddush immediately precedes the Friday evening Sabbath meal, after services at the synagogue. During the ritual the men and boys keep their heads covered, as in the synagogue. There is ordinarily some recitation and singing of hymns, followed by a brief recitation from Genesis (ch. 2, verses 1, 2 and 3) which marks the beginning of the Kiddush text proper. After this introductory the blessing over the cup of wine is uttered: "Blessed art Thou, O Lord our God, King of the universe, Who has created the fruit of the vine." The sanctification is then completed, ending with the words, "Blessed art Thou, O Lord, who sanctifiest the Sabbath," and the wine is drunk. Of the wine to be used and the procedure on this occasion, the *Shulchan Aruch* declares:

[5] Cited by Bales from the article on "Abstinence" in the *Jewish Encyclopaedia* (111).

> "It is mandatory to say kiddush upon old wine; it is also mandatory to select good wine, and if possible an effort to obtain red wine should be made. Where suitable grape wine cannot be obtained, kiddush may be said upon raisin wine. While saying 'and the heavens and earth were finished,' one should stand and gaze at the candles, thereafter he may sit down, gaze at the goblet and say the benediction 'who createst the fruit of the vine' and 'who hallowest us.' If one has no wine, he should say kiddush upon bread but not on any other beverage."

In drinking the wine, the head of the household drinks first and then passes the cup around to the various members of the household in the order of their status. The drinking is followed by the ritual washing of hands and the "breaking of the bread." There are two special Sabbath loaves which commemorate the double portion of manna that fell in the wilderness on the day before Sabbath. Everyone present partakes of the special loaves and the meal itself begins.

The second drinking ritual of the Sabbath is often called the Great Kiddush. In spite of its name, Great Kiddush is a small one. Nonetheless, its performance is essential to proper Sabbath observance. This drinking ritual takes place on the morning of the Sabbath or other festival days after the recital of prayers. It is immediately followed by the benediction over bread before breakfast. According to Bales, Great Kiddush is ritually identical with the Sabbath evening Kiddush, but the tradition of the *Shulchan Aruch* specifically permits the use of beverages other than wine on this occasion:

> "In the day time [on the Sabbath] at the morning meal, one should also say the kiddush upon a glass [of wine]. This kiddush consists in simply pronouncing the benediction 'The fruit of the vine.' This kiddush is obligatory also upon women. Before this kiddush is said it is also forbidden to partake of anything, even water, as was laid down concerning the kiddush at night, and it is fulfilling the precept in the best manner to say that kiddush also over wine. If one, however, is fond of brandy and he says kiddush thereon, he has fulfilled his obligation. He should be careful to observe that the glass contains a capacity of one and a half egg-shells and he should drink a mouthful without interruption."

In the careful specifications for drinking brandy on this occasion—a mouthful without interruption—is found the prototype for the "shot" of spirits before a meal which will later be shown to be typical of many Jews today.

The third essential drinking ritual of the Sabbath is Habdalah (literally "separation"). Like the inaugural Kiddush, Habdalah marks a transition, this time from the holy Sabbath to the secular week. The *Shulchan Aruch* emphasizes the importance of the Habdalah in these terms:

> "Just as it is mandatory to sanctify the Sabbath on its inception, so it is mandatory to sanctify the Sabbath on its conclusion upon a cup of wine that is the habdalah. Benedictions should also be pronounced upon spices and upon the light. Women are also duty bound to hear the habdalah, they should therefore listen well to the benediction."

In contradistinction to the requirement of wine for the Friday evening Kiddush, the *Shulchan Aruch* allows the substitution of other beverages at the Habdalah: "When wine cannot be procured, the habdalah should be pronounced upon another beverage which is the national drink, water excepted."

The ritual of Habdalah ordinarily takes place after dark, after the stars are out, and after evening prayers at the synagogue. During its performance the family stands at the table, the males again with their heads covered, while the father recites a prayer of separation. The usual blessing is given over a cup of wine (a special Habdalah cup may be used) and this is followed by blessings over a box of spices and over a lighted candle. The spice box is passed around the table; then all look at their fingernails by the candlelight, which symbolizes the resumption of work during the secular week. The father alone drinks, then moistens his eyes with wine and recites, "The commandment of the Lord is pure, enlightening the eyes." The *Shulchan Aruch* directs, "One should fill up the goblet of habdalah to its very brim, letting it slightly overflow as a token of blessing. . . ." After the father drinks, the remaining wine is poured on a tray and the candle is extinguished in it, thereby ending the ritual of separation. It is also quite proper for the father to repeat the Habdalah for the purpose of instructing the children: "One who had already said the habdalah may repeat it for the sake of his sons who have reached the age of religious training, in order that they may thus fulfill their obligations. . . ."

Bales (6) has suggested that the order of precedence in drinking and abstaining during the Kiddush and Habdalah ceremonies implicitly dramatizes the ideal organization of authority in the Jewish family:

> "It is interesting and important to note that the order in which the family members partake of the wine, first the father, then the lesser males, then the females, and then the domestics, emphasizes their relative status, also their relative closeness to the sacred. The same order

> in reverse is observed in the Habdalah, where first the females abstain, and then the lesser males, so that finally only the father drinks. The various members are separated from the sacred in the order of the lesser first and finally the most important."

How far this interpretation can be pressed for the Habdalah is questionable, for variations have been reported, such that others may partake of the wine after the father has completed his part of the ritual. But it is certainly important to note how alcoholic beverages and drinking are woven into these recurrent ceremonies which, in a general way, symbolize and reinforce solidarity and the organization of authority in the family, and at the same time affirm, through symbolism and ritual, the community of the entire family with the broader network of religious values.

Although Kiddush and Habdalah are properly performed in the home, they have also been performed in the synagogue since Talmudic times at the conclusion of the Friday and Saturday and festival evening services.[6] Except on the first two nights of Passover, the leader in prayer blesses over a cup of wine, but does not himself partake. Rather, he lets some of the children drink a little from the cup. While its origins are obscure, this custom probably represents a response to conditions in which it was not assured that all could observe the Kiddush and Habdalah rituals at home, necessitating their public enactment. This custom is apparently looked upon somewhat askance by the very Orthodox, since it is axiomatic among them that everyone will participate in Kiddush and Habdalah at home after the synagogue services. It is evidently on the assumption that he will later make Kiddush or Habdalah in his own home that the leader in prayer abstains from drinking in the synagogue and gives the wine to the children.

At the conclusion of Sabbath (and other formal) meals, it is also customary to say Grace, bless and partake of the Cup of Benediction. Although this custom lacks the essential character of Kiddush and Habdalah, where it is regularly observed there will be three additional drinking rituals corresponding to the three feasts required on the Sabbath. Often the third Sabbath meal is taken by the men at the synagogue, at dusk, between the late afternoon and evening prayer services—a token communal meal in which wine, beer or other beverages may be served, and this

[6] At least Dembitz (20) asserts this has been customary "since Talmudic times." Cited by Bales.

meal will be concluded by the Cup of Benediction ritual.[7] In brief allusion to this ritual, Bales says that wine drinking for the Cup of Benediction used to be part of every Jewish meal, but is generally taken only on the Sabbath or on festivals or other joyous occasions in modern times. However, in referring to Grace and the Cup of Benediction as a part of every meal, the *Shulchan Aruch* makes it clear that wine was not the only beverage used:

> "If three men ate together it is their duty to unite in saying the grace after meals, and they must say it over a glass of liquor. If possible, a glass of wine should be used; if it be impossible then beer, mead or brandy may be used, when such liquid is the common beverage of the locality, i.e., where vine culture does not obtain and one has to walk a whole day to obtain it, consequently wine is expensive and these beverages are substituted in the place of wine. Some authorities are of the opinion that even a single person is required to say Grace over a glass. Stringent people are accustomed, when saying Grace alone, not to hold the glass in their hands, but place it on the table in front of them."

It is also important to note that during Sabbath and other festival meals the drinking of wine, beer or spirits may often accompany the meal.[8]

3. *The Annual Cycle of Holy Days and Festivals*

The Orthodox Jew is commanded to honor the annual festivals as he honors the Sabbath. He must recite the Kiddush over wine before a festival meal and divide the portions of bread just as for the Sabbath meal. When a festival is followed by an ordinary weekday or by a day designated as "intermediate," i.e., between the first and last days of a week-long festival, he is also required to perform the Habdalah over a cup of wine, but omitting the benedictions of the spices and the light.

Bales has called attention to the "swing of the pendulum" in the annual religious cycle from the most serious holy days of New Year's (Rosh Hashanah) and the Day of Atonement (Yom Kippur) to the gay festival of Purim at the other extreme. While it is required that one rejoice appropriately on a joyous festival in the Jewish year, as indeed it is requisite to rejoice on the Sabbath,

[7] This point was brought to our attention by Jewish informants, and is referred to again later on.

[8] The regulations concerning blessings to be said over wine, other beverages, and foods are quite complex and need not be dealt with here.

Errata

Page ix, lines 27-28: For When, then, in the logical historical experience of the Jewish people read When, then, in the long historical experience of the Jewish people

is inappropriate for even the most festive *an Aruch* is quite explicit on this:

a festival one should not prolong in wine drinking, d say that whoever increase to do this thereby of the festival; for drunkenness, jesting and levity e foolishness, which is not according to the command. e consistent with the worship of the Creator of the 'Because thou hast not served the Lord thy God of heart,' from this may be inferred that worship serve God out of jesting, levity or drunkenness."

ive rejoicing in traditional Judaism is hardly e individual pleasure seeking or spontaneous y Americans consider as the essence of "a fun." Even the most general ideas regarding rity and enjoyment, and the norms of how and be festive, are clearly defined by the ejoicing and festivity are conceived of as nd contingent upon conformity with religious of ritual obligations. Nonetheless, there are n festivity and solemnity in the course of y days and festivals.

s in the fall with the Ten Days of Penitence, -day festival of Rosh Hashanah, the New anah is a time of judgment which anticipates n of the year, the Day of Atonement. Since stival, however, fasting is prohibited. After worship on the first day of the festival undown) a feast is held which is preceded ig ritual. On the following noon Kiddush The second day of the festival repeats the h variation in the reading from Scripture he festival is concluded with the ritual of

etween Rosh Hashanah and the Day of nergy are ordinarily devoted to settling , and, in general, to acts of penitence, tion. On the third day of this first month calendar falls the Fast of Gedaliah, com- of the last governor of Judah in the time tention from food and drink is required

The Day of Atonement (Yom Kippur) climaxes the Ten Days of Penitence. It is a day of repentance and expiation in the fullest sense, and the most solemn occasion in the annual religious cycle. Although Yom Kippur is not a day of mourning, as is Tish'ah b'Ab, a rigorous fast of some 24 hours is mandatory. The seriousness of the occasion is suggested by the fact that the Day of Atonement is the one instance in the Jewish calendar when fasting is mandatory even if the day falls on the Sabbath. During Yom Kippur all labor, eating, drinking, bathing, and even the wearing of leather shoes (in ancient times a luxury) is forbidden.

Five days after Yom Kippur comes Succot, the Festival of Booths, a 9-day period of thanksgiving and joy. Succot commemorates the days of the wandering in the Desert of Sinai. As a symbol of this period, the pious Jew constructs a kind of leafy bower (a *succah*) in which to live for a week's time during the festival. At the minimum, Jews who observe the festival will eat a token of food and recite the Kiddush over wine in the succah on the first evening. In the Orthodox tradition Kiddush will be performed on the first two days and again on the last two days. The eighth and ninth days of this period are festivals in their own right: Sh'mini Azeret and Simchat Torah, respectively. Sh'mini Azeret climaxes the thanksgiving season, which began with Succot, and is marked by the prayer for rain at the additional service in the synagogue. On Simchat Torah, the Day of Rejoicing in the Law, the annual reading cycle of the Pentateuch is completed and begun again. As its name suggests, this latter day is a particularly festive occasion. Kiddush is performed before meals during both these festivals, as on the Sabbath.

Hannukkah begins two months after Simchat Torah, and roughly coincides with the Christmas season. This 8-day festival commemorates the purification and rededication of the Temple by the Maccabees. Lights are kindled each Hannukkah evening in remembrance of the light which miraculously burned for 8 days in the Temple with oil enough to last only a day. Half of every feast is supposed to be devoted to study, the other half to eating and drinking.

Approximately 10 weeks after Hannukkah comes Purim, the most frivolous festival in the annual cycle. It is also the most secular of all the festivals, and may be thought of as the "liberal extreme" in the Jewish calendar. Purim is an occasion for especial merrymaking which commemorates the triumph of the Jewish people over Haman, as narrated in the Book of Esther. Haman is the archetype of persecutors in Jewish history and the traditional symbolic focus for pent-up feelings of aggression toward politically dominant groups. Except for Hannukkah and the intermediate days of festivals, Purim is the only festival during which business and work are permitted. It is customary for gifts to be exchanged among friends and for alms to be given to the poor. In regard to drinking, Purim is a time of relative license. The *Shulchan Aruch* declares that "it is obligatory to eat, drink and be merry on Purim" and elaborates on the importance of drinking thus:

> "As the whole miracle was occasioned through wine: Vashti was troubled in the wine feast and Esther was put in her stead; also the downfall of Haman was due to wine, therefore the sages made it obligatory on one to become drunk, until he should not be able to differentiate between 'Cursed be Haman' and 'Blessed be Mordecai.' At least one should drink more than he is accustomed to of wine or of another intoxicating beverage; one, however, who is of a weak disposition, likewise one who knows that it will cause him to despise some precept, a benediction or a prayer, or that it will lead him to levity, it is best not to become intoxicated; and all his deeds shall be done for the sake of Heaven."

In view of the ritual requirements of traditional Judaism, one could certainly not become drunk without running the risk of disrespect to some precept, benediction, or prayer, or of falling into levity.[9] Nonetheless, the idea of relative license remains in the tradition of Purim and the appearance of mild intoxication is not inappropriate. Bales suggests that the dramatization of drunkenness and the sanctioned, directed variation from the ritual and sacred uses of wine on Purim has its own "subtle educational purpose." This is because it sharpens the contrast between the ordinarily sober and dignified Jew, and the ridiculous, tipsy merrymaker in the context of the particular festival which emphasizes the hatred and dangers of the persecutor (whose downfall was due to wine). We may add that the tradition of Purim probably helps structure and reinforce the stereotypes of sober Jews and drunken Gentiles, to be discussed in Chapter 5.

Passover follows Purim by a month and at this time the pendulum swings back to more serious religious observances. Passover com-

[9] Actually, later rabbinical interpretation construed the injunction to drink until "Cursed be Haman" can no longer be distinguished from "Blessed be Mordecai" to refer to the letters in these two phrases, in each of which the numerical value comes to 502. To be unable to distinguish 502 from 502 requires little alcohol.

memorates the deliverance of the Jews from Egyptian bondage, and during its course leaven is banned from the home in accord with Biblical injunction. Although this prohibition does not extend to wine, great care must be taken to see that it is ritually pure.[10] Of the wine to be used on Passover, the *Shulchan Aruch* declares:

> "It is mandatory to acquire choice wine wherewith to perform the precept of drinking four goblets. If one can obtain red wine which is of the same quality as the white, and is also as valid for the use on Passover as the white, the former is to be preferred to the latter, for it is written: 'Do not observe wine when it becomes red,' from which it may be inferred that the value of wine lies in its being red."

However, some latitude is given in regard to alcoholic beverages for ritual use even on Passover. In the case of "one who abstains from wine during the year because it is injurious to him," the *Shulchan Aruch* rules that on Passover, "he may dilute it with water or he may drink raisin wine or mead, if this is a local beverage."

The first two evenings of Passover are *Seder* (literally, "order") nights. On the first evening certain symbolic foods are placed on the table before the regular meal. These include the *matzoth*, or unleavened bread, the "bread of affliction"; the roasted shankbone of a lamb, or a substitute, representing the Passover lamb which was annually offered up at the Temple in Jerusalem; the bitter herbs and a cup of salt water into which the herbs are dipped as a symbol of the bitterness of Egyptian slavery; the *charoseth*, a paste made of apples, almonds, spices, wine and other ingredients, representing the mortar which the Jews made for the Egyptians; and an egg, symbolizing another sacrifice made in Temple days.

The Passover ritual begins with the blessing of the children, first by the father, and then by the mother. The Kiddush is recited and all partake of the wine. The wine cups are refilled and the youngest child then asks the meaning of the festival and the special foods. A historical account of Passover is recited. Some of the special foods are passed around and all partake. Hymns are recited or sung, after which the benediction over wine is repeated and all drink the second cup. The festival meal is served, the wine cups are filled again, following which the Grace is said, ending with the drinking of the third cup. Immediately thereafter the wine cups are filled again. An extra cup, called the Cup of Elijah, is poured in expecta-

[10] The rules governing the fitness for use of wine and other beverages cannot be treated here. A summary statement is contained in the popular *Shulchan Aruch* (29).

tion of the visit of the prophet Elijah. One of the children is sent to open the door for Elijah. Then psalms and other traditional songs are sung, after which the wine blessing is repeated and the final cup is finished. After this fourth cup, no more wine may be drunk that night. To the master of the house the *Shulchan Aruch* recommends that "He should urge his household to drink at least the greater part of each cup at one time, and of the fourth cup they should drink a quarter of a cup at one time." Traditionally, then, on the first and second nights of Passover, the usual Kiddush ceremony is woven into the Seder, at which the wine is blessed and drunk four successive times. In addition there is a Kiddush in the middle of the day and a Habdalah at the close of the second day, i.e., before the intermediate days of the festival. The final two days of Passover are once again Kiddush days.

Seven weeks after the beginning of Passover comes Shavuot, the 2-day Festival of Weeks, or Pentecost, and the last festival of the year. This holiday celebrates the giving of the Torah. It is a joyous occasion and wine is used as on other feast days, the pattern of Kiddush and Habdalah being the same as on Rosh Hashanah.

The Fast of the Seventeenth of Tammuz, which occurs during the summer, commemorates the breach in the wall of Jersualem and on this day abstention from food and drink is required. From the Fast of the Seventeenth of Tammuz to the Fast of the Ninth of Ab (a period of 3 weeks) it is customary for the pious to observe some degree of mourning.[11] It is forbidden to eat meat or to drink wine during the 9 days preceding the Fast of the Ninth of Ab, or Tish'ah b'Ab, which commemorates both the first and the second destruction of the Temple. All the regulations concerning this 9-day period have to do with mourning; one should not do anything for pleasure during this time. On the Ninth of Ab one is forbidden to eat or drink, to bathe, to wear leather shoes, and so forth, from the preceding day at nightfall. The abstention from meat and drink ideally is to last until noon on the tenth of Ab. Tish'ah b'Ab is the most rigorous fast day of the Jewish year except the Day of Atonement and concludes the important occasions in the cycle of the Jewish year.

4. Later Rites de Passage

By the time the Jewish boy brought up in a traditionally religious home approaches his teens, he has experienced the rite of circumci-

[11] Tammuz and Ab are months in the Jewish year.

sion and actively participated in the Sabbath observances and festivals of which ritualized uses of alcoholic beverages are a part. It is also likely that he has been a spectator at a *Bar Mitzvah*, wedding or funeral, although he has yet to play an active or central role in these ceremonies.

The ceremony of the Bar Mitzvah marks a stage in the Jewish boy's religious education and his formal transition to adult status. The Bar Mitzvah takes place around the thirteenth birthday and makes the boy a full member of the religious community, eligible to be reckoned among the 10 men making up a minyan. There is first a religious ceremony at the synagogue, where the boy usually reads part of the Scriptures in Hebrew. This is customarily followed by a family reunion and celebration. Speeches may be given, the boy is blessed by the rabbi and receives gifts from family and friends. There is no special use of wine or alcoholic beverages on this occasion as at the circumcision, but these beverages will be sanctified and used as a part of the meal of celebration.

Ordinarily, the next important status transition after the Bar Mitzvah occurs with marriage. Marriage is held in great reverence among Jews, for the founding of a family is accounted a religious duty as well as a social ideal. The traditions and rules for the preparation and conduct of an Orthodox wedding are much too elaborate to be outlined here. However, the central significance of wine and drinking in the wedding ceremony itself must be noted. During the ceremony the rabbi utters the benediction over a cup of wine and hands it to the bridal couple who partake of it. They may then pass it on to their nearest relatives who also drink. The procedure thereafter is this:

> "... The person performing the ceremony continues as follows: 'Blessed art thou, O Lord, our God, King of the universe, who has sanctified us with Thy commandments concerning forbidden connections, and hast forbidden unto us those who are merely betrothed and hast permitted unto us those lawfully married to us through "canopy" (*huppah*) and "betrothal" (*kiddushin*). Blessed art Thou, O Lord, who sanctifiest Thy people Israel through huppah and kiddushin,' after which the groom hands to the bride a ring or some object of value (not less than a perutah, the smallest current coin), saying, 'Be thou betrothed (or consecrated) unto me with this ring (or object) in accordance with the laws of Moses and Israel.' ... This act of betrothal is at present combined with the rite of hometaking; and after the placing of the ring upon the finger of the bride, the marriage contract (*ketubah*) is read, to form an interval between the two acts. The recitation of another benediction over wine and

of the customary seven wedding benedictions forms the completion of the wedding ceremony."[12]

It is also customary for the groom to break a wine glass on the floor or crush it beneath his feet. Although a number of interpretations have been offered for this custom, the original meaning is obscure.

The last of the rites in the life cycle is, of course, the funeral. Jewish tradition prescribes that full mourning be limited to the death of a father, mother, son, daughter, brother, sister, wife or husband. It is also appropriate for a student to mourn for his teacher. As might be expected, during the initial period of grief, that is, until the time of burial, abstention from eating in company, from meat and from wine is enjoined (Sabbath and holy days excepted). As to the positive uses of alcoholic beverages at this time, the *Shulchan Aruch* prescribes that wine be used to wash the head of the corpse:

> "Then they beat an egg with some wine, and the egg should be beaten in its shell, indicating thereby the wheel of fortune that makes revolutions in this world (and where wine is unobtainable water may be substituted), and wash the head of the dead therewith. And the custom prevailing in some places that each one takes a little from this mixture and sprinkles it upon the dead, is improper; such custom should be abolished because it resembles the customs of other peoples; his head only should be washed therewith."

From the point of view of structuring cultural definitions of drinking in the personality, rites de passage cannot, in their nature, have the repetitive impact of the Sabbath ceremonies on the personality of the Jew. Perhaps, also, rites like the wedding, which are adult experiences, thereby lose some effectiveness as occasions for socialization. Nevertheless, the rites de passage are events of great significance to the individual which redefine his social status and relationships. Moreover, from the vantage point of membership in the community these rites have a recurrent character. The individual may participate in them variously as candidate, groom, father, relative, member of the congregation, fellow Jew, and so forth. More broadly, the rites de passage are tangible expressions and reinforcements of the ideal structure and solidarity of the extended family and social community. And they are occasions for expressing and reinforcing the overriding symbolism and sentiments of the religious community in the broadest sense. The fact

[12] Cited by Bales from the article on "Betrothal" in the *Jewish Encyclopaedia* (111).

that alcoholic beverages and drinking have either a prominent or ancillary role in all these ceremonies implies (*1*) the further impact of cultural definitions of drinking upon the individual, and (*2*) a strengthening of the links between drinking and the most powerful norms, ideas and sentiments of the group in "outer" social expression and "inner" structure of the personality. It also testifies to the consistency with which traditional Judaism incorporates these beverages and drinking in its core symbolism, sentiments and activities.

5. Other Uses and Basic Meanings of Alcoholic Beverages and Drinking in Orthodox Culture

In brief conclusion to his documentary study of drinking among Orthodox Jews, Bales notes that early rabbinical writings contain references to drinking for other than religious ritual purposes. These usages, he says, seem largely to have disappeared with the exception of the drinking of *schnapps*, originally a strongly alcoholic drink made by pouring *aqua vitae* over fruit and allowing the whole to stand, now any spirits. Schnapps, according to Bales, is sometimes taken by the master of the house before a meal or is occasionally taken as medicine. The rationale for the custom is "medicinal," although for schnapps, as indeed for any drinking, a short blessing is required.[13] In regard to specifically medicinal usages, whether at mealtime or any other time, the *Shulchan Aruch* specifies that "One who partakes of food or drink as medicine, if it be something savoury which he relishes, even if it is forbidden food, he should say the preceding and concluding benedictions appropriate thereto . . ." The clear implication of the Orthodox tradition is that even in otherwise secular situations the drinking is drawn into the realm of religious ideas and sentiments by the extension of religious symbolism. As we shall see, however, the use of schnapps in religious contexts—quite clearly provided for by the *Shulchan Aruch*—and in other situations is far more widespread among Jews than Bales' comments would suggest.

It is nonetheless pertinent to reiterate the basic meanings of alcoholic beverages and drinking in Orthodox Jewish culture as these have been summarized by Bales:

"... the essential uses of wine and other alcoholic beverages as they have existed to the present time are quite uniform: wine is symbolic of the

[13] The short benediction (*brachah*) for schnapps is "Blessed art Thou, O Lord our God, King of the Universe, at Whose word everything came into being."

sacred source of moral authority, God and the commandments of God, the law, the moral community and those who stand for it, such as the father; the act of drinking has the ritual significance of *creating, manifesting, or renewing a union* between the individual and the source of moral authority; and conversely, a degree of separation of the individual from the sacred things represented by the wine is symbolically initiated, manifested, or perpetuated by an *abstention* from, or prevention of the act of drinking in certain ways . . . Virtually all of the drinking which takes place in the Orthodox Jewish culture has these socially defined meanings, and furthermore, it can be assumed that practically every Orthodox Jew associates the act of drinking (consciously or not) with these profoundly moving ideas and sentiments regarding the sacred and his relationship to it, because of the intimate integration of the meaningful act with the earliest processes of socialization, the rites de passage, the weekly and yearly cycle of religious events, and the relationships of individuals within the family."

The concept of a "ritual attitude" toward drinking, which Bales believes is at the root of the low rates of drinking pathologies among Jews, was referred to in Chapter 1. But, against the background of rituals and ceremonies which we have described, the above summary statement articulates the content of Orthodox Jewish attitudes toward drinking and the ways in which these are structured and sustained in the individual personality.[14] Elaboration of these ideas and their possible significance for the low rates of drinking

[14] It is pertinent to spell out here more fully than in Chapter 1 the formal characteristics of ritual drinking as defined by Bales and as found, empirically, in Orthodox Jewish culture. In its ideal-type form, ritual drinking embodies these characteristics: "*1.* The ends of the act are non-empirical, that is, it is not possible to determine scientifically whether or not they are achieved, because they refer to entities and states of the 'other world'—the world which is articulated in terms of religious ideas and sentiments. The purposes, although entertained by an individual, are also the joint purposes of a 'moral community' in Durkheim's sense, not simply of the individual as an individual. The purposes are supposedly achieved in the act itself, not in further empirical effects which the act brings about. The purposes are expressive and communicative rather than procurative. *2.* Employment of the act of drinking as a means to the end is successful, not by reason of its empirical, physical character or effects, but by reason of its symbolic socially arbitrary definition. The empirical function of the act lies in the control and manipulation of the cognitive and moral modes of orientation of the participants, not of the affectional, hedonic or goal directive modes. *3.* The conditions of success lie in the proper symbolic performance of the act itself, as socially defined by the tradition of the group, rather than in conforming to any physical conditions of cause and effect. The act must be performed in the presence (real or imagined) of others who understand and concur in the meaning and purpose of the act." Bales defines the characteristics of ritual drinking as point for point opposed to utilitarian (or hedonistic) drinking, the prevalence of which in Irish culture he sees as a factor predisposing toward high rates of drinking pathologies. Compare Snyder and Landman (91).

pathologies among Jews must be postponed, however, until the actual drinking behaviors and attitudes of contemporary Jews are given fairly extensive consideration.

Patterns and Variations in Contemporary Jewish Drinking

The transition from a brief description of traditional patterns to a consideration of the full range of contemporary Jewish drinking patterns necessarily involves some abruptness. This stems partly from differences in modes of exposition appropriate to materials from documentary sources and to data from actual field research. But it also reflects the variation among contemporary Jews from the drinking norms, ideas and sentiments embodied in traditional codes. As we shall presently show, variation in its turn is indicative of more than isolated instances of deviation from traditional patterns. It also reflects shifts in basic cultural ideals and practices among vast segments of the American Jewish populace. Although essential from the point of view of our research design, variation immensely complicates the tasks of description and analysis. In beginning systematic study, only limited aspects of current Jewish drinking can be treated, e.g., frequencies of drinking, types of beverages, and contexts of drinking. Choosing aspects for measurability and analytic purposes, and treating them separately, gives an incomplete, momentarily distorted picture of reality. Nonetheless, from such study of current Jewish drinking, continuities in traditional patterns and significant areas of divergence from these patterns should eventually become clear.

1. Incidence and Frequency of Drinking

A popular and tenacious notion about Jewish drinking is the idea that "Jews don't drink." This assumed fact is often thought to account for the rarity of drinking pathologies in the Jewish group. Many people feel either that the traditional patterns we have described are "not really drinking," or that these no longer exist in the Jewish community. Others who acknowledge these patterns look upon them as a dying vestige of ancient times when drinking and drunkenness were common. These ideas shade into another and subtler version of the same theme, namely, that although some Jews drink, drinking is generally a rare occurrence. Those who adhere to the latter belief often assert that there must be "a tendency toward abstinence" in the Jewish group. The presupposition that drinking simply cannot be associated with sober and righteous living generally lies behind beliefs of this kind. That many Americans find it difficult to conceive of a group of people who drink alcoholic beverages with few undesirable consequences is hardly surprising in view of the prevalence and intensity of abstinence attitudes in our culture (61). And it is extremely difficult to convey the facts of drinking and drinking pathologies among Jews to people imbued with the abstinence tradition.

The idea of infrequent drinking among Jews is nonetheless supportable by the research of social scientists, provided Bales' work (7) is considered esoteric and the studies of Glad (31) and of Landman (58) are ignored. The results, for instance, of Riley and Marden's (78) useful national survey can easily be interpreted as showing the infrequency of drinking by Jews. Riley and Marden estimate that 13 per cent of American Jews are abstainers. Still more important, they designate 64 per cent of American Jews as "occasional drinkers." However, in their study occasional drinkers were defined as persons who neither abstain nor drink three times a week or more. Obviously this definition is broad enough to admit the possibility that a majority of Jews drink rarely, perhaps once or twice a year, if at all. A similar conclusion about Jewish drinking might be drawn from Straus and Bacons' (96) report on student drinking. Theirs is the only rigorous study, aside from Riley and Marden's, which essays broad comparisons of drinking among Jews and other groups. Straus and Bacon even suggest the infrequency of Jewish drinking in discussing their findings on the extensiveness of drinking. Noting that Jews have the greatest percentage of users of alcoholic beverages, they further comment that Jews "fall well behind both Catholic and Protestants in their extent of drinking . . ." However, Straus and Bacon refer to ratings of Jews and other religious groups on a quantity-frequency index of drinking behavior in speaking of the "extent of drinking." Ratings of groups on the index (Table 1) depend upon quantities of alcohol ordinarily consumed and frequencies of drinking. By making their only measure of extent of drinking contingent upon quantity, as well as frequency, Straus and Bacon left the way open for the inference that drinking is a rare occurrence for many Jewish students. Indeed, it would appear from their data that in extent of drinking Jewish students are more like Mormons, who come from an abstinence background, than either Catholics or Protestants.

Adding to misconceptions about Jewish drinking is the common

TABLE 1.—*Quantity–Frequency Index of Drinking, Male College Students, by Religious Affiliation (in Per Cent)**

Q–F Index†	Catholic	Jewish	Mormon	Protestant
1	16	31	33	28
2	17	13	17	14
3	10	22	18	21
4	29	25	25	23
5	28	9	7	14

* From Straus and Bacon (96).

† Higher indexes indicate more extensive drinking.

belief among Jews themselves that "Jews don't drink." This idea was often expressed in our interviews with New Haven Jewish men. Indeed, at the beginning of their interviews several men insisted, "I never drink, I never touch the stuff," or "A smell of the cork is enough for me." Later on, the same men readily acknowledged drinking, some as often as two or three times a day. This tendency to deny "drinking" has important implications and is related to the cultural stereotypes of Jewish and Gentile drinking which will be discussed in Chapter 5. But for the moment, two themes must be stressed. On the one hand, denials of drinking by these men ought not to be construed as deliberate falsifications. The very term "drinking" was often associated at first with drunkenness and drunkards. Many men were simply trying to impress upon the interviewer that they were not drunkards or prone to drunkenness. On the other hand, the belief that "Jews don't drink" in this sense often obscures from Jews themselves the realities of Jewish drinking which they know from personal experience and daily observation.

Because of the confused state of belief and knowledge, it is especially important to clarify in some detail both the incidence and frequency of drinking among Jews. In respect to incidence there were no lifetime abstainers among the 73 Jewish men in our New Haven sample. All the men interviewed reported having had alcoholic beverages to drink.[15] Among the Jewish students included in the College Drinking Survey, the incidence of drinking is also high. Only 6 per cent of these students professed to be abstainers in classifying themselves in regard to current use of alcoholic beverages.[16] In comparable groups of Irish Catholic and British Protestant

[15] The one current abstainer is a diabetic under doctor's orders not to drink. He drank frequently in the past and would prefer to drink now were it not for his physical condition.

[16] It should be borne in mind that the term "students," in all citations herein from the College Drinking Survey, refers to male college students only.

students, there are significantly higher proportions of abstainers.[17] Moreover, it seems likely that the proportion of abstainers among Jewish students is actually lower than 6 per cent. Thirty-eight (6 per cent) of the Jewish students classified themselves as abstainers in checking the question dealing directly with this point. But in answer to subsequent questions six of these reported having had an alcoholic beverage to drink during the past year, and five more reported drinking from one to four years prior to the survey. Thus 6 per cent abstainers is probably an exaggeration for Jewish students.[18]

The proportions of drinkers in these samples of Jewish men and students (99 and 94 per cent, respectively) are higher than the 87 per cent suggested for American Jews by Riley and Marden (78). The latter did include women in their survey, among whom there are generally more abstainers. However, Straus and Bacon (96) found little difference in the incidence of drinking between Jewish men and women students. It may be supposed that Riley and Marden's interviewers were sometimes greeted with, "I never touch the stuff" in briefly questioning Jewish men and women on drinking. Had the drinking phase of their research been more detailed, they would perhaps have found the proportion of drinkers among American Jews to be more than 90 per cent. Nevertheless, the national, New Haven, and student samples all point to a higher incidence of drinking among Jewish men than American men in general, among whom Riley and Marden estimated 75 per cent drinkers.[19]

Determining frequencies of drinking for a time span such as a year, which encompasses seasonal and other special variations, is more difficult than determining the incidence of drinking. Few people

[17] The samples of Irish Catholic and British Protestant students to which we refer were specially selected from the records of the College Drinking Survey and are often used for comparisons in this study. They are defined as follows: The Irish Catholic sample is composed of the 828 male college students who listed the "dominant nationality" of their parents as Irish and their own religious affiliation as Roman Catholic. The British Protestant sample is composed of the 1,007 male college students who listed the "dominant nationality" of their parents as British (including Scotch or Welsh) and reported religious affiliation with any of the Protestant denominations. Abstainers comprise 15 and 20 per cent of the Irish Catholics and British Protestants, respectively. Chi-square of the difference (drinkers versus abstainers by religioethnic group) is 57.76, P is less than .001.

[18] These 38 students are hereinafter treated as abstainers, even though a few might better be classed as drinkers. Where they appear in tables and computations the inclusion of "abstainers" is specified. Otherwise, data refer to students who definitely considered themselves drinkers at the time of questioning.

[19] Evidence of a high incidence of drinking among Jewish children has been presented by Landman (58) and is briefly discussed below.

TABLE 2.—*Frequencies of Drinking among New Haven Jewish Men, and Jewish, British Protestant and Irish Catholic Students, including Abstainers (in Per Cent)*

Frequency of Drinking	Jewish Men	Jewish Students	British Protestant Students	Irish Catholic Students
Never drink (abstainers)	1	6	20	15
1 to 5 times a year	5	20	17	9
6 to 12 times a year	10	27	20	17
2 to 4 times a month	27	35	26	34
2 to 3 times a week	32	11	14	21
4 or more times a week	25	1	3	4
Number reporting	(73)	(605)	(944)	(795)

keep track of exactly how often they drink and the men and students questioned in our research were no exception to this rule. Those who seldom drink may vividly recall their few drinking experiences, but frequent drinkers may not remember with much precision. In view of this situation, students in the College Drinking Survey were simply asked "How often during the past year did you have one or more drinks?" They were then given a list of frequency intervals from which to choose, which required less fine discriminations at higher frequencies of drinking. The resulting lack of precision in frequency estimates does not detract from their value in differentiating modes and extremes of drinking. In our interviews with New Haven Jewish men it was possible to reconstruct more exact estimates of frequencies of drinking during the previous year.[20] But even with the added time and detailed inquiry of the New Haven interviews, the frequencies obtained can only be regarded as approximations. For purposes of comparison, then, these latter data have been reclassified according to the broad intervals used in the College Drinking Survey.

A general picture of frequencies of drinking among New Haven Jewish men and Jewish students is presented in Table 2, together with comparative frequency data on Irish Catholic and British Protestant students.[21] Certain aspects of these findings bear special comment: It is seen, firstly, that the percentages of Jewish, Irish

[20] When drinking is confined within a cycle of ritual and ceremonial activities, as among some Jews, frequencies are easily reconstructed.

[21] "Frequencies of drinking," as used throughout, refers to estimates of the number of occasions or situations in which alcoholic beverages were used during the past year, that is, from the time interviews and questionnaires were administered. These are ordinarily expressed as percentages at different frequency intervals. In the

Catholic and British Protestant students at the highest frequency of drinking, that is, four or more times a week, are lower and much more alike than the percentages of Jewish, Catholic and Protestant students who are the most extensive drinkers according to the Q–F index referred to above (Table 1). Moreover, the mode for Jewish students is in the center of the distribution of Table 2, while their mode is the minimum extent of drinking when measured by the Q–F index. The modal frequency for Jewish students is drinking two to four times a month, which is also the mode for Irish Catholic and British Protestant students. There is thus fair similarity among these three categories of students in modes and extreme highs of drinking when frequency alone is considered. Secondly, it appears that there are far more frequent drinkers among New Haven Jewish men than among any of the student categories shown. These findings also indicate more frequent drinking among New Haven Jewish men than American men in general, or the Jews incorporated in Riley and Marden's (78) national survey.

The inclusion of abstainers is desirable in presenting a first picture of drinking. However, a balanced perspective on frequencies of drinking among the categories shown in Table 2 requires consideration of drinkers only. The exclusion of abstainers can little affect the patterns of drinking frequencies for Jewish men and Jewish students since there are so few abstainers among them. But it does slightly increase the proportions of Irish Catholic and British Protestant students at the higher frequencies of drinking, even though their mode remains drinking from two to four times a month.[22] To check on the significance of differences among drinkers only, Jewish men, and Jewish, Irish Catholic and British Protestant students were divided into "frequent" and "infrequent" drinkers, the frequent drinkers being defined by the criterion of drinking twice a month or more. Chi-square tests yielded these results: There is a significant difference in numbers of frequent and infrequent

---

tables throughout, column, row and table totals are ordinarily omitted to conserve space. Where tabular data are given in per cent (and this is only where the table total exceeds 99), the numbers upon which percentages are based are included in parentheses. In categories which appear more than once the numbers reporting may vary somewhat from table to table and from stated sample totals where equivalence might be expected. This is because of differences in numbers of respondents giving sufficient information on particular items. Unless otherwise indicated, respondents giving insufficient information are excluded from consideration.

[22] The data are presented fully in Snyder (90).

drinkers among students according to religioethnic groups. This is primarily because there are substantially more of frequent drinkers, as defined, among Irish Catholic than among either Jewish or British Protestant student drinkers, whose frequency patterns are much alike. Jewish men, however, significantly exceed even the Irish Catholic students in this respect.[23]

That Jewish and British Protestant student drinkers hardly differ in frequencies of drinking is particularly important because students of British Protestant background exemplify "culturally dominant" drinking patterns. There is wide variation in drinking patterns among American college students, and among students of British Protestant background specifically; it is therefore erroneous to think of a single college drinking pattern (96). But, as much as any single group can, students of British Protestant background may be taken as embodying American norms. Over-all similarities in drinking frequencies between these students and Jewish students suggest convergence of Jewish drinking practices with dominant cultural patterns. Quite aside from this possibility, however, the negligible difference in drinking frequencies makes it difficult to sustain the idea that drinking is, in relative terms, a rare occurrence among American Jewish students.

Before turning to other aspects of Jewish drinking, the difference in drinking frequencies between Jewish men and Jewish students must be briefly considered. Partly this may mirror more accurate reconstruction of drinking frequencies in New Haven interviews, or it may reflect higher frequencies of drinking among older age levels in the population at large. But it seems likely that two further facts have a bearing on this difference. The first is that regular schnapps drinking is associated in the Jewish tradition with the status of household head. The prevalence of this type of drinking, common among New Haven men, implies more frequent drinking by older than younger Jews. The second is that New Haven men are generally closer to Orthodox traditions than are Jewish students.[24]

[23] Chi-square of the difference (frequent versus infrequent drinkers) among students is 54.06, P is less than .001. Chi-square for Jewish men versus Irish Catholic students is 8.10, P is less than .01. Chi-squares are corrected for continuity when N is less than 100.

[24] This is the case even though the latter sample was weighted to include Orthodox students in disproportionate numbers. The reasons for this situation are complex, having to do principally with the impact of the social class system on successive generations. This is discussed in Chapter 4.

The more widespread involvement of the men in traditional ceremonials and rituals requires their more frequent drinking.

2. Early Drinking Experiences

The traditional patterns of drinking which we have briefly described are still solidly woven into the more varied patterns of drinking among contemporary Jews. Wine figures prominently in ceremonial and ritual, although Jewish custom is flexible enough to allow the use of schnapps or other beverages in many instances. The significance of traditional drinking can be readily seen in the current practices of New Haven men and Jewish students, but it is especially clear in their remembrances of drinking in childhood.

Among the 73 Jewish men interviewed in New Haven, 66 recalled taking their "first drink" on a religious occasion with the presence and approval of their parents. Only one man remembered first drinking in a nonreligious situation, although three men could not recall the circumstances of their first drinking. Wine was associated with the first drink in most instances, but two men mentioned drinking schnapps on ceremonial occasions and others referred to schnapps on "occasions" in childhood after their first drinking experiences. Moreover, these recollections of drinking on religious occasions often run back to very early years. The men who recalled their first drinking experiences reported their ages as follows: 11 were less than 6 years old at the time, 45 were between 6 and 10, 10 between 11 and 15, and only one man recalled being over 15 years at the time of his first drink.

As reconstructions of the actual circumstances of first drinking, these data cannot be taken literally, for there are certainly selective processes which often obscure memories, and particularly those of childhood. Actually, there are reasons for believing that many of these men had their first alcoholic drinks even earlier than their remembrances suggest.[25] The important consideration, however, is not that drinking first occurred exactly as described but that most Jewish men recalled drinking in childhood and that these early experiences left vivid impressions in the form of ideas and sentiments about drinking on religious and ceremonial occasions which carried through into later life.

[25] Our reference is not just to the custom of giving a child a taste of the wine at his circumcision but to the findings of Landman (58) on the high incidence of drinking among Jewish children in the youngest age group.

Although less detailed, further evidences of a high incidence of childhood drinking and an early emphasis on the ritual use of wine among Jews are contained in College Drinking Survey data. To the question on drinking before the age of 11, 85 per cent of all Jewish students responded affirmatively, compared to 52 per cent of the Irish Catholic and 33 per cent of the British Protestant students.[26] Among the Jewish students, 82 per cent reported drinking wine before their eleventh year, but only 32 per cent reported drinking spirits and 31 per cent beer before this age. In response to a check list of reasons for drinking wine in childhood, a majority of Jewish students indicated that their drinking was "part of a regular family, social, or religious custom." There are differences along religious lines among Jewish students in the extent and type of the use of wine and other beverages before the age of 11. To explore these, however, requires brief digression into variations in Jewish student religious affiliation and practice.

Jewish students in the College Drinking Survey were asked to identify themselves as Orthodox, Conservative or Reform, or, if unaffiliated or irreligious, to specify this fact. To the three familiar nominal religious divisions of modern Judaism may be added, then, a fourth category of "Secular" students, composed of the unaffiliated and irreligious.[27] Although discussion of differences and characteristics of these nominal groups will be deferred until later, two points must be stressed here: First, on the basis of general historical considerations, these nominal religious divisions—in the order, Orthodox, Conservative, Reform and Secular—roughly correspond

[26] Chi-square of the difference is 411.51, P is less than .001.

[27] Of the 644 male Jewish students in the Survey only 335 were questioned on details of their religious affiliation. This was because the original questionnaire failed to include specific questions on religious affiliation among Jewish students. At about the halfway point in the Survey the questionnaire was slightly altered to include more detailed information on Jewish religious affiliation. Thus, in treating nominal religious affiliation of Jewish students in relation to drinking and other variables, it is necessary to use the smaller sample of 335 Jewish students. This sample, in turn, is composed of 103 Orthodox, 91 Conservative, 72 Reform and 69 Secular students. Of these 335 students, 318 are definitely drinkers. Among the drinkers, 100 are Orthodox, 86 Conservative, 67 Reform and 65 Secular. Where nominal religious affiliation is considered, then, our reference is ordinarily to the 318 Jewish student drinkers, from the total male sample of 644 whose affiliation was determined.

To avoid more cumbersome expressions, "Secular" students are often referred to as among the "nominal religious divisions" or "four religious categories," as if they were a definite religious group, which is not intended. A few Jewish students classified as Secular do participate in religious activities, but we refer to Secular students as among the religious groups for expository convenience only.

TABLE 3.—*Frequency of Participation in Organized Religious Activities of Jewish Students, by Nominal Religious Affiliation (in Per Cent)*

	None to Four Times a Year	Five Times a Year to Twice a Month	About Once a Week or More	Number Reporting
Orthodox	11	14	75	(100)
Conservative	47	37	13	(86)
Reform	76	16	8	(67)
Secular	84	11	5	(64)

Chi-square = 181.23, P < .001

to a gradient of adherence to traditional Jewish values and religious practice, ranging from maximum to minimum. Second, these divisions actually mirror an orderly decline in religious participation among the Jewish students sampled in the College Drinking Survey, as shown in Table 3.[28]

On the question of extent and type of childhood drinking among Jewish students by nominal religious affiliation, only 6 per cent of the Orthodox reported no use of wine before the age of 11, compared to 13 per cent of the Conservative, 17 per cent of the Reform, and 10 per cent of the Secular. While the proportion of Jewish students indicating no wine drinking before the age of 11 rises from Orthodox to Reform, the proportion who experienced it as a regular family, social or religious custom shows a corresponding decline. Of the Orthodox students, 78 per cent checked wine drinking in childhood as a regular custom, compared to 68 per cent of the Conservative and 47 per cent of the Reform students. The Secular students fall between Conservative and Reform in this respect, 65 per cent indicating customary wine drinking before age 11.

These data on customary drinking in childhood have a specific reference to drinking as "part of a regular family, social, or religious

[28] Since the College Drinking Survey was designed for American students in general, no attempt was made to survey the particular practices of different religious groups. "How often do you participate in organized religious activities?" was the key question on religious behavior. While the data in Table 3 cannot be taken as accurately reflecting religious participation in the American Jewish population at large, they are probably indicative of wider tendencies toward differentials in participation among the four nominal divisions. (Differences among these religious categories are more fully treated in Chapter 4.) Quite apart from this problem, however, the gradient of decline in religious participation according to nominal affiliation evident in this sample makes these data especially useful to us for purposes of relating religious and other behaviors, since the nominal categories, which imply systematic differences in participation, are simpler to work with than measures of participation, as the College Survey materials are presently arranged.

TABLE 4.—*Specification of Customary Religious Drinking Before Age 11 among Jewish Students, by Nominal Religious Affiliation*

	Specification		No Specification	
	Per Cent	*Number*	*Per Cent*	*Number*
Orthodox	55	(55)	45	(45)
Conservative	52	(45)	48	(41)
Reform	27	(18)	73	(49)
Secular	26	(17)	74	(48)

Chi-square = 23.34, P < .001

custom." This item, in turn, was one among a check list of possible kinds of drinking in childhood included in the Survey questionnaire. Students were asked to choose from this list the kinds of drinking which applied to their own childhood experience. Those checking customary drinking in childhood were also asked to specify (in writing) the religious, social or other nature of their drinking, for wine and other beverages as well. Some students ignored this request for more detailed information, but the distribution of specified "religious" drinking among Jewish students as a custom in childhood is pertinent to our purpose. As Table 4 shows, specification of customary religious drinking in childhood declines systematically moving through the nominal religious divisions, Orthodox, Conservative, Reform and Secular.

There is substantial evidence that the recollections of New Haven men and of Jewish students concerning wine and other ceremonial drinking in childhood are more than figments of the imagination. Landman's recent study (58) revealed the quite common experience of drinking in three different age groups of boys and girls attending Jewish religious schools in the same city. Of the children between the ages of 5 and 7, 88 per cent said they had had an alcoholic beverage to drink. In the group aged 12 to 14 years, 96 per cent had used some alcoholic beverage. Among the older children, aged 15 to 17, 93 per cent recalled drinking at one time or another. Because of certain limitations of method, the importance of ritual wine and other ceremonial drinking in the total drinking of these Jewish children cannot be finally determined. Nonetheless, the evidence points to a preponderance of this type of drinking, as Landman's summary statement of the matter suggests:

> "That familiarity with alcoholic beverages cannot be attributed solely to the Kiddush ceremony [i.e., the Friday evening Kiddush] may be seen from the findings.... Roughly 50 per cent of all the children come from

homes in which Kiddush is performed [regularly], while the percentage of those who had been introduced to alcoholic beverages is closer to 90. It is nevertheless probable that many of the children whose parents do not perform Kiddush regularly had their introduction to alcoholic drinks at some ritual occasion."

Landman's cautious conclusions are quite in accord with the findings from our New Haven study and the College Drinking Survey. Certainly, in recalling their early drinking experiences, a few Jewish men mentioned drinking beverages other than wine in nonreligious situations. Also, about a third of the Jewish college students reported drinking beer or spirits before the age of 11, and some gave reasons other than custom or religion for their drinking. But the findings from all three samples, Jewish men, students, and children, suggest the prominence of ceremonial drinking, and especially wine drinking, in childhood, and the likelihood of first drinking on a religious occasion.

More important, these data testify to the widespread and powerful impact of traditional cultural definitions of drinking as a consequence of the integration of the act itself in the Sabbath observances, festivals and rites de passage of Orthodox Judaism. The deep and abiding linkage of the very idea of drinking with ceremonial and religious contexts is easily brought to present consciousness in the minds of many Jews by questions about their drinking experiences in the past. Evidently, the impact of the traditional culture has left an indelible residue of ideas and sentiments about drinking in the personalities of many Jews who are far from Orthodox in their current religious practice. And it is clear that these are intimately bound up with the most reverenced ideas and sentiments regarding parents, family and religion.

Further evidence on the importance of these early and repeated experiences of ceremonial and ritual drinking and the resulting structure of attitudes in countering intoxication and drinking pathologies is presented and discussed in later chapters. Here we wish merely to highlight this role by reference to the contrasting early drinking experiences of addictive drinkers. Ullman (102) has recently called attention to different types of first drinking experiences as possible factors in the etiology of alcohol addiction. By comparing the memories of first drinking among samples of addictive and nonaddictive drinkers, he has tentatively shown that more addictive than nonaddictive drinkers became intoxicated at the time of their first drink, and that more of the addictive drinkers had their first drink at later ages, in places outside the home, and in the company of persons other than the family. Also, there was ordinarily a greater time lapse between the first and second drinking experiences of the addictive than of the nonaddictive drinkers. Apparently the typical circumstances of the first drinking recalled by alcohol addicts are point for point opposed to the usual circumstances of first and early drinking among New Haven Jewish men, Jewish students and Jewish school children.[29] However, it is essential to note that with the modification or abandonment of traditional religious practices there is less assurance of (*1*) an early introduction to beverage alcohol within the family on a ceremonial or religious occasion, and (*2*) repeated experience of familial and ritual drinking. The gross effects of such changes seem already to be reflected in the minds of Jewish students insofar as their reports on drinking in childhood indicate a growing dissociation of drinking from family and religious custom as religious participation declines and affiliation changes from Orthodox, to Conservative, to Reform and Secular. The continued vitality and impact of the traditional culture in the modern Jewish community is nonetheless evidenced by Landman's findings of extensive drinking among New Haven Jewish children.

3. Importance of Different Beverages and Drinking Contexts

The ritualized uses of wine run like a red thread through current Jewish drinking patterns. In terms of incidence, wine is the most used alcoholic beverage. Of the 73 Jewish men interviewed in New Haven, 72 currently drink wine,[30] while 69 drink spirits and 60 drink beer. Of the students in the College Drinking Survey, 85 per cent currently drink wine, while 81 per cent drink spirits and 81 per cent drink beer. But although wine dominates in incidence and in childhood remembrances, it is used less frequently than spirits and beer.

Among the 72 Jewish men who drink, 25 drink spirits more often than either beer or wine, 22 drink wine more often, 16 beer, and 9 drink two or more of these beverages with about equal frequencies.

[29] There is no intention of implying that a few childhood experiences with ceremonial or familial drinking are necessarily preventive of addiction in later life, or that introduction to beverage alcohol under conditions such as Ullman describes for addicts will necessarily produce addiction. We intend only to suggest that the social circumstances surrounding first drinking experiences and drinking in the formative years may favor or impede the development of alcohol addiction.

[30] The sole exception is the diabetic, noted above.

In this sense, wine follows closely on the heels of spirits, and well ahead of beer, in the drinking of New Haven men. With a low measure of frequency as a criterion, however, 53 Jewish men drink spirits at least six times in the year, 43 drink beer, but only 37 drink wine with at least this minimum frequency. At a higher frequency of drinking, twice a month or more, 29 men designate spirits, 23 beer, but only 19 wine.

A clear distinction in regard to frequency of wine drinking can be drawn between Jewish men who adhere to the traditions of the Sabbath and those who have abandoned these customs. Forty-six men indicated that when they were children their parents faithfully observed the Friday Kiddush ritual, but only 13 continue this custom regularly today. This means, of course, that these 13 men drink wine at least weekly. Among Jewish men who no longer regularly observe the Kiddush, 33 drink wine less than six times a year, 13 six times a year to once a month, 8 once a month to once a week, but only 4 as often as once a week. Evidently, as regular observance of the complex of Sabbath customs declines, the frequency of wine drinking drops sharply. For the most part, however, the wine drinking of the less ritually observant is confined to vestiges of traditional Jewish ceremonial and ritual, which respondents often subsumed by the term "occasions." A few examples from interviews with less ritually observant men will indicate the nature of this drinking:

> "I rarely drink wine; just on holy days and festive occasions and some other times when it happens to be available. It's ritual or festive occasions, at home or visiting with a meal." [15][31]
>
> "Wine? Just at Passover, but sometimes at social gatherings." [20]
>
> "I drink wine at Passover, a few little glasses. Otherwise, I don't have any opportunity to drink wine." [10]

Ideas of just drinking on "occasions" or "occasionally" ("at social gatherings" or "to be sociable") are deeply embedded in current Jewish drinking attitudes. This applies to wine and other beverages as well. Occasional drinking or drinking on occasions, in the sense in which Jewish men commonly speak of it, refers to more than a meas-

[31] Numbers in square brackets after excerpts refer to case numbers assigned to the 73 men in our New Haven study. We will generally speak of these men as "respondents" and use the term "informants" for Jewish men who were not specifically included in the New Haven or college student samples.

ure of drinking frequency. It implies the real or quasi ceremonial character of situations in which drinking is deemed appropriate. There may often be an implication of moderate or infrequent drinking, but the basic meaning is that drinking is subordinate to, or an aspect of the occasion. This generally refers to family gatherings, often on the Sabbath or holy days, or ceremonials in which the individual's ties with the larger group and its symbolism are affirmed. Both in its normative sense and in its actual social expression this attitude implies that most Jewish men should not and do not create an occasion for drinking. Rather, the occasions require drinking as a sign of social conformity and solidarity:

> "The only time I take a drink is in company or occasions such as weddings, engagements, anniversaries, births." [16]
>
> "Sometimes I drink at a wedding or other occasions and people offer you a glass. My drinking is as rare as the festive occasion." [31]
>
> "I very seldom drink unless there's a party or people come. If we invite company to the house we have a little drink. I have no desire for it, wouldn't touch it for months unless some occasion comes." [34]
>
> "I seldom drink liquor except at a gathering or affair." [36]
>
> "I'm an occasional drinker, I drink on occasions. There has to be a reason for it when I drink." [49]
>
> "I drink on special occasions: Bar Mitzvahs, anniversaries, holy days." [56]

The ideas and sentiments in these excerpts, which refer to various beverages, could be duplicated by statements from a majority of the men interviewed in our New Haven study. Their statements seem to mirror conceptions of drinking hardly a step removed from the Orthodox attitudes in reference to which Bales (7) concluded that "the act of drinking has the ritual significance of creating, manifesting or renewing a union between the individual and the source of moral authority. . . ."

The frequency of spirits drinking exceeds wine drinking among New Haven Jewish men, but this by no means indicates their wholesale abandonment of traditional drinking patterns. Kiddush is not necessarily performed with wine, although wine is certainly preferred for the ceremony which inaugurates the Sabbath. However, excepting also the rituals' of the Passover seder and the wedding ceremony, schnapps is often used in preference to wine on festivals or other ritual occasions. Schnapps, nowadays usually whisky or brandy, is very likely to be used at the "lesser Kiddushes," as one informant classified them in speaking of the Great Kiddush and the circumcision ceremony.[32] This is particularly important because if ideas and sentiments associated with ritual drinking are to counter drinking pathologies, as Bales (7) suggests, there cannot be a total symbolic and contextual division between wine and other frequently used alcoholic beverages. And this is indeed the case among New Haven Jewish men. A sense of the interchangeability of beverages together with the special sacredness of wine can readily be gained from the interviews with these men:

> "I keep a five gallon bottle of wine for Kiddush. Everything from beer upwards is an alcoholic beverage; beer and wine have a small alcohol content. I drink occasional beer or wine or Kiddush schnapps. Wine a couple of times a week—Kiddush wine; beer once or twice a month with meat, to go with a heavy meal at home. Wine I drink for Kiddush and religious celebrations, like Kiddush in *shul* [synagogue] or weddings. Wine is for religious demands, otherwise, I don't like it. I drink schnapps for religious celebrations, only for religious observances. I wouldn't buy it. [He also drinks schnapps in tea when he has a cold.] I drink Kiddush and schnapps right before meals, beer during meals. I eat after schnapps to remove the taste. I never drink more than one or two, it doesn't agree with me anyway." [01]

This respondent's references to "Kiddush schnapps" and to "schnapps for religious celebrations" are indicative of the incorporation of spirits in the pattern of religious and ritual drinking. Similar tendencies are evident in the following excerpts which emphasize the significance of wine for Sabbath and schnapps for other ceremonial occasions:

> "I only use Kosher wine, for Kiddush and Habdalah. When I was working I used to have a couple of schnappses daily. [He doesn't drink beer.] Now I have schnapps only in shul, at *Yarhzeit*, or Bar Mitzvah, or at home occasionally with a guest."[33] [73]
>
> "Every Friday, when my father-in-law says Kiddush, I have a glass of wine. Wine is for Sabbath purposes, with the family. When I go out, I have some rye but the amount of hard liquor [he means frequency] depends on how many occasions I go to. I enjoy the taste of hard liquor only when I have a cold. [But he adds later] I only have hard liquor on occasions like a wedding or a birth. Beer? Very seldom, only two or three times a year on visits. I'd never buy it for myself." [16]

[32] These practices are, of course, quite consistent with the *Shulchan Aruch's* liberal allowances for the use of beverages other than wine.

[33] *Yarhzeit* refers to the day annually commemorating the death of a parent, when it is customary to serve schnapps to men in the synagogue after the morning service.

It is not just the ceremonial schnapps drinking, however, which accounts for the high frequency of spirits drinking. The home ritual of schnapps before meals and other less frequent uses of schnapps as medicine are prevalent among Jewish men and an important factor in their total drinking. Historical models for drinking schnapps before meals are to be found in the rituals of Kiddush and Great Kiddush (for the latter, schnapps is common) and in the closely related ancient customs of drinking wine before ordinary meals with the appropriate benediction. But certain points must be borne in mind in considering the mealtime schnapps drinking of New Haven men as ritual. On other than special occasions, such as Great Kiddush, this drinking is not in the nature of a sanctification even though a benediction is required among the Orthodox. Among the less Orthodox, schnapps drinking has often lost its connection with explicit religious symbolism. Also, there are utilitarian "medicinal" and "stimulant" rationales for schnapps, although this drinking can hardly be considered purely utilitarian.[34] Even with these qualifications, schnapps drinking before the meal among New Haven men has attributes of ritual as broadly defined by Bossard and Boll (13): "a prescribed procedure . . . involving a pattern of defined behavior, which is directed toward some specific end or purpose, and acquires rigidity and a sense of rightness as a result of its continuing history."

Numerous references to mealtime schnapps drinking are contained in our New Haven interviews of which these excerpts are typical:

> "I take a drink and start my meal. I have a drink before dinner mostly during the winter." [10]
>
> "I drink on Saturday before meals for appetite. I eat my dinner better." [38]
>
> "In the winter I like to have a shot every night before I eat, just one." [40]
>
> "I have one shot of whisky before my meal. I drink whisky on cold days or before a meal for an appetizer." [69]
>
> "When I was working I used to drink schnapps twice a day; in the morning before I went out [before breakfast] and before supper, especially in the winter. [He now drinks schnapps two or three times a week, mostly in the synagogue.]" [71]

[34] This is because of the specific tradition of extending religious symbolism to these usages, and broader religious ideas of the importance of health and the sacredness of the body. A general distinction from the utilitarian can be drawn in terms of the degree to which health considerations are integral with the purposes of the moral community, as opposed to being conceived of as primarily individual concerns.

This type of drinking must not be confused with "cocktails" in the American pattern. Spirits, usually brandy or whisky, are taken "straight" and the emphasis is on "a shot," "one," "just one," or "one or two little drinks."[35] This emphasis is quite reminiscent of the *Shulchan Aruch's* specifications for drinking a mouthful of brandy at the ritual before breakfast on the Sabbath. Also, the regular use of schnapps is a prerogative of men. Women may be present, and the younger men and boys may occasionally partake in the company of fathers, grandfathers or other relatives; but as a regular practice, schnapps drinking is linked with the status of ritual head of the household, as Bales (7) suggested was true of wine before the meal in ancient times. Apparently, also, the custom is more characteristic of the older generation, comparatively Orthodox Jews.[36]

The medicinal and stimulant rationales for a little schnapps have been especially well stated by two New Haven Jewish men:

> "A little liquor, I think, is good for any person, especially at my age [53 years old]—just a little—at my own table, just before a meal. When I do take a little drink before my meals it gives me a better appetite to eat. I feel much better. For the last 10 years I really don't care for liquor except at my own table for my health. I think any doctor would advise taking a little every day." [02]
>
> "The doctor told me that I should take one or two drinks, usually when I get home, to relax, before dinner. I drink when I have to entertain also, but I'm not a habitual drinker. [He observes Sabbath Kiddush regularly.] I can do without it, thank God." [32]

It is questionable how much the advice of the doctors weighed in the decisions of these men to drink a little schnapps before meals, for the custom is widespread irrespective of such prescription. Ideas of the medicinal value of small amounts of alcohol are of long standing in the Jewish tradition, antedating distilled spirits, and have the sanction of the physician in the popular mind. That Jewish physicians have not been averse to such usages is evidenced by the medical opinions of Maimonides. Schweisheimer (85) notes the recommendations of this eminent twelfth-century Jewish physician and philosopher to the effect that "The older a man gets . . . the better is wine for him, and the very old need it most. Small quantities of wine are good for the digestion. Wine may be considered a tonic and even a remedy for many diseases." In the cases cited above, the beverage

[35] On the amounts of spirits ordinarily consumed, see below.

[36] As will be seen in Chapter 4, generation of itself is not the primary determinant in Jewish drinking customs.

might as well have been wine and the prescribing physician Maimonides.

Unfortunately our data are inadequate to specify the incidence with which traditional benedictions or vestiges of religious symbolism are connected with schnapps drinking. Some ritually observant men mentioned the benedictions in connection with schnapps and a few reported drinking "a shot" every evening and also every morning, before breakfast, with appropriate blessings. (Other Jewish informants tell us that this morning drinking was a prevalent custom "in the old days.") We know definitely, however, that among some Orthodox men drinking is always explicitly connected with religious symbolism. Even in unusual drinking circumstances, e.g., apart from home or synagogue and with Gentiles present, the observant man may quietly utter the benediction. An abstract from a conversation with a New Haven Jewish informant will illustrate these latter points:

Q. Do you ever make Kiddush on Friday evening with schnapps?

A. No, always with wine. Schnapps is for Kiddush, Saturday morning after service.

Q. Suppose I've been away for a long time and I come back and walk into your store and you bring out a bottle of schnapps to celebrate with a drink.[37] Would you say a blessing under your breath? [The investigator is non-Jewish and this is known to the informant.]

A. A brachah? Always! You don't shout it, but the object is to get the other fellow to join in with Amen. I'd murmur it.

The explicit religious symbolism which may have been associated with schnapps by fathers and grandfathers has been abandoned in many instances, but a brief toast, such as "*l'chaim*" (to life), which has definite Jewish and religious connotations, is often continued in place of the benediction. Changes of this kind are well summarized in this recollection, by a secular informant in his early twenties who prefers his spirits straight:

"We never made Kiddush in my home; that is, my father. But I remember Kiddush at relatives'. The wine was prominent but the schnapps was always there in the background. In my mind they stressed it [schnapps] less, but it was always there. There was always a bottle of schnapps around. Even on Passover, when the use of wine is ritually prescribed, the men would take a drink of slivovitz [plum brandy] which was on the Seder table, and my grandfather would say a blessing. My

[37] In another conversation this informant had mentioned the custom in the Jewish tradition of celebrating the return of a traveler by a drink.

uncles I'm not sure of, because they weren't Orthodox. But they'd at least say 'l'chaim'."

This abstract also suggests what seems plausible generally, namely, that the ideas and sentiments associated with the contexts of wine and schnapps drinking for Sabbath rituals and other ceremonial occasions generalize (consciously or not) to schnapps before meals among Jews socialized in more Orthodox traditions. It also seems reasonable to assume that such generalization is facilitated and strengthened through observance of the Orthodox requirement of the short blessing. But with or without the benediction, the custom of schnapps before meals is continued by many Jewish men according to the behavioral models of their fathers:

"My father always had a small drink [spirits] before any meal—breakfast, lunch, supper." [60]

"My father drank schnapps to stimulate his appetite." [62]

"My father always drank schnapps as an appetizer." [63]

And the importance of these repeated parental examples of drinking small amount of distilled spirits cannot be overestimated in effectively socializing Jews to norms of moderate drinking and sobriety. As Straus and Bacon (96) have concluded from their comprehensive study of student drinking, "The influence of parental drinking *practices* upon those of sons and daughters cannot be stressed too strongly."[38]

Still there are contexts of drinking often mentioned by New Haven Jewish men which cannot be equated with the situations thus far described. Very often these are also contexts which involve the use of beer and mixed drinks in preference to wine or schnapps. By far the most important of these is the "business situation," the significance of which is suggested in the words of these respondents:

"Food and drink are an important part of business associations. I go out to drink for sociability. I wouldn't want a customer to drink alone. [His customers are mostly non-Jewish.]" [07]

"I only drink if I have company or for business purposes." [21]

"I drink when I'm entertaining a customer at business luncheons and dinners. It's the customary thing in sales." [19]

"I drink with business associates. I go along with them to make them feel as pleasant as possible. [Most of his business associates are non-Jewish.]" [32]

"I have a glass of beer, if a customer or friend comes in, or at an Association meeting." [34]

[38] Italics supplied.

Although business drinking suggests their frequent use, there is little patronage by Jewish men of bars, taverns or other commercial establishments for drinking in connection with purely social or recreational purposes. There is some attendance of night clubs, especially by the younger single men and married couples, but nothing comparable to the bar and tavern patronage described by Macrory (65) for other groups. In their business roles, however, some Jewish men are frequent patrons of bars and taverns for clearly defined business purposes:

> "I have liquor for sales meetings and guests. I never go to bars and taverns for pleasure, only for business. I don't like beer but I drink it out of courtesy to my customers. I sell to a lot of taverns. [He is a beverage salesman.]" [30]
>
> "Occasionally I go to a tavern and have a drink with business companions. I'll drink one beer at the Bar Association meetings." [52]
>
> "I drink whisky in bars or taverns with business associates about 15 times a year." [50]
>
> "I go to a bar about once a week with business associates and have one drink, usually beer." [67]
>
> "I go to bars or taverns occasionally with business associates and have a cocktail or highball." [69]

Business drinking will be dealt with more fully in Chapter 5, where ingroup–outgroup relations are considered as they bear on Jewish sobriety. But it is useful to anticipate that discussion with some general comments here.

Business drinking for most of the New Haven Jewish respondents is superimposed on the foundation of socialization to traditional Jewish drinking norms. Traditional attitudes are already firmly structured in the personality before drinking in association with business begins. More often than not these attitudes are being reinforced in later life by periodic or regular drinking in family and ceremonial contexts which alternates with business drinking. It is interesting to note in our interviews how the more religious men reiterate the norms of "just one," "one little drink" or "only one or two drinks" for business as for any other drinking. And it is to be noted again that the secular character of the business situation does not obviate the requirement of the brachah for the ritually observant. Then, too, there is stress on the necessity of drinking to comply with custom and to be sociable in business.[39] This accords with the

[39] See the allusions in the above excerpts to sociability, courtesy, and "the customary thing in sales."

traditional Jewish attitudes on drinking insofar as it is an expression of social conformity. However, business situations are not authentic Jewish occasions for drinking during which the individual's solidarity with the group and its symbolism are affirmed. And there is a marked ambivalence about drinking in business stemming from the opposition of this fact to traditional attitudes which require abstention from drinking on other than ritual or ceremonial occasions, or for "medicinal" purposes. This ambivalence was concretely expressed by several men as a definite aversion to any drinking in business situations. In expressing their aversion, some said that they would nonetheless take a drink for "sociability." With others, however, the conflict was so strong that they insisted they would "just hold on to the glass for sociability."[40] Drinking in business apparently represents an uncomfortable compromise between practical and religious demands which is rationalized by the social conformity or sociability aspects of the traditional drinking attitudes.[41]

There is seldom any indication of drinking to satisfy the immediate pleasurable or self-regarding need of the individual. That this is true is the more surprising at first glance in view of the fact that business is a specialized role bringing some Jewish men into frequent contact with Gentiles whose drinking is not always moderate. But there is evidently a definite "instrumental" structure and heightened sense of ethnic difference (Jew versus Gentile) in many of these situations.[42] As will be suggested in detail later, these latter elements in the social structure of the business drinking situation may further constrain Jewish men precisely where their drinking might otherwise take a more convivial or hedonistic turn.

Among the younger and less Orthodox New Haven Jewish men beer drinking is quite common. This is not to imply that beer is unused by the more Orthodox, for beer may sometimes be taken with meals, on an "occasion," or perhaps for "business purposes." Reports from Jewish informants suggest that during the early 1900's

[40] This is often a glass containing a mixed drink or beer, which they otherwise might not use.

[41] That drinking can be so rationalized probably makes Jews less anxious than persons with an abstinence background in business and other common drinking situations. Very likely this is related to the fact that a sobriety norm can be more easily sustained in practice among the former. (Liabilities of intoxication and more extreme drinking pathologies among persons of Jewish, abstinence and other background will be considered in later Chapters.)

[42] These elements are suggested in the respondent's phrase, "I go along with them to make them feel as pleasant as possible," cited above.

beer drinking with meals (Sabbath, festival or other meals) was fairly prevalent among Jews in New York City. One New Haven man vividly recalled beer being used by Orthodox men in a New York synagogue as a part of the third meal of the Sabbath. An Orthodox New Haven informant reported that beer is occasionally used in this same connection in the synagogue to which he now belongs. Apparently, as is the case generally, beverage preference among Jews is the most flexible aspect of drinking customs.[43] It is nonetheless safe to say that the more Orthodox New Haven men make extensive use of wine and schnapps with only occasional use of beer, while beer has made strong inroads among the less observant. For instance, only 2 of the 13 men who nowadays observe the Friday evening Kiddush drink beer twice a month or more; 9 of the 34 whose parents observed the Kiddush but who are no longer observant themselves drink beer twice a month or more; but 13 of 24 men whose parents were nonobservant and who are nonobservant themselves drink beer with at least this frequency.[44] Similar tendencies are suggested by our data in regard to preferences for mixed drinks as opposed to wine or spirits taken "straight." Seen in the context of their use, these preferences for beer and cocktails appear to be definite signs of acculturation to wider American patterns. Apart from business usages, the less Orthodox typically associated beer with drinking contexts suggested by "with the boys," "with the fellows after a ball game," "playing poker," and "in the pub," while cocktails were referred to in connection with "parties" or "night clubs."

A distinction is to be drawn between this latter drinking and the drinking of the more Orthodox. The difference cannot be expressed solely in terms of beverages or even of a specific structural aspect

[43] In this connection, the Falashas of Ethiopia, racially similar to neighboring Negro tribes, present an interesting case of Jewish beer drinking. The Falashas, as described by Leslau (59), have no wine but use a native beer extensively. The beverage and its drinking are woven into their religious life somewhat as wine and schnapps are incorporated in the holy days and festivals of eastern European Jews. According to Leslau the Falashas are noted for their sobriety among surrounding Ethiopian tribes (personal communication). An informant has suggested that the widespread use of schnapps by New Haven men is related to the majority's background of residence in regions of eastern Europe where wine was difficult to obtain. For Sabbath purposes raisin wine frequently had to be made at home, often with almost unpalatable results. Schnapps was therefore substituted for lesser ritual purposes, or before the meal. (Whatever its historical merits, this interpretation accords with the *Shulchan Aruch's* outlook regarding the use of local beverages.)

[44] Kiddush background is uncertain in two cases.

TABLE 5.—*Value Ratings of Selected Reasons for Drinking among Jewish Students, by Nominal Religious Affiliation (in Per Cent)*

	To Comply With Custom	Number Reporting	To Get High	Number Reporting	To Get Drunk	Number Reporting
Orthodox	27	(87)	4	(83)	1	(82)
Conservative	23	(76)	9	(76)	1	(75)
Reform	20	(63)	10	(61)	3	(60)
Secular	15	(58)	11	(59)	5	(59)

of the drinking group.[45] What can be said is that beer and cocktails and their contexts tend to be dissociated from the weight of Jewish tradition, and especially from the drinking norms embodied in Orthodox religious institutions and vitalized through relations with parents, extended family and Jewish community. The less Orthodox Jews' abandonment of traditional cycles of religious ceremonial means the loss of routine and clearly defined drinking occasions. Lacking a new and comprehensive calendar of occasions, there is increased participation in segmented, loosely structured, "pleasure seeking" groups which Bacon identifies as traits of modern society.[46] The drinking in these groups may be highly social and by no means invariably leads to drunkenness. The context and the drinking, however, are more closely connected with individual needs, conceived apart from the purposes of the moral community, and drinking itself is sometimes paramount. We might say, then, that among less Orthodox Jews there is a tendency to create occasions for drinking in contrast to drinking on foreordained occasions.

That there actually are variations in drinking attitudes of this kind which correspond to changes in religious affiliation and participation, and do not depend solely on age or other differences, is suggested by data on Jewish students' reasons for drinking. As the value ratings in Table 5 show, the proportion of these students rating "to comply with custom" as an important reason for drinking (relative to other reasons) declines through the nominal religious

[45] The incidence of drinking in all male or in family groups, for example, is insufficient to express the difference. The Orthodox may drink schnapps in male groups on Yarhzeit days or at the third meal of the Sabbath in the synagogue with quite different connotations from drinking "with the boys" as understood by nonobservant Jews, or in American culture generally, or by a "bottle gang." Less Orthodox Jews, as many other Americans, may become intoxicated at "parties" in the home, while observant Jews drink at home without similar effect.

[46] In "Alcohol and complex society," Lecture 13 in Alcohol, Science and Society (113).

TABLE 6.—*Beverage Most Frequently Used by Jewish, British Protestant and Irish Catholic Students (in Per Cent)*

	Wine	Beer	Spirits	Number Reporting
Jewish	23	46	31	(530)
British Protestant	7	74	19	(700)
Irish Catholic	4	79	17	(648)

divisions. By contrast, the proportion of Jewish students rating "to get high" and "to get drunk" as important tends to rise.[47] Of course, "to comply with custom" is a somewhat ambiguous phrase. One may drink in various ways to comply with the customs of particular groups and situations. Nonetheless, compliance with custom as an explicit reason for drinking suggests social and traditional drinking conceptions contrary to the individualistic attitudes implied by "to get high" or "to get drunk." The additional fact that 85 per cent of the Orthodox but only 64 per cent of the Secular students list "to comply with custom" as an important reason, cannot be ignored as an indication of differences in essential conceptions of the purpose in drinking.[48] These variations among Jewish students, as well as the contextual differences suggested for New Haven men, are probably conditioned by class and generation factors, but their more direct dependence on extent of participation in traditional religious patterns is certainly suggested. The importance of religious influences will become clearer, however, when variations in types of beverages and contexts of drinking for Jewish students are considered below in relation to religious affiliation, and this in relation to other aspects of drinking patterns in Chapter 3.

Wine ranks behind both beer and spirits as the beverage of most frequent use by Jewish college students (Table 6). This should not obscure the prominence of wine drinking among these students as

[47] On value ratings: Students were asked to assign considerable, some or no importance to each of a check list of 13 reasons for drinking. Since the over-all importance assigned to reasons varies (e.g., Reform have a greater propensity than Conservative students to check reasons as important), these data are expressed as proportions of the number of students in each religious category assigning some or considerable importance to all reasons listed. Value ratings were computed according to the formula $2a + b \div \Sigma(2a + b)$, where a is the number of students selecting a reason as the most important reason for drinking, and b the number who selected a reason as of some importance. This follows Straus and Bacon's (96) convention for analyzing students' reasons for abstaining.

[48] This value for the Secular students (64 per cent) is the same as for all male students in the College Drinking Survey.

TABLE 7.—*Beverage Most Frequently Used by Jewish Students, by Nominal Religious Affiliation (in Per Cent)*

	Wine	Beer	Spirits	Number Reporting
Orthodox	62	24	14	(84)
Conservative	24	45	31	(71)
Reform	24	37	39	(59)
Secular	16	48	36	(59)

compared to Irish Catholic or British Protestant students. Table 6 also shows that wine is far more often the most frequently used beverage among Jewish students than among students in these latter groups.[49]

The correspondence between a decline in the relative importance of wine drinking and variations from traditional Jewish patterns is suggested by the data in Table 7 on the beverages most frequently used. Nearly two thirds of the Orthodox students drink wine the most, but less than a fourth of the students in each of the other religious divisions drink wine more often than either beer or spirits.[50] Among Conservative and Secular students, beer takes precedence over wine or spirits, while spirits rank ahead of beer and wine as the beverage most frequently used among the Reform. The outstanding fact in Table 7, however, is the substantial difference in the relative importance of wine in the drinking patterns of Orthodox and non-Orthodox students. Variation is most pronounced between Orthodox and Secular students, representing the two extremes of the religious spectrum. This corresponds to the sharp decline in the use of wine among less ritually observant New Haven Jewish men.

While these data indicate something of the relative importance of each type of beverage in the drinking patterns of Jewish students, they do not render an accurate comparative picture of the frequencies of their use. The percentage measure of beverages most frequently used is based on rankings by each student of the frequency of use of wine, beer and spirits. And such ranking must not be confused with direct measures of frequency. To guard against mistaken impressions, data are needed on the frequencies with which Jewish students drink these beverages. Questions on precise frequencies of drinking different beverages were not included in the College Survey

[49] Chi-square of difference (wine versus other beverages) by religioethnic group is 124.84, P is less than .001.

[50] Chi-square for wine versus other beverages along religious lines is 42.76, P is less than .001.

TABLE 8.—*Jewish Students who Used Wine, Beer or Spirits More than 10 Times During the Previous Year, by Nominal Religious Affiliation, Including Abstainers (in Per Cent)*

	Wine	Beer	Spirits	Number Reporting
Orthodox	71	50	39	(101)
Conservative	32	40	26	(90)
Reform	18	51	52	(71)
Secular	35	55	49	(69)

questionnaire. Students were asked, however, whether or not they had used wine, beer or spirits more than 10 times during the previous year, and a rough impression of frequencies can be gained from their responses to these questions.

The proportions of Jewish students in each religious division who drank wine, beer or spirits more than 10 times during the previous year are shown on Table 8. In some basic ways the pattern of these data is similar to that in the preceding table. Orthodox students surpass the others in wine drinking whether this is measured by percentage who drink wine most often or percentage who use wine more than 10 times yearly. Also, the Orthodox ranking of the different beverages is the same in either case, wine being most important, followed by beer and spirits, respectively. However, the data on drinking frequencies in Table 8 rank Secular ahead of Conservative and Reform students in the use of wine. This does not mean that Secular students necessarily drink wine extensively for religious purposes or in the family. Their infrequent religious participation (Table 3) suggests other purposes and contexts for wine drinking. Actually, only 64 per cent of the Secular students who drink wine list family members as their most frequent wine drinking companions. By contrast, more than 80 per cent of Orthodox and Conservative wine drinkers report the family as their usual companions. Evidently, the rather extensive wine drinking of Secular students is not strictly confined to the family circle, which is the focus of traditional religious ceremonies of a regular character. Therefore, a substantial portion of the wine drinking of Secular students must be exempt from religious and familial sanctions. These findings together with data on religious participation also indicate that Conservative students do rank next to the Orthodox in the ritual use of wine in the family.

The four divisions of Jewish students are quite similar in the proportions who drink beer more than 10 times yearly. Thus beer is not inconsequential to Orthodox students even though wine drinking predominates among them. Conservative students may drink beer somewhat less often than the rest but, on the whole, beer is probably the most important beverage for this group. In our opinion, much of the beer drinking among Jewish students reflects an accommodation to prevailing college drinking patterns which accord first-rank importance to beer drinking in male fellowships.[51]

Spirits are evidently rather frequently used by higher proportions of Reform and Secular students than Orthodox and Conservative ones. Subsequent data will show that this difference is related to more frequent drinking in mixed company, other than the family, among the former.[52] But the modest, although not insignificant, spirits drinking of Orthodox students stands in sharper contrast to the frequent use of spirits by the more ritually observant men in our New Haven sample. As suggested earlier, this difference between students and men stems primarily from the customary association of schnapps drinking with the status of head of the household. It is not, we believe, until later life that the more Orthodox students, who drink spirits rather infrequently, will drink spirits as regularly as their fathers and grandfathers. From the point of view of the life cycle, this drinking follows repeated ritual use of wine in childhood and adolescence, perhaps occasional use of schnapps or other beverages, and, very likely, observation of regular schnapps drinking by the father.[53]

4. Variations in Drinking Frequencies along Religious Lines

The findings in Table 8 point to less frequent drinking by Conservative and Reform than by Orthodox and Secular students. For each type of beverage Conservative students show smaller percentages drinking more than 10 times yearly. Reform students, while perhaps drinking beer and spirits more often than the Orthodox, fall far behind the Orthodox in the use of wine. The percentage pattern of the Secular students suggests relatively frequent use of all three types of beverages.

The possibility of high frequencies of drinking at the extremes of

[51] On prevailing college patterns see Straus and Bacon (96). Accommodations of other aspects of Jewish drinking to social pressures and patterns in college and military service will be discussed in Chapter 5.

[52] Compare Table 10, below.

[53] Also to be considered in the difference in frequency of spirits drinking between more Orthodox men and students is the apparent preference for spirits among men in the business world at large, which differs from the emphasis on beer drinking in college.

TABLE 9.—*Frequency of Drinking (All Types of Beverages) among Jewish Students, by Nominal Religious Affiliation (in Per Cent)*

	One to Five Times a Year	Six to Twelve Times a Year	Two to Four Times a Month	Two or More Times a Week	Number Reporting
Orthodox	18	28	36	18	(89)
Conservative	17	37	41	5	(76)
Reform	20	33	36	11	(64)
Secular	21	20	31	28	(61)

Orthodox and Secular is given some support by the frequency data in Table 9 based on each student's estimate of his drinking during the past year, regardless of type of beverage. While the percentages at the lowest frequency are fairly constant among all four categories, Secular and Orthodox students have the highest proportions who drink two or more times a week.[54] When divided at the approximate median frequency, these data show the following percentages of students in the various nominal religious divisions who drink alcoholic beverages twice a month or more: Orthodox 54, Conservative 46, Reform 47, and Secular 59. The difference along religious lines is not statistically significant but there is a tendency toward higher frequencies of drinking at the extremes.

An analogous tendency toward high frequencies of drinking at the extremes of maximum and minimum religious participation is suggested by our data from interviews with New Haven men. When all types of beverages are combined into a single measure of frequency, Jewish men who observe the Friday Kiddush regularly have the highest mean frequency of drinking, averaging 226 times a year. Men brought up in a home where Kiddush was regularly observed but who are no longer regularly observant themselves have a mean drinking frequency of 106 times a year. Among Jewish men with no regular past or present Kiddush experience the mean frequency of drinking rises again to 146 times a year.[55]

Collectively these data suggest (*1*) that somewhat lower frequencies of drinking among Conservative and Reform students and men

[54] The proportion of Orthodox at the highest frequency of drinking (Table 9) is nonetheless below what might be expected. This probably is due to the circumstance that an Orthodox student who faithfully observes the Sabbath ceremonies could reasonably class himself in either of the two higher intervals. If he counts the Sabbath as a single drinking occasion, he might well choose the lower of these two intervals.

[55] Within each of these categories of religious observance there is a wide range of variation in drinking frequencies. For the Kiddush observant, a lower limit of drinking about once a week is set by the requirements of religious ritual. Among the others, the range is from drinking once or twice yearly to twice daily.

TABLE 10.—*Most Frequent Beverage and Drinking Companions of Jewish Students, by Nominal Religious Affiliation (in Per Cent)*

	Wine in the Family	Beer in Small Male Group	Spirits in Small Mixed Group	Other Combinations	Number Reporting
Orthodox	54	18	9	19	(71)
Conservative	19	27	16	38	(62)
Reform	13	30	28	29	(54)
Secular	8	42	19	31	(52)

of intermediate ritual experience result from declining adherence to Jewish traditions of drinking for religious purposes, and (*2*) that these same categories lag behind Secular students and the least religiously observant men in adopting new patterns of drinking. As manifestations of continuity or discontinuity in the Orthodox culture, frequencies of drinking apparently drop to some extent among Jews socialized in the traditional religious pattern who are no longer very observant, but rise again among the least observant in background and practice. That drinking frequencies are in fact relatively high among observant Orthodox Jews has significant implications for the discussion of Jewish sobriety in later chapters.

5. Variations in Beverages and Drinking Contexts along Religious Lines

While the New Haven data are more detailed, the data on Jewish students are better suited to statistical demonstration of variations in drinking patterns which correspond to changes in religious affiliation and practice. Perhaps the best way to express these variations with the available data is to consider two aspects of the drinking situation simultaneously: (*1*) the most frequently used beverage, and (*2*) the companions or social group with whom this beverage is often used. Data on these points are summarized in Table 10, where it is clear that the relative importance of wine in the family in the drinking patterns of each religious division diminishes in the order, Orthodox, Conservative, Reform and Secular.[56] By contrast, beer drinking in small groups outside the family gains steadily in importance moving through these same nominal religious divisions.[57] The percentage of students for whom spirits drinking in small mixed

[56] Chi-square for wine in the family versus all other beverages is 42.70, P is less than .001.

[57] Beer in small male groups is far more often the most frequent beverage and drinking situation for British Protestant and Irish Catholic than for Jewish students. The family is comparatively more important for the latter, even disregarding types of beverages

groups, other than family, is most important also rises through the Orthodox, Conservative and Reform categories. Among Secular students, however, drinking beer in male fellowships takes precedence over drinking spirits in small mixed groups.[58]

Seen in the perspective of nationwide college drinking, these data are especially indicative of the nature and direction of changes in Jewish drinking patterns. In the larger sample of American male college students, beer drinking in male fellowships is of foremost importance, followed by drinking spirits in mixed company and, least important, wine in the family (96). For Orthodox Jewish students the rank order of these beverages and contexts is exactly the opposite. But the ranking of these drinking contexts by Jewish students undergoes a reversal along nominal religious lines. Moving through the religious divisions from Orthodox to Secular, there is a closer and closer approximation of the general college pattern, so that Secular Jewish students actually conform to the widest statistical norms in their choices of most frequent beverage and companions. Of course, these data only show trends toward situational conformity in the drinking patterns of Jewish students and do not signify the adoption of modes of drinking which necessarily go beyond the college setting. Nevertheless, there is variation among Jewish students and a definite trend in the choice of beverages and companions. The trend is toward conformity with the most general college drinking norms and it corresponds with changes in Jewish religious affiliation and practice from Orthodox to Secular.

[58] On companions or social groups in Table 10: "Small male" refers to groups of less than 15 members composed of males other than family members; "small mixed" refers to groups of less than 15 composed of males and females other than family members. Of course there are possible types of groups other than the three shown, as the percentages for other combinations of groups and beverages suggest. However, family, small male, and mixed groups are the three most important types of drinking groups, statistically speaking. The phrase "most frequent beverage and drinking companions" in Table 10 refers to whichever of the beverages—wine, beer or spirits—a student ranked as most frequently used, and to the most frequent drinking companions or groups with that particular beverage. It is possible that social groups other than those most frequently associated with the most frequently used beverage should be more frequent drinking companions when the individual's total drinking pattern is considered. Nevertheless we believe that these measures, the only ones available, are good indicators of priorities in beverages and contexts and their variations. Moreover, our data show that if drinking contexts are considered irrespective of the particular beverage, the family declines as the most frequent context, as follows (expressed in per cent): Orthodox 54, Conservative 29, Reform 13, Secular 12. Chi-square for family versus all other contexts along religious lines is 35.57, P is less than .001.

It is pertinent also that the decline in familial wine drinking cannot be simply attributed to "going to college" or to separation from the family while in college. Prolonged separation from home may, of course, result in a temporary discontinuation of traditional Jewish drinking just as continuation of these patterns presupposes participation in family activities. But from popular impressions of Orthodox family solidarity it might be supposed that these students are less often separated from their homes than are Reform and Secular students and that the inaccessibility of the family determines the infrequent familial wine drinking of the latter. The fact is, however, that access to the family is no guarantee of the continuation of familial wine drinking. Our data show that only 54 per cent of the Orthodox students live at home, compared to 72, 58 and 60 per cent of the Conservative, Reform and Secular students, respectively.[59] Nevertheless, familial wine drinking declines in importance moving in sequence through these nominal religious divisions. Thus, the change in these drinking patterns cannot result solely from leaving home to go to college or from the impact of college experience on drinking behavior. It must be related as well to other factors affecting systematic variations along nominal religious lines in Jewish family and religious structures.

The significance of these findings on beverages and drinking contexts is, therefore, not only that changes occur in the direction of conformity with wider collegiate patterns. More important is the discovery that both the relinquishment of traditional drinking patterns and the acquisition of new patterns become more pronounced as participation in Jewish religious practices declines and affiliation changes from Orthodox, to Conservative, to Reform and Secular. Also important to the present study is the clarification and support these data give to our suggestions regarding the greater separation of drinking from core social institutions and its reemergence in less stable, segmented social groupings as religious affiliation changes and participation declines.[60]

[59] The difference in home residence along religious lines is not significant (P = .08). Further data on residence patterns are given in Snyder (90).

[60] The percentages in these data cannot, of course, be immediately applied to nominal religious groups in the Jewish population. The relations evident in these data may nonetheless aid our understanding of sociocultural factors influencing the noteworthy sobriety of Jews.

6. Amounts of Alcohol Ordinarily Consumed and Variation along Religious Lines

Since drinking pathologies among them are rare, it is to be expected that the quantities of alcohol which Jews ordinarily drink are small even though drinking is high in incidence and by no means infrequent. The ordinary use of alcohol in small amounts by many Jewish men and students has been implicit or explicit at several points in our discussion, but a closer consideration of amounts has definite values. Similarities and differences in alcohol consumption in the form of different beverages can be delineated. Comparisons can be made of this aspect of drinking in the Jewish and other groups which have not previously been made directly. And the range of variation among Jews can be determined so that related sociocultural factors may be systematically explored.

The estimation of amount of alcohol ordinarily consumed in the drinking situation presents difficulties analogous to those encountered in determining frequencies of drinking. People seldom consider the absolute alcohol content of their drinks, the tendency being to think of broad classes of beverages, such as wine, beer and spirits, whose alcohol content varies widely. As Straus and Bacon (96) observe:

> "Beer usually contains from 3 to 6 per cent alcohol by volume. The alcohol content of wines may range from around 8 per cent for some homemade varieties to 12 per cent for common commercial brands of table wines and from 18 to 20 per cent for the aperitifs (sherry, vermouth) which have been fortified by the introduction of distilled alcohol during their manufacture. Distilled spirits contain from around 30 to 50 per cent alcohol by volume."

The tendency also is to think of drinking from glasses, bottles and other containers without being cognizant of their volumes or the precise relations between volumes and amounts of absolute alcohol. Because of this situation, the only practical method of gathering comparable data must begin by letting each person express in his own way how much he usually drinks. These reports may then be translated into standardized classifications of beverage and volume in terms of quantities of absolute alcohol.

Converting reports on amounts into estimates of absolute alcohol is not difficult where detailed information is available and the kind of beverage and container are clearly fixed by custom.[61] But often such data are not available, and the translation into amounts of absolute alcohol requires some intervening assumptions. This is especially true of the reports on amounts from students in the College Drinking Survey. When asked to disregard extreme experiences and indicate the average amount of wine, beer or spirits ordinarily consumed at a sitting, students frequently answered with statements such as "three glasses" of beer, "a couple of glasses" of wine, or "two drinks" of spirits. Thus we have adopted Straus and Bacon's (96) conventions that the average wine glass contains 3.5 ounces, the average beer glass 8 ounces, and the average jigger, "shot" or drink of spirits 1.5 ounces. Additional criteria are needed, however, for distinguishing smaller and larger amounts of absolute alcohol. The basic requirement in this respect is the feasibility of reducing different types of beverages and containers to comparable units of absolute alcohol. To this end, Straus and Bacon (96) have proposed the following rules of convenience, which are also adopted here:

> "Smaller amounts would contain less than 1.4 ounces of absolute alcohol; medium amounts between 1.4 and 3 ounces; and larger amounts 3 ounces or more. Translating the terms used by the students, smaller amounts include up to 3 glasses or 2 bottles of beer, up to 2 glasses of wine, or 2 drinks containing spirits; larger amounts include more than 8 glasses or 6 bottles of beer, 6 glasses of wine or 4 drinks containing spirits."

When the amounts of alcohol which Jewish students ordinarily drink are compared with amounts consumed by British Protestant and Irish Catholic students, substantial differences appear (Table 11). Jewish students usually drink considerably less alcohol in the form of beer and spirits than students in either of the other categories.[62] With respect to wine there is little difference between the groups. This may be so because among college students in general wine drinking tends to be associated with the family social group context where controls on drinking may be strongest (96). Perhaps some of the wine drinking reported by British Protestant students is in connection with religious communion. But in any event, wine

[61] Among the Orthodox Jews, for example, schnapps is ordinarily taken "straight" in a small glass containing about an ounce and a half of the beverage, or 0.7 ounce of absolute alcohol.

[62] Chi-squares for differences by religioethnic group in amounts ordinarily consumed in beer and spirits are 216.61 and 51.01, respectively (P is less than .001 in both instances). To simplify presentation, only percentages are given in Tables 11 and 12; the numbers reporting may be found in Snyder (90).

TABLE 11.—*Amounts of Alcohol Ordinarily Consumed in Beer, Wine and Spirits by Jewish, British Protestant and Irish Catholic Students (in Per Cent)*

Amounts	Jewish	British Protestant	Irish Catholic
Beer			
Smaller	71	47	28
Medium	27	45	56
Larger	2	8	16
Spirits			
Smaller	54	41	33
Medium	27	33	39
Larger	19	26	28
Wine			
Smaller	79	80	81
Medium	20	14	18
Larger	1	6	1

drinking figures far less prominently in the drinking patterns of Irish Catholic and British Protestant students than among the Jewish students. The two most important findings in Table 11 are these: First, a majority of Jewish students drink only smaller amounts of alcohol regardless of the type of beverage, while significantly more British Protestant and Irish Catholic students drink medium and larger amounts of beer and spirits. Second, there is variation within the Jewish student group; although a majority of Jewish students usually consume smaller amounts, some ordinarily drink medium and larger amounts of alcohol.

The fact of a range in amounts consumed by Jewish students leads to the question whether or not this varies systematically with other sociocultural factors. The data in Table 12 indicate that this is, indeed, the case. Moving through the nominal religious divisions, Orthodox, Conservative, Reform and Secular, the proportion of Jewish students who ordinarily drink smaller amounts of alcohol declines for each type of beverage.[63]

It is apparent that within any particular religious division and for any particular beverage, a majority of Jewish students ordinarily drink smaller amounts of alcohol. However, the consensus among Orthodox students regarding drinking all types of beverages in

[63] Chi-square and probability values for differences by nominal religious affiliation in amounts of alcohol (smaller versus medium and larger) consumed in beer, spirits and wine, respectively, are as follows: 26.29, P less than .001; 9.26, $P = .03$; 8.20, $P = .05$.

TABLE 12.—*Amounts of Alcohol Ordinarily Consumed by Jewish Students in the Form of Beer, Spirits and Wine, by Nominal Religious Affiliation (in Per Cent)*

Amounts	Orthodox	Conservative	Reform	Secular
Beer				
Smaller	93	88	67	61
Medium	7	12	33	35
Larger	0	0	0	4
Spirits				
Smaller	77	62	57	55
Medium	15	31	31	17
Larger	8	7	12	28
Wine				
Smaller	91	86	75	75
Medium	9	13	23	23
Larger	0	1	2	2

smaller amounts is striking when viewed alongside the variability among Reform and Secular students in this respect.

New Haven Jewish men are not unlike Jewish college students in the amounts of alcohol which they ordinarily drink, although they apparently drink even more moderately. Of the sample of 73 men, 53 of the 69 who currently use spirits indicated that they ordinarily drink smaller amounts, while 70 of the 72 who use wine ordinarily drink smaller amounts. Some of the more typical comments of Jewish men in response to questions on how much wine, beer and spirits they ordinarily drink are illuminating:

Wine:

"I drink a glass of wine for Kiddush at home and for religious celebrations." [01]

"I just take a sip of Kiddush wine." [07]

"I drink a couple of glasses of wine on Passover and on other festive occasions. I like sweet ritual wine." [29]

"I drink a little cup or glass of wine for ritual purposes and for Passover occasions." [43]

"I drink six or seven ounces of wine at a time, for special occasions, Kiddush on holidays, seder, et cetera." [58]

"I drink one or two glasses of wine for ritual purposes and with the meal." [63]

"I drink one glass of wine for ceremonials with the family." [69]

Beer:

"I drink a glass of beer with a heavy meal now and then." [01]

"I drink a couple of glasses of beer when I'm with a friend or go to a dance or a night club with my wife." [04]

"I drink a bottle of beer with my meals in the summer." [09]

"I drink a can of beer at one time. Occasionally I'll have three or four glasses." [35]

"I drink a bottle of beer almost every day during July and August when it's hot." [49]

"Occasionally I have a glass of beer with a salesman." [55]

Spirits:

"I'll take a highball or a straight shot of liquor at a party. I can tolerate a shot of rye whisky." [16]

"One is enough, one little glass." [17]

"I drink a shot of whisky at one time, just a little." [20]

"I may have a highball or two, or maybe just whisky." [34]

"One drink is my limit." [36]

"I have one shot of whisky at a time, at parties or weddings." [38]

"Sometimes before dinner I have just one shot of whisky." [40]

"I may have a taste of liquor in company, but I don't care for it, just a taste." [51]

"On the holy days I drink a water glassful of wine. Of hard liquor I may take two at a time, cocktails or highballs, or a shot or two of whisky." [56]

"I have one shot of whisky before meals." [69]

In addition to the general tendency toward very moderate drinking among Jewish men, an important feature of our data is that variation from the pattern of drinking smaller amounts occurs most often among men of less ritually Orthodox background. This situation can be readily illustrated by dividing Jewish men into two categories of Orthodoxy according to the extent of their experience of ritual drinking: a "More Orthodox" category including Jewish men who either now observe the Friday evening Kiddush regularly or were brought up in homes where the Kiddush was regularly observed; and a "Less Orthodox" category including men whose parents did not observe the Kiddush ceremony regularly and who do not do so themselves. It is evident, in Table 13, that variation from the

TABLE 13.—*Amounts of Alcohol Ordinarily Consumed in the Form of Spirits by More Orthodox and Less Orthodox New Haven Jewish Men**

	Smaller Amounts	Medium or Larger Amounts
More Orthodox	38	6
Less Orthodox	14	9

Chi-square = 5.64, $P < .05$

* Two cases are excluded from the table because of insufficient information on Orthodoxy.

norm of ordinarily drinking smaller amounts of alcohol in spirits is more pronounced among the Less Orthodox men. Among users of beer, which is less important than spirits in the drinking patterns of Jewish men, all four men who ordinarily drink more than smaller amounts fall in the Less Orthodox category. Similarly, the two men in our New Haven sample who reported ordinarily using wine in more than smaller amounts are both in the Less Orthodox group.[64]

These findings clearly point to more uniform acceptance among comparatively Orthodox Jews of norms restricting the ordinary use of all types of alcoholic beverages to smaller amounts. As traditional religious observance declines and nominal affiliation changes, the norms governing amounts evidently become increasingly variable. True, many relatively secular Jews usually drink only smaller amounts of alcohol. But among the less religious the range of variation in this specific aspect of drinking appears to be related to the dissolution of a broader complex of traditional religious values and practices.

7. *Attitudes Toward Drunkenness and Drunkards and Variations along Religious Lines*

A discussion of amounts of alcohol ordinarily consumed quite naturally leads to the question of the actual extent of intoxication in the Jewish group. Before treating this behavior, however, some attention needs to be given to Jewish attitudes toward "drunkenness" and "drunkards," variations in these attitudes, and the ways in which they parallel or diverge from the common attitudes of other groups.

[64] It must be noted that for a few men, who are infrequent drinkers, Passover is the principal wine drinking occasion. Tradition calls for the drinking of the better part of four cups of wine on Passover. These men might therefore be classed as drinking medium rather than smaller amounts by the criterion given above. But in practice the Passover wine is often only partially consumed, tasted or touched to the lips. Also, the wine used is usually not fortified but a mild homemade or commercial table wine. Even when all four cups are taken in full, it is doubtful that the alcohol content exceeds 1.4 ounces. Moreover, the Passover ritual drinking is divided into two parts (before and after the meal) and can be thought of as two distinct sittings. For these reasons it seems appropriate to classify Passover drinking as drinking in smaller amounts. How the classification of Passover drinking would affect the distribution of amounts of wine ordinarily consumed by Jewish students (Table 11) is indeterminable because Passover drinking was not specified in the student questionnaire. It seems likely, however, that a few students who drink wine principally on Passover may have listed four cups (drinks or glasses) as their ordinary amount. If so, the data in Table 11 probably overestimate the proportion of Jewish students who drink medium in contrast to smaller amounts of alcohol.

There has been considerable speculation in the literature on Jewish drinking as to the content of Jewish attitudes toward drunkenness and drunkards. Different writers have ascribed different origins to these attitudes as well as different roles in accounting for the rarity of drinking pathologies. Bales (7), for instance, believes that among Orthodox Jews drunkenness is viewed with "disgust" and as an "abomination." He suggests that this attitude derives from the basic configuration of religious ideas and sentiments which underlie the ritual use of wine, and which, in his opinion, thwart the development of alcohol addiction. Immanuel Kant (48), in noting their sobriety, remarked that intoxication would be a "scandal" for Jews, and related this to the sectarian's need for caution in the face of community censure. As a further instance, Myerson (70, 71) emphasized the "hatred" of drunkards in the Jewish tradition. This he saw as particularly characteristic of the older Jews and as fundamental to the low rates of alcoholism.[65] Myerson failed to make clear, however, just why the "older" Jews should have such strong feelings on the matter. He commented that among the younger generation of Jews these attitudes are weakening as a consequence of acculturation, and in a gross sense this is descriptively true. But as will be shown hereinafter, there are younger Jews who probably censure drunkenness and drunkards as strongly as the older generation to whom Myerson referred.

Glad (31) is one of the few students of Jewish drinking who has presented evidence on Jewish attitudes toward drunkenness, the only others being Straus and Bacon (96). By comparing samples of Jewish, Irish Catholic and Protestant adolescents Glad showed both the prevalence of moral censure of drunkenness among the Jews and greater censure than among the Irish Catholics. In interpreting his

[65] For singling out "hatred" of the alcoholic to account for the rareness of alcoholism, Myerson has been properly criticized by Bales (7) on the grounds that the negative sanctions stemming from such an attitude neither cure nor prevent the disease. Moreover, in instances of alcoholism among Jews which have come to our attention, families—even communities—rallied to support rather than ostracize the individuals concerned, albeit with great emotional ambivalence. But when Myerson speaks of the attitude toward drunkards as a factor in Jewish sobriety we believe he is correct with these provisos. To be relevant, hatred of the drunkard cannot be insulated from other attitudes and focused in its social expression on the obviously incipient or confirmed alcohol addict. Rather, this attitude must reflect, reinforce and be integral with a wider nexus of attitudes regulating individual behavior in the drinking situation itself. These distinctions are considered more fully in Chapter 5, where attitudes toward drunkenness and drunkards are discussed in relation to the broader network of Jewish religious ideas and sentiments.

findings Glad minimized these attitudes as factors in the low Jewish rates of inebriety. The implications of his discussion are somewhat contradictory and involved and need not be dealt with here.[66] For the present purpose, the important feature of Glad's study is not his interpretation but his findings that Jewish adolescents quite regularly condemned drunkenness.

The impressions of Immanuel Kant, Myerson and Bales, and the findings of Glad as to the general content of Jewish attitudes toward drunkenness and drunkards, are consistent with attitudes expressed by many New Haven Jewish men. Moral condemnation of drunkenness and drunkards was not given in response to a particular question or set of direct questions in our interviews. Rather, it was explicit at one point or another in many of the interviews and implicit in most of them. Now and again the basically censorious attitude toward the drunkard came into conflict with rational concepts of a "sick person" or a person with "emotional problems." But many Jewish men who at one moment speak of the drunkard as a medical or psychiatric problem will at another moment say there is absolutely no excuse for anyone being a drunkard. In a similar vein, when asked how much others should drink, Jewish men will often say that they can drink as much as they want to, only to add later that "every man should know his limit and I never take more than two drinks." In answer to objective questions on the drinker, drunkenness and other topics, value-toned answers were often given which were not solicited by our questions. The following excerpts are illustrative:

"[On responsibility of a person who sometimes gets drunk] I can't see any reason for anybody ever to get drunk. It is degrading to a person. I wouldn't trust a man who gets drunk. He's not responsible." [1]

"[About a drinker, interpreted as an excessive drinker] If I see him drunk enough, it disgusts me. They never know when to stop. On New Years's Eve there's always someone who makes a pig of himself." [6]

"[Discussing a drunkard] A disgusting, pathetic person who is missing out on enjoying life." [12]

"[Defining drunkenness] Pigs have more intelligence than drunken human beings. It's the most disgusting thing you can see. [On the person who gets drunk occasionally] I would say that a fellow that gets drunk can't be trusted." [18]

"[Asked to describe someone who was drunk] I think it's awful, I can tell by his way of talking. I wouldn't want anyone to see me like that. I think it's terrible." [38]

[66] These are given fairly extensive consideration in Snyder (90).

"[When asked whether Jews should drink less than Gentiles] It's a matter of individual taste. But you have a racial pride and don't like to see your people like that." [39]

"[On drunkenness] Even in the old country [Poland] I saw people intoxicated on the streets; it was rotten. I didn't even like the smell of whisky. I hated it when I was a kid and I hate it now." [64]

"[On the drunkard] I have very little sympathy for a drinker. To me a drinker is a coward. He's trying to find the easiest way out of his troubles. I really don't think there's any excuse for a man to be an habitual drunk no matter what the circumstances." [66]

"[On Jewish and Gentile drinking] A Jew who is a drunkard should never have been born. [Asked to describe someone who is drunk] It means he is good-for-nothing. I didn't have to be taught [about the consequences of excessive drinking]. I could see for myself that the Gentiles frequently drink in excess and start fighting and beating each other. [Asked whether he would consider a man who got drunk occasionally to be responsible] No, he can't be responsible. You can't talk to him. He has no understanding." [71]

Pigs, degenerates, obscene, disgusting, rotten—the nouns and adjectives chosen by these Jewish men to describe drunkards and drunkenness leave little to the imagination in regard to their attitudes. Bales' term "abomination" would seem to summarize the matter aptly. Also to be observed in some of these excerpts is the linkage of sobriety with Jewishness and "racial pride."

It is a startling fact, however, that Straus and Bacon (96) discovered virtually no differences between the attitudes of Jewish and non-Jewish students toward drunkenness in other men. In their questionnaire, Straus and Bacon asked the students to indicate their strongest reaction to drunkenness in other men on a check list composed of 10 items: indifference, tolerance, pity, desire to help, disgust, intolerance, scorn, loss of respect, amusement, and fear. Generalizing their findings on these attitudes by students of different religions, Straus and Bacon comment: "No marked differences in attitude toward drunkenness in men appear among Catholic, Jewish, and Protestant men. Mormons, however, as compared with the other three, are significantly less tolerant . . ."

This conclusion, as it applies to Jews, warrants careful scrutiny. Straus and Bacon apparently based this particular conclusion on a 10-per-cent sample of all students included in the College Drinking Survey. To check their findings in this respect, we compared the reactions to drunkenness of all 644 Jewish students in the Survey with the reactions of all male students, and found negligible differ-

TABLE 14.—*Reactions of Students to Drunkenness in Other Men, by Nominal Religious Affiliation*

	Disgust, Intolerance, Scorn, Loss of Respect		Tolerance or Indifference	
	Per Cent	*Number*	*Per Cent*	*Number*
Orthodox Jewish	49	(44)	16	(14)
Conservative Jewish	48	(40)	31	(26)
Mormon*	47		21	
Reform Jewish	46	(29)	24	(15)
Protestant*	39		36	
Catholic*	34		36	
Secular Jewish	29	(18)	39	(24)

*From Straus and Bacon (96).

ences.[67] In short, it would appear that in their attitudes toward drunkenness in other men, Jewish students are hardly distinguishable from other students.

When the Jewish students are divided by nominal religious affiliation, however, the picture of their attitudes toward drunkenness changes radically. In Table 14, attitudes are grouped, following Straus and Bacon, into categories of tolerance versus disapproval or rejection, and data on students in other religious groups are included for purposes of comparison. It is clear from these data that proportionately more Orthodox Jewish students express disapproval and intolerance of drunkenness in other men than any of the religious categories shown. At the opposite end of the scale, Secular Jewish students most often express tolerance and least often outright disapproval. In regard to both tolerance and disapproval, Orthodox Jewish students appear to be most like the Mormons, who are significantly less tolerant than Protestants or Catholics. Considering disapproval only, there is an orderly percentage decline among the Jewish students through the nominal religious divisions, Orthodox, Conservative, Reform and Secular, although the first three categories are quite similar.[68] The percentages showing tolerance increase from Orthodox to Conservative to Secular, but fewer Reform than Conservative Jewish students express tolerance or indifference toward drunkenness in other men.

To some extent, however, the similarities in percentages disapproving drunkenness among Orthodox, Conservative and Reform

[67] The data are presented fully in Snyder (90).

[68] The orderly difference is important, but as between any two of these first three categories the differences are not significant.

Jewish students, as well as the lesser tolerance of Reform than Conservative students, are artifacts of classification. The classification devised by Straus and Bacon and used in Table 14 fails to exhaust the list of attitudes in the student questionnaire and a substantial proportion of the attitudes held by Jewish students. For instance, pity and amusement are the strongest expressed reactions to drunkenness of about a fourth of all Jewish students. To encompass Jewish attitudes more fully and to exploit differences along nominal religious lines, addition and reclassification are needed, even at some risk of ambiguity.

Of the two important reactions, pity and amusement, which were omitted from Straus and Bacon's tolerance and disapproval classification, pity has, we believe, more often than not, connotations of moral censure. Pity, according to Webster's New International Dictionary, "sometimes regards its object as not only suffering, but weak and inferior," while the Oxford Dictionary regards pity as "sometimes implying slight contempt for a person on account of some moral or intellectual inferiority . . ." By contrast, amusement suggests a less censorious, mildly approving attitude. Amusement may contain an element of aggression and sometimes merges with scorn and ridicule. But given the choices of attitudes in the original list, it is doubtful that students with definitely disapproving attitudes would indicate amusement as their strongest reaction to drunkenness. Desire to help, however, is certainly an ambiguous category. Students expressing this attitude may be motivated by abstract concerns of welfare, genuine personal concern, or guilt feelings compensating for an underlying contempt of the drunken person. As for fear, which was checked by less than 1 per cent of Jewish students, we suspect, on the basis of New Haven interviews, an association with strong moral censure. In reclassifying the attitudes, then, pity and fear were included with the disapproving attitudes, amusement with tolerance and indifference, while desire to help has been classed with "unknown."

Using this modified classification, the attitudes of Jewish students toward drunkenness in other men are shown in Table 15. With these slight classificatory changes, the differentiation along nominal religious lines becomes more pronounced. The decline in attitudes of disapproval is retained and sharpened, while the attitudes of relative tolerance show a systematic increase moving through the nominal religious divisions, Orthodox, Conservative, Reform and Secular.

TABLE 15.—*Reaction of Jewish Students, by Nominal Religious Affiliation, to Drunkenness in Other Men (in Per Cent)*

	Disgust, Intolerance, Scorn, Loss of Respect, Pity, Fear	Tolerance, Indifference, Amusement	Number Reporting
Orthodox	76	24	(75)
Conservative	59	41	(76)
Reform	55	45	(56)
Secular	44	56	(52)

Chi-square = 13.94, P < .05

In view of these findings and the differences in religious participation among these categories, strong and uniform moral condemnation of drunkenness by Jews would appear to be intimately bound up with their identification with and participation in the traditions of Orthodox Judaism.

The burden of the evidence from the sample of New Haven men and the nationwide sample of college students is that attitudes strongly censuring drunkenness and drunkards are common in the Jewish group. More important, however, is the indication that these attitudes are most prevalent among the more Orthodox and religiously observant Jews. Insofar as these attitudes represent projections of ideas and feelings about the self, the more Orthodox must quite consistently feel great anxiety about drinking to the point of intoxication. Externalized as social expectancies and sanctions, these attitudes undoubtedly help to create an atmosphere favoring moderate drinking and sobriety. That Myerson was descriptively correct in associating these attitudes primarily with older generation Jews seems reasonable. But this is not because of age or generation differences per se. Where religious Orthodoxy prevails among younger Jews, strong censure of drunkards and drunkenness will also be found. Further discussion and related evidence on the latter topic will be presented in later chapters.

8. *Definition, Incidence and Frequency of Intoxication*

The extent of intoxication remains as the final aspect of Jewish drinking patterns for consideration in the present chapter. Intoxication among Jews has been the subject for much, often contradictory, speculation, for there is no real agreement regarding its incidence, frequency and distribution in the group. The reason for the confusion is not difficult to find: with the partial exception of Straus and

Bacon's report, there are no systematic studies of intoxication among Jews.[69] Statistics on more extreme drinking pathologies have often led to the conclusion that intoxication is rare, but a tenuous chain of inferences links these data to propositions about intoxication and its control among Jews. A knowledge of the actual extent of intoxication seems essential before speculating further about Jewish sobriety. With the facts in hand we may begin to theorize more confidently about the bases of sobriety, intoxication and drinking pathologies. To present our findings on intoxication among Jews unambiguously, it is necessary to dwell first on a few points of method involving problems of definition.[70]

Behind the task of estimating the extent of intoxication from respondents' reports lies the problem of defining this behavior so as to permit classification, comparison and analysis. It is a poor procedure to ask "How many times have you been drunk?" if by drunk the interviewer means being on the verge of unconsciousness, while the respondent refers to the "stimulation" experienced after a third drink of schnapps. A common basis for understanding is required if behavior is to be classified and compared. The New Haven Jewish men were therefore asked in the interviews for their own definitions of three terms widely used to designate degrees of intoxication: high, tight and drunk. Their definitions of these terms, or such others as they chose to substitute, and their reports of behavior were then translated into standard classifications from the College Drinking Survey. High, tight and drunk were defined in the College Drinking Survey as follows:

"*High* would indicate a noticeable effect without going beyond socially acceptable behavior, e.g., increased gayness, a slight fuzziness of perception, drowsiness and the like.

"*Tight* would suggest an over-stepping of social expectancies, or noticeable aggressiveness, or oversolicitousness, or loss of control of social amenities or of verbal accuracy, or slight nausea.

"*Drunk* would suggest an over-stepping of social expectancies, loss of

[69] Straus and Bacon (96) present data on the incidence of intoxication among students of Jewish and other religions. Some attention has been given to gross differences in frequencies. The problem has been reviewed in Chapter 1.

[70] Selective recall and biases influencing these findings are discussed in Snyder (90). In the same work, procedures used to circumvent these factors are outlined and their success is evaluated by checks for internal consistency in respondents' reports.

control in ordinary physical activities, and inability to respond to the reactions of others."[71]

What, if anything, did high, tight and drunk mean to the 73 Jewish men in our New Haven sample? Everyone used the word "drunk" and there was fair agreement as to its meaning. Some Jewish men referred to behavior as "drunk" which we would classify as tight, but the same men also labeled as "drunk" behavior which is such by our definition. However, 30 of the Jewish men said that they had "never heard of," or were "not familiar with" or "never used" the word "tight"; and 15 made similar statements about both "high" and "tight." Twenty-three respondents who were familiar with these terms differed with the standard definitions as to their meanings; some used "tight" for the extreme forms of intoxication, which we would call drunkenness; others considered "high" to be more extreme than "tight"; still others considered the three terms to be synonymous. Only 18 of the 73 Jewish men interviewed used high, tight and drunk with meanings equivalent to the definitions given above. These findings clearly testify to the need for definition prior to classification and analysis of reports on intoxication.

Apparently there is a broader significance to the rather common lack of familiarity with or use of conventional terms for intoxication among the Jewish men. Most of the men who did not use either tight or high were relatively Orthodox in religious practice or background. A few of these men were not especially fluent in English, and this may bear on the paucity of terms for intoxication. But only two interviews in this study were conducted in Yiddish; the other respondents were sufficiently conversant with English to complete interviews lasting 2 to 3 hours. Moreover, in Yiddish there are no special terms for different stages of intoxication. For virtually all purposes, the one term *shikker* (from the Hebrew *shikur*, meaning drunkard or drunk, as noun or adjective) appears to be sufficient. Thus the idea of a language barrier seems inadequate to account for the sparse use of terms for intoxication. Rather, fine discriminations about intoxication were unnecessary, even inadmissible, to many Jewish men. As one man remarked when queried about the term tight:

> "I don't use it. I heard it, but I don't use it. My only word is drunk. Either he's sober or drunk." [32]

[71] These definitions were included in the Survey questionnaire after pretesting for currency of use and meaning among college students.

This remark exemplifies a tendency to dichotomize sobriety and intoxication which is prevalent among these men. A sharp division between these two states is based on a consideration of whether or not the individual is definitely "in control of himself," mentally and physically, and behaving in accord with social conventions which apply irrespective of drinking. Evidently this dichotomy is a part of traditional cultural concepts of drinking, and is linked both with the sparsity of terms and very limited experience of intoxication.[72]

A clear distinction between tight and drunk could not always be maintained in translating Jewish men's reports of their own experiences into standard classifications. This partly reflects the fact that the more extreme instances of intoxication were often of the "once in a lifetime" variety; consequently many men had a few or no reference points for subjectively scaling their severity. There was a tendency among the New Haven men to designate these episodes as "drunk," even though a careful behavioral description (which could not always be obtained) would lead us to classify some of these episodes as tight. Because of this situation, tight and drunk are combined into a single category of intoxication for the New Haven men.

This poses the further question of whether these latter behaviors could be reasonably distinguished from the mild reactions to alcohol designated by high in the standard definitions. Our affirmative answer to this question stems from the point brought out above, namely, that in spite of confusion in terms, many Jewish men sharply distinguish the state of intoxication when the individual shows signs of being "out of control." As inspection of the above definitions will show, this cultural criterion is essentially the criterion by which tight and drunk are distinguished from high in the standard classification. It seems reasonable to assume, then, that many, if not most, men made sufficient distinctions between the more extreme reactions to alcohol and the mild ones classified as high. On

[72] More detailed evidence is presented in Snyder (90). The general significance of the lack of terms may be pointed up, however, by considering a radically contrasting case. In describing the Aymara of Bolivia, La Barre (57) comments: "The old Jesuit father Bertonio gives in the second volume of his vocabulary between two and three pages of terms for drinking and for the minutely discriminated stages of Aymara drunkenness, so it is evident that the modern natives come by their drinking habits quite normally. . . . All travellers have remarked on the quantities of alcohol the Aymara can consume, and the states of intoxication to which they can attain, and I can only confirm that I have never anywhere seen American Indians more thoroughly intoxicated than at the usual Aymara fiesta."

the other hand, much behavior which could hardly be considered intoxication was perforce classified as high because of the propensity of many of the men to describe their slightest reactions to the smallest amounts of alcohol. Among persons who drink as frequently as these Jewish men, "noticeable effects"—e.g., a sensation of warmth in the stomach or momentary dizziness—are bound to occur even if drinking is strictly limited. Moreover, in a few instances some men obviously confused the atmosphere of festive occasions, which customarily call for "high spirits," with specific reactions to the drinking of alcoholic beverages. In these circumstances it seemed advisable to include all sorts of miscellany in the "high" classification and tabulate them accordingly. To have included them in an index of intoxication would have been a dubious procedure.

On the basis of these considerations, high has been excluded as a measure of intoxication for the New Haven Jewish men. The mild reactions to drinking subsumed by this classification are presented below, but intoxication, as used hereinafter, refers to behavior which has been designated and defined above as tight and drunk only.

These findings and considerations concerning the New Haven men bear on the definition and measures of intoxication which are used for the Jewish students in the present study. High, tight and drunk were, of course, included in the College Survey questionnaire on which the Jewish students classified and reported their own intoxication experience according to the definitions of these terms given above. However, only tight and drunk are used as indices of intoxication for Jewish and other students. These might preferably have been combined into a single index for the students as for the New Haven Jewish men, but the student reports on these behaviors were classified and coded in intervals of different sizes and increasing magnitudes which prohibit this. Thus, data on tight and drunk among Jewish and other college students will be presented separately. This is done with the recognition that in all probability Jewish students often failed to make precise distinctions between these stages of intoxication.

The incidence and frequencies of intoxication and mild reactions to drinking among the New Haven Jewish men are shown in Table 16. In view of the high incidence and frequency of drinking, the mere fact that nearly half of these men (44 per cent) have never been intoxicated is striking.

It would be fortunate if these findings could be directly compared with the incidence and frequency of intoxication among men in

TABLE 16.—*Frequencies of Intoxication and Mild Reactions to Alcoholic Beverages among New Haven Jewish Men*

Frequency (lifetime)	Intoxication (Drunk and Tight)	Mild Reactions* (High)
Never	32	26
1–5	24	15
6–10	5	9
11–20	5	2
21–35	4	8
36–50	2	3
Over 50	1	3

* Seven men are excluded from consideration: five known to have been high, but frequency indeterminate; two unknown.

other religioethnic groups, but data are not available for this purpose.[73] However, data on arrests involving "drunkenness" and being "under the influence" of alcohol, recently reported by Skolnick (89), are suggestive of the comparative status of New Haven Jewish men in this connection. These data are especially pertinent because they are based on all charges arising from arrests in New Haven during January and July 1951, the year in which our New Haven interviews were begun. Among the eight ethnic groups considered by Skolnick, the Jewish group contributed the least number of arrests for inebriety. The Jews also had the lowest ratio of observed to expected arrests for inebriety.[74] Finally, the Jewish group ranks about in the middle in arrests for other causes, indicating that group differentials in liability to arrest are not responsible for their infrequent arrest on charges of inebriety. Together, these findings point to relatively little intoxication among Jewish men in New Haven during the period of our research.

More direct and decisive evidence of the infrequency of intoxication among Jews is to be found through comparison of Jewish with other groups of college students. While contrasts with specific groups will be made in later chapters, the patterns of incidence and frequency for tight and drunk behavior among Jewish and all students included in the College Drinking Survey are shown in Table

[73] An exception is the information on intoxication among Italians being gathered by G. Lolli, G. G. Golder and their associates in research in progress at the Yale Center of Alcohol Studies.

[74] Expected arrests were determined according to the proportionate representation of various ethnic groups in the New Haven population as described by Hollingshead (42).

TABLE 17.—*Lifetime Frequencies of Intoxication among Jewish and All Male College Students*

	Jewish Students		All Male Students*
	Per Cent	*Number*	*Per Cent*
Drunk			
Never	55	(281)	38
1–5	34	(174)	40
6–10	4	(21)	8
11–20	3	(14)	5
Over 20	2	(11)	4
Undetermined	2	(9)	4
Tight			
Never	33	(182)	20
1–5	31	(171)	25
6–15	16	(86)	18
16–50	11	(59)	17
51–100	2	(12)	5
100 or more	1	(8)	4
Undetermined	5	(29)	11

* From Straus and Bacon (96).

17. It is clear from these data that Jewish student drinkers are consistently below the majority in incidence and in proportions at various frequencies of intoxication.

Seen in different perspective, these findings on intoxication among Jewish men and college students contradict assertions that Jews never get drunk, as well as mystical notions that Jews are somehow impervious to the ordinary effects of drinking large amounts of alcoholic beverages. The range of variation in intoxication within the group is too broad to sustain any such notions. In fact the important contribution of these data is not simply confirmation of the impression that Jews are on the whole a sober people. Of greater importance for our research purpose is the establishment of a range of variation in intoxication among Jews. This range provides the essential points of contrast against which sociocultural factors influencing Jewish sobriety may be systematically explored in forthcoming chapters.

Chapter 3

CEREMONIAL ORTHODOXY

DIFFERENCES along religious lines have been shown in Chapter 2 to influence Jewish drinking patterns significantly. It is thus obviously relevant to explore the role of ceremonial Orthodoxy in structuring and vitalizing in the personality those attitudes toward drinking which thwart the development of drinking pathologies.[1] This possibility was originally stressed by Bales (6, 7), who, in contrast to most other investigators, gives priority to the integration of drinking in religious forms, and to underlying religious ideas and sentiments, in accounting for Jewish sobriety. Substantiation of this view would dispose of a variety of alternative speculations or at least highlight the need to reassess their significance. Moreover, quite definite inferences as to the sociocultural sources of differences among Jews in intoxication and drinking pathologies can be drawn from Bales' ideas, while other hypotheses are either ambiguous or offer no logical grounds for anticipating differences in these respects.[2]

The general validity or sensitizing value of Bales' ideas may be thought of in the present context as hinging on the empirical confirmation or negation of one implication in particular. This is the implication of a change in Jewish responses to drinking alcoholic beverages corresponding to the relative decline of ceremonial Orthodoxy in America. Theoretically, diminished adherence to the Orthodox religion should be accompanied by a weakening of those highly controlling attitudes on drinking which are presumably crystallized

[1] "Ceremonial Orthodoxy" refers to the entire body of ritual and ceremonial observances of traditional normative Judaism, most completely exemplified at present in the lives of certain nominally Orthodox Jews. (Restricted operational meanings are given where appropriate.) In speaking of "Jewish sobriety," there is no intention of suggesting either that sobriety is uniquely Jewish or that there is a special kind of Jewish sobriety. These phrases are used to avoid more cumbersome expressions.

[2] Hereinafter our reference to Bales' study is to his original work (7). In referring more generally to Bales' views it is recognized that these directly presuppose the ideas of others, notably Cheinisse (18). Certainly the value of different theories concerning Jewish sobriety is contingent upon their ability to encompass the fact that all Jews are not equally sober. The conditions for sobriety which a satisfactory explanation supposes must be absent or modified where intoxication occurs most frequently.

in the personality through religious participation, and should facilitate their replacement by other attitudes. While we have shown differences in other aspects of drinking, the question remains whether or not the modification or abandonment of the religious traditions is in fact accompanied by increases in intoxication and the more extreme drinking pathologies. Before presenting evidence which bears directly on this problem, it is pertinent to examine more closely than hitherto the factual foundations for Bales' claim of relative sobriety among Orthodox Jews, as well as the basis for contrary assertions in the recent literature.

Conflicting Observations

At the outset of his study, Bales suggested that an increased incidence of intoxication among Jews and a convergence of the Jewish alcoholism rate with the American norm would occur as "assimilation" proceeds and Orthodoxy declines. Actually, he presented no evidence for these changes apart from the clinical impressions of Fishberg, Bernheimer and Myerson, together with a few statistics from Malzberg. The relevant data from Malzberg are these:

> "Though the general level of alcoholic addiction is still fortunately very low among Jews, we can see some premonitory statistical signs of the change. In 1920 there were no Jewish admissions with alcoholic psychoses to the New York civil State hospitals. In 1930 there were 4 such admissions, representing 0.4 per cent of all Jewish first admissions. In 1940 there were 11 cases, or 0.7 per cent. These are still at a very low level, but they point to a definite change."[3]

These statistics and judgments, plus a few case histories pointing to the deviance of Jewish alcoholics from the Orthodox religion, constitute the evidence bearing on this crucial point.[4] While it is reasonable to infer from these data that increases both in intoxication and in rates of alcoholism are related to the relative dissolution of Orthodox religious practices, there is no direct evidence that this is so, and other inferences are possible.

[3] Cited by Bales (7) from a lecture by Benjamin Malzberg, "Statistics of Alcoholic Mental Disease," Summer School of Alcohol Studies, Yale University, July 1943.

[4] Indeed, Bales did not use data on changes accompanying the decline of religious Orthodoxy to check the implications of his views. Instead, he used these rather sketchy data as a rationale for restricting his study to Orthodox Jews—first-generation immigrants from Eastern Europe of lower class status in America—for purposes of comparison with Irish of equivalent status and in preference to treating the nominally Jewish group as a whole, or different types of Jews within the nominal group.

The assumption of differences between religiously Orthodox and non-Orthodox Jews, as noted previously, was definitely disputed by Glad (31). In proposing his "instrumental drinking" hypothesis to account for the low Jewish "rates of inebriety," Glad was at pains to show that low rates apply to Jews in general, not to any particular classes or groups of Jews, and regardless of religious Orthodoxy. To support this position Glad drew inferences from nine European and American studies which merit somewhat fuller consideration here than was given in Chapter 1. We stated there that the statistics are too crude to provide an adequate basis for determining the connection between Orthodox religious practices and the notable sobriety of Jews. Glad's controversy with Bales, however, is important not only because of the differing implications regarding the role of Orthodoxy and the possible consequences of changing Jewish religious practices for intoxication and drinking pathologies. It is important also because the rather impressive list of studies cited by Glad has led later writers to accept uncritically his assertion of no difference between rates of inebriety among Orthodox and non-Orthodox Jews.[5] There is, consequently, a double need to clarify the factual background of Glad's reasoning.

One of the principal grounds for the assertion of no differences among particular groups or classes of Jews is the finding of rather similar low rates of inebriety among Jews in countries where, Glad assumed, " 'there are hardly any Orthodox Jews . . . '. "[6] He reasoned, for instance, from studies made in Germany at the turn of the century and in Poland in the late 1920's, that "Jews, regardless of Orthodoxy, are not likely to be found in classifications of inebriety." Two closely related points must be kept in mind in evaluating this conclusion. On the one hand, in none of the studies to which Glad refers is there a definite measure of the extent of traditional Jewish religious practice or its impact on the populations considered. On the other hand, there is good reason for holding that there were substantial Orthodox Jewish elements in these populations. That

[5] For example, Thorner (101) at one point comments on little or no difference between Orthodox and non-Orthodox Jews, and cites Glad in support. Also, in discussing the breakdown of the traditional Jewish religious community, Glazer (32), apparently on the basis of Glad's citations, would have us believe that ". . . Jewish suicide rates began to leap upward at the beginning of the 20th century: indeed Jews of pre-Hitler Germany had some of the highest suicide rates ever recorded for any group. But at the same time, as we have seen, Jews did not show any greater propensity for drunkenness and its consequences."

[6] The quotation is from a personal communication from E. M. Jellinek to Glad.

the statistics cited by Glad may well have been based on Jewish populations including sizable observant Orthodox elements is suggested by the following considerations. Glad cites three German studies showing low rates of inebriety among Jews in support of his position: Sichel (88), reporting in 1908 for the years 1897 to 1905; Guttman (37), reporting in 1909, and Rüden (81) in 1903. All of these studies were made at the peak of Jewish immigration from eastern Europe into Germany. As Lestschinsky has noted: " . . . the peak was reached in the first years of the 20th century—there was little emigration *from* Germany but considerable migration *into* Germany by Polish and Russian Jews."[7] Since eastern Europe was the stronghold of Jewish Orthodoxy, there was evidently a steady influx of traditionally religious Jews to buttress the declining German Orthodox population at precisely the time when these studies were made.[8] Glad also cites Becker's (9) study for the year 1929 showing few Jewish "alcoholic admissions" to psychiatric institutions in Poland, but Poland was a great center of Jewish Orthodoxy even as late as 1929. Glad refers to two other European studies mentioned by Jellinek in a personal communication—by Pohlisch in 1938 and Schatsky in 1937—with no further identification. Bibliographic search yielded this statement from Pohlisch (76): "The rarity of alcoholism among Jews of various countries has been a striking observation for a long time and, insofar as Poland is concerned, has also been demonstrated by statistics."[9] Beyond this observation Pohlisch offers nothing in the way of evidence on Jewish rates. The work of Schatsky in this field could not be found, but perhaps the intended reference was to Schottky (84), who in 1937 summarized some of the early studies showing differences between Jews and non-Jews in drinking pathologies. Schottky, however, presented no new material. With respect to France, Cheinisse's study apparently contradicts Glad's assumption of no differences among Jews.[10] With

[7] J. Lestschinsky, "Jewish migrations, 1840–1946," in Finkelstein (26).

[8] Religious and other cultural differences between the Jews of eastern and western Europe are briefly discussed and documented in Chapter 4.

[9] Translation mine.

[10] Cheinisse (18) emphasized the cohesion of the traditional, religious community (presupposed by Bales) as the important element in Jewish sobriety. He wrote, in part, "Judaism has in general conserved up to the present time this characteristic of collective and social ties which the other churches have lost little by little, and it is precisely this force of cohesion and concentration of the religious community which has kept the great Jewish mass from alcoholism. But wherever the traditional tie is weakened, one immediately sees the alcoholic contagion open a fissure and penetrate this milieu which previously appeared absolutely refractory." Supporting evidence

regard to the United States, Glad acknowledges that Hyde and Chisholm, as well as Faris and Dunham, "suggest that their statistics [showing low Jewish rates of inebriety] refer particularly to Russian Jews." These studies, therefore, suggest underlying differences along lines of religious observance, as well as the obvious difference between American Jews of eastern and western European origin. But instead of bringing out this possibility, Glad turns to Malzberg's findings on alcoholic psychoses in New York City. These, says Glad, "took socioeconomic status into account by including data from public as well as private hospitals," and he evidently interprets Malzberg's restricted findings of no obvious socioeconomic differences as supporting his assumption of no differences among Jews. In the work to which Glad refers, however, Malzberg (66) gives his own opinion of Jewish "antipathy to alcoholic indulgence" as follows: "In eastern Europe intemperance is rare among Jews as a result of the influences of their religious and family structures. In the western world, where life is more secularized, the Jewish attitude toward alcohol is beginning to resemble that of other people."

Thus, careful consideration of the many studies cited by Glad to support his idea of no differences in rates of inebriety among Jews shows that these by no means rule out differences along religious lines. On the contrary, they can easily be reinterpreted to support the view that Jewish sobriety is related to religious Orthodoxy. The most that can be said with assurance is that different interpretations are possible, as in the case of the data cited by Bales. As we suggested previously, the most effective means of beginning to resolve the dilemmas posed by competing hypotheses and inconclusive findings is the direct study of the relations among different Jewish patterns of religious affiliation and practice, sobriety, intoxication and drinking pathologies. For this purpose, in this and succeeding chapters, the range of variation in intoxication among Jews is used as the initial variable against which to test associations with religious and

cited by Cheinisse for these ideas is as follows: "According to M. Zadoc-Kahn the Jewish population of the Rothschild hospital can be divided into two classes: 1. the more numerous, consisting of recent immigrants to Paris, having arrived in the majority from Russia or other Slavic countries; 2. the less numerous, which comprises the Jews established in Paris for at least five years. The first category does not furnish, so to speak, a single alcoholic, not one patient presenting signs of mild or severe intoxication. It is otherwise with the second category, where the alcoholic contagion has already opened a small fissure." (Translation mine.)

other factors, in preference to using rates of alcoholism or other extreme drinking pathologies. However, since intoxication cannot be equated indiscriminately with more extreme drinking pathologies, some measures of the latter are given special attention in Chapter 6.

Evidence on Orthodoxy and Sobriety

1. New Haven Jewish Men

The main question of fact is whether or not the implications of Bales' views can account for the established range of variation in intoxication within the nominal Jewish group. As an initial test, lifetime frequencies of intoxication among Jewish men in our New Haven sample were related to a key aspect of participation in the Orthodox ceremonial pattern. In classifying men according to ceremonial Orthodoxy, we used the respondents' reports of their own and their parents' participation in the Kiddush ceremony—the Friday ritual of sanctification and wine drinking which inaugurates the Sabbath. The data permit the construction of a series of types based on the extent of ritual drinking both in childhood and in current practice. Of the 4 logically possible types, 3 describe all but 3 of our 73 cases. The first of these types is the "Most Orthodox," composed of Kiddush-observing men whose parents were also observant. The second, and most frequent, is an "Intermediate" type, consisting of those respondents who no longer observe the Kiddush ritual, although it was regularly observed in their parental homes. In the third and "Least Orthodox" type, ranking second in frequency, the weekly Kiddush was observed by neither the respondents nor their parents. When these types, ranging from greater to lesser experience of ceremonial drinking, are plotted against lifetime frequencies of intoxication, the pattern of the data clearly supports the view that ceremonial Orthodoxy is associated with sobriety (Table 18).[11] The evident relationship is made even more striking by the fact that the ritually observant men in our sample have markedly higher frequencies of drinking than men in either of the

[11] Two men with no history of intoxication are ambiguous with respect to ceremony and have been omitted from Table 1. These latter are also omitted from subsequent tables in which ceremonial Orthodoxy, as here defined, is considered. One Kiddush-observing man whose background is uncertain has been classed with the Most Orthodox. The dividing criterion for intoxication used in Table 18 is the approximate mean frequency of intoxication for the sample. This criterion is used throughout in presenting data on intoxication for New Haven Jewish men.

TABLE 18.—*Intoxication Experience of New Haven Jewish Men, By Degree of Ceremonial Orthodoxy*

	Five Times or Less	More Than Five Times
Most Orthodox	13	1
Intermediate	29	5
Least Orthodox	12	11
	Chi-square = 9.9, P = .008	

other two categories.[12] This fact, together with the data in Table 18, is consistent with Bales' paradoxical contention that drinking may serve as a barrier to drinking pathologies, provided it is drinking of a very special kind.

Much of the current drinking by Jewish men is nonetheless of a secular rather than of a sacred ceremonial character. For given individuals, fairly extensive business or other drinking may alternate with occasional ritual drinking; their drinking may be largely of a secular character or it may be confined to vestiges of the Orthodox ritual. And the varieties of current drinking are hardly exhausted by the above classification.[13] In this connection, it is worthy of note that only 3 of the 23 men who gave evidence of a preponderance of ritual drinking in their current patterns have been intoxicated more than 5 times in their lives. This is consistent with Bales' assumption concerning the significance of continued solidarity or community of feeling with members of the religious community in sustaining sobriety.[14] It is pertinent to ask, however, whether those men who currently exhibit preponderantly secular drinking patterns are differentiated in degree of sobriety according to early experience of ceremonial drinking. The assumption behind this question is that Jewish sobriety cannot be conceived of solely in terms of the sup-

[12] As was previously shown (Chapter 2), the Most Orthodox men drink alcoholic beverages an average of 226 times a year, Intermediate men 106 times, and the Least Orthodox 146 times.

[13] For instance, the fact that a man fails to observe the Kiddush ceremony regularly (or even that his parents never did) is no sure sign of the importance of ceremonial compared to other modes of drinking in his particular pattern. The Friday evening Kiddush is not the only Jewish ritual drinking occasion. Moreover, a man who occasionally observes the Kiddush, or participates now and then with relatives, would be excluded from the Most Orthodox category.

[14] Bales states the matter this way: "On the social level the act of drinking has symbolic and emotional ties with other acts and objects, as an integral part of an established network or system of meanings and values. The individual is able to internalize these ideas and sentiments fairly early in the process of socialization primarily through the aid of emotionally significant persons in the group, and the continued effectiveness of these ideas and sentiments *at the source of impulse* depends in significant degree upon his continued effective solidarity or community of feeling with these persons or their later substitutes."

porting power of the social milieu but involves the early internalization of normative attitudes toward drinking which militate against hedonistic drinking. Although presenting no supporting evidence, Bales expresses his ideas on these points as follows:

> "It [alcohol] is not forbidden in general, as something which should be avoided and ignored: if it were, it is likely that the individual, under pressure, would find it possible to regard it as a means of aggression, or in other utilitarian ways, and in all likelihood the control would not be nearly so effective as it is. For as the social definitions stand, they not only permit, but *require* the active expression, on the overt level, of ideas and sentiments toward the act and the object which are directly *counter* to, and take the place of, ideas and sentiments of a utilitarian type. Because these counter sentiments are required to be expressed in action they are much more likely to be thoroughly and deeply internalized, accepted without question, than if the requirements were for complete avoidance, because the attitudes which the individual is expected to internalize are positively structured and 'stamped in,' not simply left to the individual to work out for himself by a process of implication."

This view implies that Jews reared in the Orthodox tradition may be relatively immune to intoxication and especially to addiction, as compared with other Jews, even when confronted with changes in typical drinking situations. The inner resistance built up in the course of socialization should carry over to some extent—consciously or unconsciously—even though drinking shifts from a sacred to a secular pattern.[15] The data in Table 19, where the intoxication experience of predominantly secular drinkers is compared to their background of ceremonial drinking (based on "Kiddush background"[16]), support this expectation. The fact that some consistently

[15] The distinction between preponderantly "sacred" and "secular" drinkers is necessarily gross, and for a few men could not be made with sufficient accuracy to warrant its use. Alternation of sacred and secular drinking is present in most cases. Classification as sacred drinkers rests on evidence of explicit religious symbolism in a majority of drinking situations. Secular thus includes considerable "traditional drinking" which otherwise has a ritual character, as broadly defined, e.g., much schnapps drinking as described in Chapter 2. Obviously, there are variously socially structured secular drinking situations, and these are not all equally conducive to sobriety. Some of these are discussed in Chapter 5, where it is shown that Jewish students of all degrees of Orthodoxy yield to social pressures toward intoxication in certain unusual situations, such as military service. It is also shown, however, that the response of the more Orthodox is probably less marked even in these circumstances.

[16] "Kiddush background" refers to regular Sabbath observance of the ceremony of sanctification in the respondent's parental home. "No Kiddush background" (as in Table 19) does not necessarily preclude occasional or isolated experiences of this kind but does preclude regular observance.

TABLE 19.—*Intoxication Experience of Preponderantly Secular Drinkers among New Haven Jewish Men, by Extent of Past Ceremonial Drinking Experience*

	Five Times or Less	More Than Five Times
Kiddush background	22	4
No Kiddush background	10	10

Chi-square = 5.2, P = .03

sober Jewish men report no regular past experience of ceremonial drinking does not necessarily contradict Bales' views. The significant aspect of Table 19 is the indication that a background of extensive ceremonial drinking in the family helps insure sobriety by strengthening ideas and sentiments antithetical to hedonistic drinking. Possibly the extra increment of control stemming from those experiences in which drinking is of central significance is sufficient to account for some of the observed difference between Jews and other groups in respect to intoxication and drinking pathologies.

But how far can these findings be taken as proof that repeated ritual or ceremonial drinking in and of itself contributes to the sobriety of the Jews? The data from our New Haven sample are consistent with the assumption of such a relationship, but they by no means prove it. In Chapter 4 it will be shown that consistent sobriety among Jews is more intimately related to adherence to traditional religious practices than to other important sociocultural factors (nationality, generation and class), but subsequently evidence will be adduced pointing to broad features of the traditional religious complex and the Jewish situation other than ritual drinking which play an important role in sustaining norms of moderate drinking and sobriety. The question here, however, is whether or not the specific customs of ceremonial drinking are as closely connected with sobriety as other behavioral features of Orthodox Judaism. If so, the significance of these concrete practices in mitigating intoxication and drinking pathologies will be more firmly established.

There are certain obvious limits to the process of isolating specific aspects of a complex religious system.[17] Several questions included in the New Haven interview schedule, however, were designed to bring out different aspects of religious practice which are variously

[17] The difficulty in weighing the contribution which extensive ceremonial drinking makes to Jewish sobriety lies in the fact that Jewish Orthodoxy is an integrated sociocultural system. As in other such systems, various patterns of ideas, sentiments and behaviors are to some degree functionally and meaningfully interdependent, and there is no way of completely isolating the effect upon sobriety of each and every

observed in the Jewish community. Observance and nonobservance of these practices were then related to the sobriety–intoxication range. Of the different religious practices considered, the frequent ceremonial drinking indicated by regular Kiddush observance is as closely associated with sobriety, and as negatively associated with intoxication, as any other. But there are other aspects of religious practice which bear a similar relation to the sobriety–intoxication range among Jewish men. Daily use of phylacteries in prayer, or daily attendance at the synagogue (by the respondent or his father) are examples of such practices. By contrast, observance of certain annual holy days (e.g., Passover) and the rites de passage (e.g., Bar Mitzvah) is quite general among nominally Jewish men and accordingly does not vary with the sobriety–intoxication range.

A distinction can be made, however, between observances which tend to vary inversely along the sobriety–intoxication range and those which show little or no relation to the incidence and frequency of intoxication. The essence of the difference lies in the regular, demanding nature of the religious behavior on the one hand, and its infrequent, almost token nature on the other. The data suggest that sobriety is most characteristic of Jews who are committed to the daily and weekly observance of traditional rituals and ceremonials and, secondarily, of Jews who have been socialized in this tradition. Men who recite the prayers daily, attend synagogue frequently, and regularly observe the ceremonials of the Sabbath are likely to be sober even though they drink alcoholic beverages frequently. These men also participate in the round of annual holy days and rites de passage still observed by the less religious. But Jews who are removed from daily and weekly religious activities do not adhere to norms of moderate drinking and sobriety with equal consistency. Most of these men still participate in the less frequent and less personally exacting ceremonies which signify continuing identification with the larger Jewish community, and apparently remain quite sober during the course of their lives. But intoxication is statistically more frequent among them than among the more strictly observant Jews.

---

feature of this complex. An association between sobriety and frequent ceremonial drinking implies associations with other behavioral features of the religious system, yet these are not all equally interdependent. Among American Jews, some practices are abandoned or modified without immediately noticeable effects on others; some traditions change quickly while others persist tenaciously. Because of this capacity for differential change, the range of aspects of Jewish religious ritual and ceremonial associated with sobriety can be somewhat narrowed.

The particular behaviors which typify the soberest Jews indicate commitment to a system of religious norms, ideas and sentiments whose principal function is the total regulation of life, even in its minutest details. The ceremonial and ritual use of alcoholic beverages and the extension of religious symbolism to other drinking is an integral part of this broader religious pattern. It is not possible to state quantitatively just how much it contributes to the prevention of intoxication and extreme drinking pathologies. On the basis of our evidence, however, the noteworthy sobriety of the Jews appears to be primarily associated with the culture of Orthodox Judaism—a religious culture with a ritualistic emphasis, prescribing frequent drinking which is integrated with familial religious practices.

2. Jewish College Students

Additional confirmation of the findings on the relations of religious Orthodoxy to Jewish sobriety, and of the implications drawn from them, is much to be desired. In this respect, data from the College Drinking Survey[18] offer several possibilities. It will be recalled that past and present ritual observances were not measured as directly in the College Drinking Survey as in the New Haven study; nor did the Survey attempt to probe the details of religious observance, either in the Jewish or other groups. But the nominal religious affiliation—Orthodox, Conservative, Reform or Secular—and frequency of participation in organized religious activities were determined in a large number of Jewish students. As was shown above, participation in religious activities among Jewish students declines significantly moving in order through these four nominal religious divisions. However, certain general differences between the various nominal divisions of Judaism require more specific comment here, although extended discussion will be postponed until Chapter 4.

A basic issue between Reform and Orthodox Judaism centers on the extent to which traditional ritual and ceremonial should be retained in modern society. Proponents of the Reform movement have contended that ritual and ceremonial observances are secondary to cultivating the spirit of Judaism. Reform Jews have been willing to sacrifice many aspects of Jewish tradition which conflict with full participation in American life. By contrast, the Orthodox see in traditional Jewish ritual and ceremonial an end in itself as well as a

[18] See Straus and Bacon (96). The limitations of these data for purposes of generalization, discussed in Chapter 1, must be borne in mind.

means of Jewish survival. The Conservatives take a compromise position intermediate between the Orthodox and Reform with respect to retaining these traditions. Thus, in the present context, these nominal divisions not only reflect diminished participation in religious activities but, probably, differences in the ritual content of current student religious activity as well as experience of religious ritual in childhood in the parental home.[19] For our immediate purpose, then, these nominal divisions can be ordered from maximum to minimum adherence to traditional ceremonial and ritual practice as follows: Orthodox, Conservative, Reform and Secular.[20]

To substantiate the theoretical considerations and findings on Jewish men presented above, increasing frequencies of intoxication should be evident among Jewish students, moving progressively from Orthodox to Secular in the four nominal divisions. Marked differences in intoxication should appear between Orthodox and Reform students, with Conservative students in between. There is no special reason for anticipating much difference between Reform and Secular students, although the latter might show somewhat higher frequencies of intoxication because of a more complete break with Jewish traditions. These expectations are fully confirmed by the data on intoxication in Table 20. Not only does the predicted order of increase in intoxication ("tight" or drunk[21]) by nominal religious affiliation obtain, but the differences along religious lines are statistically highly significant. Moreover, these differences in intoxication cannot be attributed to differences in frequencies of drinking. As was shown in Chapter 2, Orthodox students tend, if anything, to drink more often than either Conservative or Reform

[19] The systematic decline in specification of customary religious drinking in childhood (shown in Chapter 2) is indicative in the latter connection. This is not to say that in each individual instance membership in a particular nominal division is a perfect indicator of the content and extent o ritual observance. A Jewish student may observe much or little of traditional ritual within the framework of any one of these nominal categories. Our reference is only to general tendencies.

[20] For a general discussion of these subdivisions of Judaism, see M. Davis, "Jewish religious life and institutions in America," in Finkelstein (26).

[21] Definitions of tight and drunk, as used throughout this study, are given in Chapter 2, tight being a less extreme form of intoxication than drunk. The criteria (drunk twice or more, tight more than five times) used throughout to divide these distributions are as close to the medians for all students as the system of classification permits. "Frequency of intoxication" by students, throughout the tables, is expressed as percentage above the criteria; "number reporting" is the base upon which percentages were computed.

TABLE 20.—*Frequency of Intoxication among Jewish Students, by Nominal Religious Affiliation (in Per Cent)*

	Drunk Twice or More	Number Reporting	Tight More Than Five Times	Number Reporting
Orthodox	10	(74)	13	(86)
Conservative	20	(66)	24	(67)
Reform	38	(58)	36	(61)
Secular	42	(52)	45	(56)
	Chi-square = 23.59, $P < .001$		Chi-square = 20.31, $P < .001$	

students, although Secular students may drink somewhat more often than members of these religious groups.

To further clarify the relations between drinking and intoxication, frequencies of intoxication were plotted against frequencies of drinking for students in each of the nominal religious divisions (Figure 1).[22] These data are especially useful representations of the consequences of changing patterns of drinking among Jewish students accompanying the decline of ceremonial and ritual observance. In preparing the data for Figure 1, it was anticipated that little or no association would appear between frequencies of drinking and intoxication among Orthodox students. Moreover, a progressive increase was expected in the association between frequency of drinking and frequency of intoxication, moving through the nominal religious divisions, although little difference was anticipated between Reform and Secular students.

The marked differences in the slopes of the lines in Figure 1 decidedly support these expectations. The increasing, positive association between frequencies of drinking and intoxication is evident from the increase in the slopes moving from Orthodox to Conservative to Reform and Secular students. As expected, the slopes for Reform and Secular students are practically alike.[23] From the flatness of the Orthodox lines in Figure 1 it seems safe to say that there is no positive association between the frequencies of their drinking and intoxication. But for the progressively less religious, in the traditional sense, the rarity of intoxication depends more and more on reduced frequencies of drinking.

[22] The lines in Figures 1 and 2 were fitted by least squares using arc sine transformations.

[23] It may, therefore, be inferred that some of the difference between Reform and Secular students (Table 20) results from somewhat higher drinking frequencies among the latter, rather than from differences in the effectiveness of sanctions in the drinking situation.

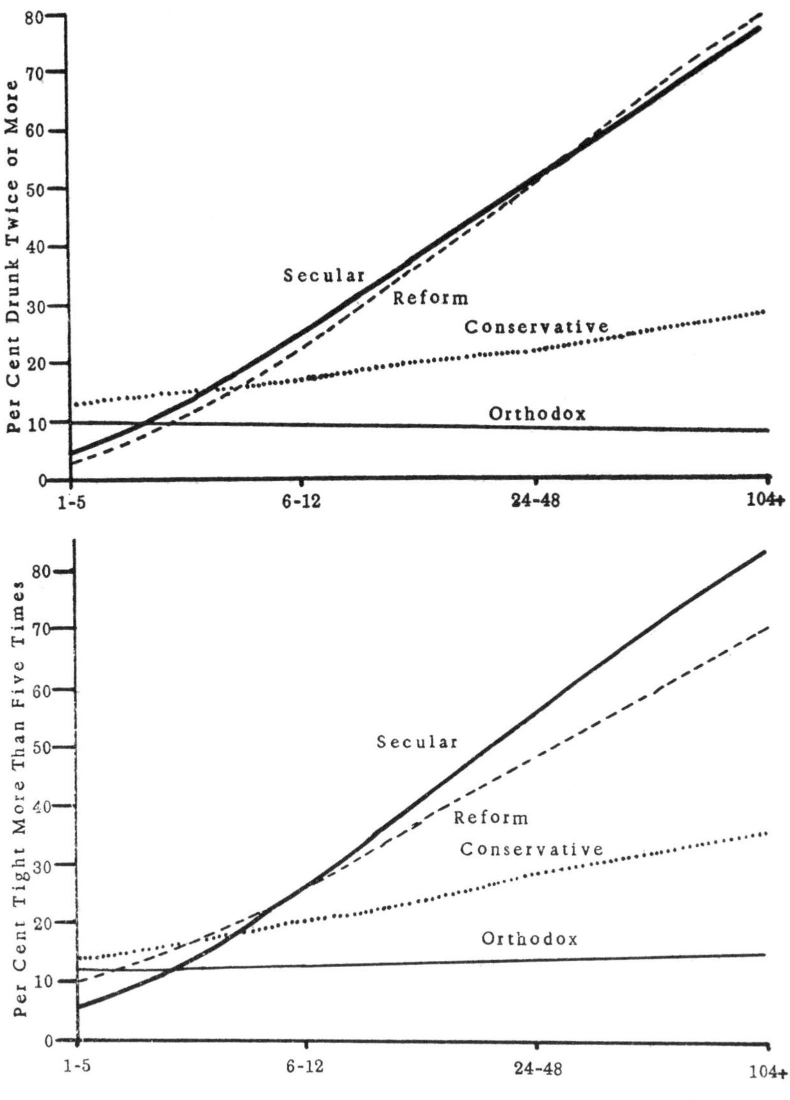

FIGURE 1.—*Frequency of Drinking and Frequency of Intoxication among Jewish Students, by Nominal Religious Affiliation.*

These data on intoxication and drinking among Jewish college students of different religious affiliation are entirely consistent with the findings on Jewish men in the New Haven community. The close correspondence in the results from these two independent samples strongly favors theoretical positions which associate Jewish sobriety primarily with the values and practices of Orthodox Judaism.

Convergence with Wider Societal Norms

Recognition of the variations in frequency of intoxication among Jews along religious lines still leaves two interrelated problems: (*1*) Is the pattern of intoxication of less Orthodox Jews converging with patterns typical of the larger society? (*2*) Do Jews who have largely abandoned the Orthodox traditions continue to be distinguished by their sobriety from much the rest of the American populace? To answer these questions it is necessary to determine broad group similarities or differences in patterns of intoxication, but this is by no means easy. Attention was previously called to the dearth of direct information on intoxication among groups of men with whom the New Haven Jewish sample might be compared. All that can be done here is to reiterate the conclusion that intoxication is probably relatively infrequent in the latter. This conclusion is of little value for understanding variations within the nominally Jewish group or trends toward its convergence with, or divergence from, wider societal norms. More can be done in this connection with the college data, as a consequence of the scope and inclusiveness of the College Drinking Survey. However, the broad range of variation in intoxication and the existence of a fair proportion of abstainers among non-Jewish students must be remembered, over and above the intrinsic limitations of the student sample for the purposes of generalization. These circumstances complicate comparisons and restrict generalization. Nonetheless, the college student data are useful for further intergroup comparisons as long as these limitations are borne in mind.

Insight into trends in intoxication among Jewish students may be gained by comparing frequencies of intoxication within the four nominal religious divisions with those among students of Irish Catholic and British Protestant background. The proportions of all students, including abstainers, in each of these religioethnic categories who have been intoxicated above the criteria are shown in Table 21. It is clear from these findings that there is substantially less intoxication among Jewish Orthodox and Conservative students than among Irish Catholics and British Protestants. But between the latter groups and the Jewish Reform and Secular students there are no

TABLE 21.—*Frequency of Intoxication of Jewish Students, by Nominal Religious Affiliation, and of Irish Catholic and British Protestant Students, Including Abstainers (in Per Cent)*

	Drunk Twice or More	Tight More Than Five Times
Jewish Orthodox	9	12
Jewish Conservative	18	22
Jewish Reform	35	33
Irish Catholic	35	35
Jewish Secular	39	42
British Protestant	39	42

such marked differences. Table 21 shows quite similar frequencies for Jewish Reform, Irish Catholic, Jewish Secular and British Protestant students; indeed, Jewish Secular students actually exceed Irish Catholic students in percentages above the criteria.

These data refer, however, to all students, including current abstainers. If abstainers are excluded from consideration the percentages are slightly altered.[24] Nonetheless, the relative position of the six religioethnic groups remains the same whether abstainers are included or excluded, with one exception: when abstainers are excluded, British Protestants exceed Secular Jews in intoxication. Also, as might be expected, Jewish Orthodox and Conservative students are even less often intoxicated, in percentage terms, than the Irish Catholics and British Protestants, when drinkers alone are considered. Moreover, analysis of the relations of drinking and intoxication by the graphic technique used above shows closely corresponding patterns of association between frequencies of drinking and intoxication among Irish Catholic, British Protestant, Jewish Reform and Jewish Secular student drinkers.[25] These comparisons suggest that among Jewish Reform and Secular students not only frequencies of intoxication, but also relations between drinking and intoxication tend to converge with typical patterns of the larger society.

A major inference to be drawn from these data is that there is a decided change in drinking responses and growing convergence with wider societal norms among those Jewish students who have relinquished traditional ceremonial and ritual practices most thor-

[24] The data are reported fully in Snyder (90).

[25] These data are also presented in full in Snyder (90). The outstanding feature of the graphs is that all four groups show roughly similar progressive increases in intoxication with more frequent drinking. There are no flat lines, indicating little or no association, comparable to the lines for Jewish Orthodox students in Figure 1.

oughly.[26] Apparently, sanctions on intoxication are about equally effective among Jewish Reform, Jewish Secular, Irish Catholic and British Protestant students. It seems, therefore, unnecessary to assume special inner or outer controls on intoxication which distinguish the Reform and Secular students from students in these other groups. However, such factors may be postulated legitimately for Jewish Orthodox and, to a lesser extent, Conservative students. Our findings strongly suggest that the sobriety for which Jews have long been noted depends upon the continuity and vitality of the Orthodox religious tradition, and that participation in Orthodox religious activities substantially insures moderation in drinking regardless of frequency.

Influences of Religious Participation and Membership

The data presented thus far strongly support the view that religious participation among Jews is related to sobriety. It has been shown that the most ritually observant New Haven Jewish men are the soberest, in spite of their extensive drinking. Among Jewish college students, intoxication increases through the nominal religious divisions of Orthodox, Conservative, Reform and Secular. This phenomenon was assumed to correspond with a decline in religious participation, since such participation decreases moving through these religious categories. To obviate this intervening assumption, direct evidence of growing intoxication with declining religious participation among Jewish students is presented in Table 22. These latter data, however, suggest the important possibility that it is any religious participation, or at least participation in the principal Western religions, which is conducive to sobriety. According to Straus and Bacon (96), the infrequent religious participants among college students in general are more often intoxicated than the frequent participants. Summarizing their findings on the influences of religious membership and participation, they comment that " . . . extent of participation in a denomination is itself a significant factor, perhaps as important in its way as membership." Perhaps, then, there is nothing especially sobering about participating in traditional Jewish religious activities as such. The more observant Orthodox Jews may be comparatively sober because they are religiously active,

[26] Judging from the positive association between frequency of drinking and frequency of intoxication among these students, Bales' (7) concept of "convivial drinking" would seem adequate to describe their drinking. The situational character of this trend, and similar trends in other aspects of drinking, must be borne in mind.

TABLE 22.—*Frequency of Intoxication of Jewish Students, by Frequency of Participation in Organized Religious Activities (in Per Cent)*

Religious Participation	Drunk Twice or More	Number Reporting	Tight More Than Five Times	Number Reporting
0–4 times a year	38	(296)	41	(293)
5 times a year to twice a month	27	(118)	27	(124)
About once a week or more	11	(84)	11	(99)
	Chi-square = 24.21, $P < .001$		Chi-square = 31.90, $P < .001$	

and not because they adhere to specific religious customs which foster sober attitudes toward drinking. Many of the religious denominations included in the College Drinking Survey, however, advocate total abstinence. It is likely that regular participation in these religious communities helps curtail drinking itself—and intoxication only incidentally. The influences on sobriety which traditional Judaism exerts on its members must be seen against the background of extensive drinking by the more Orthodox Jews, and hence can best be evaluated through comparisons with other religious groups which also permit drinking.[27]

1. *Catholic and Jewish Participation*

To begin to assess the relative significance for sobriety of religious participation in general and participation in Orthodox Judaism, comparisons must be made with religions which ideally allow drinking but do not countenance intoxication.[28] For this purpose, Roman Catholicism provides a good model. Normatively, Catholicism stands for temperance in the sense of the use of alcoholic beverages in moderation. Drunkenness is condemned, but abstinence is not prescribed, although abstinence movements have emerged from time to time within the framework of Catholicism in Ireland, America and

[27] Later on (Chapter 6) comment will be made on the possible role of abstinence attitudes in enhancing drinking pathologies in our society where drinking is prevalent. Here only comparisons free of the complications which the abstinence factor introduces are undertaken.

[28] Perhaps the most cogent way to highlight the effects on sobriety of participation in Jewish Orthodoxy, as opposed to participation in other religious activities, would be to compare Reform and Orthodox students. The object would be to show that frequent participation in Orthodox Judaism is more closely related to sobriety than is frequent participation in Reform religious activities. This cannot be done at present because the number of Jewish Reform students in the sample at higher frequencies of religious participation is insufficient for the necessary analysis.

elsewhere.[29] In these essential respects, Catholicism and traditional Judaism are much alike in "official" attitudes toward drinking. They differ in that Catholicism does not ordinarily incorporate beverage alcohol into the sphere of ritual, except in the Communion Sacrament of the priest, while Orthodox Judaism does so most extensively. If, then, participation in the activities of the Catholic religious community, which ideally permits drinking but censures intoxication, is a powerful deterrent to intoxication, certain consequences must follow: Religiously active Catholics should be differentiated from the inactive by their sobriety, as religiously observant Jews are distinguished from the nonobservant, and little difference in intoxication is to be expected between religiously participant Jews and Catholics.

Some signs of less intoxication among Catholics who are religiously active are to be found in data gathered by Lolli and his associates from Italians in New Haven and Rome.[30] Although the findings have yet to be fully analyzed, pertinent facts on the intoxication experience of 212 Italian men of Catholic affiliation suggest decreasing intoxication with more frequent religious participation. The difference, however, is not nearly so marked as in the case of the Jews.[31] From the writer's inspection of the data, it appears that the highest proportion of Italian men who have been "intoxicated" frequently (25 times or more) is to be found among the very infrequent participants in religious activities.[32] But of the New Haven Italian men who participate at least weekly in Catholic religious activities 11 per cent have been "intoxicated" at least 25 times in their lives. While the data from the Italian and Jewish studies are not strictly comparable, certain tentative conclusions are suggested: (*1*) There is some tendency for intoxication to vary inversely with participation in Catholic religious activities; (*2*) stronger sanctions

[29] Generalizations about the normative position of Roman Catholicism regarding beverage alcohol and its uses are based in part on a lecture by the Rev. J. C. Ford, "Moral Philosophy, Alcohol and Alcoholism," Yale University Summer School of Alcohol Studies (July 1951). See also Bainton (5).

[30] We are especially indebted to Giorgio Lolli, M.D. and Grace Golder, R.N., M.A., of the Yale Center of Alcohol Studies, for making available these comparative data from studies of drinking patterns of Italians which are now in progress. Cf. Lolli, Serianni et al. (60).

[31] The data are presented in Snyder (90). The difference among Italians does not quite achieve statistical significance, but in our opinion is worthy of attention, especially for future research.

[32] The quotation marks indicate lack of strict comparability between our own definition of intoxication and that used in the Italian study.

TABLE 23.—*Frequency of Intoxication of Students of Irish Background, by Frequency of Participation in Catholic Religious Activities (in Per Cent)*

Religious Participation	Drunk Twice or More	Number Reporting	Tight More Than Five Times	Number Reporting
0–4 times a year	61	(51)	49	(47)
5 times a year to twice a month	47	(47)	42	(50)
About once a week or more	42	(327)	42	(327)
	Chi-square = 6.01, P = .05		Chi-square = 0.52, P = .75	

on intoxication appear to be consequent upon regular participation in Orthodox Jewish ritual and ceremonial than in Catholic religious activities.

To explore these ideas further, the responses of Catholic college students of Irish background to questions on frequencies of intoxication and religious participation have been assembled in Table 23.[33] The results are somewhat ambiguous. There is a moderately significant increase in drunkenness with less frequent religious participation, but in the milder forms of intoxication (tight) the difference by religious participation is negligible. Evidently the relation between frequent religious participation and sobriety is less pronounced for Irish Catholic than for Jewish students. This is clearly shown by a comparison of the data in Table 23 with those in Table 22. Of the Irish students who participate weekly in religious activities, 42 per cent have been intoxicated above the criteria, in contrast to 11 per cent of the Jewish students who are equally religiously active. This difference is consistent with the indication of greater intoxication among Italian than among Jewish men who are the most frequent participants in Catholic and Jewish religious activities, respectively. Hence, the idea of more effective sanctions on intoxication consequent upon participation in Jewish religious activities gains support. Nevertheless, the data in Table 23 point to a tendency for intoxication to vary inversely with Catholic religious participation when more decided drunken behavior is taken as the index.

[33] For technical reasons, having to do with the use of different questionnaire forms and corresponding variations in punch card arrangement, slightly less than half of the sample of Irish Catholic students is included in Table 23. Inclusion of all these students would have required a hand sorting of original questionnaires. Such a sort was made for Jewish students but was not deemed worth while in the case of the Irish Catholic students, since the half-sample is fairly large and there is no reason to assume bias.

Still further problems must be considered before the meaning of this latter tendency becomes clear and before the differential effects of participation in Jewish and Catholic religious activities can be appreciated. For instance, does frequent participation in Catholic religious activities contribute an increment of control over intoxication in the drinking situation which distinguishes religiously observant from more secular students of Irish Catholic background? Or are different frequencies of drinking responsible for differences in intoxication among more and less observant Irish Catholic students? How, then, do Jewish and Irish Catholic students of similar degrees of religious participation compare in intoxication at different frequencies of drinking? In point of fact, the picture of the sanctioning effects of Catholic religious participation is decidedly altered when frequencies of drinking are taken into account. Similarities emerge in the intoxication patterns of the more and less observant Irish Catholic students. Also, the contrasting influences on sobriety of participation in Catholic and traditional Jewish religious activities becomes apparent.

In Figure 2, the extent of intoxication at different frequencies of drinking is shown for Irish Catholic and Jewish students representing various frequencies of religious participation. A comparison of the graphs shows a marked difference in slopes of the lines for those Irish Catholic and Jewish students who participate most often in religious activities, that is, about once a week or more. The percentages intoxicated above the criteria mount quite sharply for the most religiously active Irish Catholic students as frequencies of drinking rise. In contrast, there are only slight percentage increases in intoxication among religiously active Jewish students with increasing frequencies of drinking, as the gradualness of the slopes for these students indicates.

There is little difference in intoxication between more and less religiously active Irish Catholic students at higher frequencies of drinking. At lower frequencies of drinking, there is a definite difference in drunkenness between Irish Catholic students who seldom or never participate in organized religious activities and all other Irish Catholic students.[34] Otherwise the slopes of the lines for Irish Cath-

[34] The relatively high proportion of "secularized" Irish Catholic students drunk above the criterion at lower frequencies of drinking is actually somewhat spurious. From inspection of the individual questionnaires it is evident that there are several problem drinkers in this category, some of whom are currently "on the water wagon." This partly explains the higher lifetime frequencies of drunkenness at currently lower

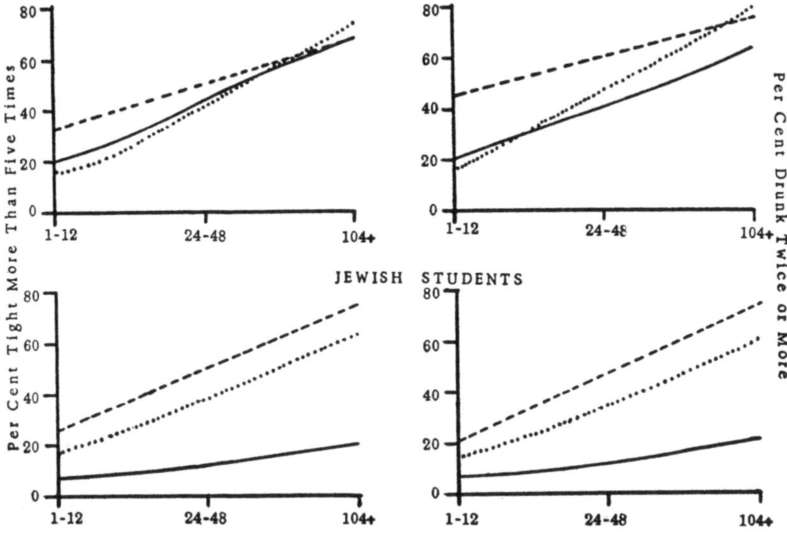

FIGURE 2.—*Frequency of Drinking and Frequency of Intoxication among Irish Catholic and Jewish Students, by Frequency of Religious Participation.* Broken lines = never to four times a year; dotted lines = five times a year to twice a month; solid lines = about once a week or more.

olic students are much alike. While religiously observant Irish Catholic students may become intoxicated somewhat less often than Catholics who seldom participate in church activities, much of the difference is attributable to different frequencies of drinking rather than to more effective controls on intoxication in the drinking situation.[35] In the drinking situation, then, the religiously active

frequencies of drinking among Irish Catholic students. An early and marked deterioration in religious participation among problem drinkers and incipient and confirmed alcoholics has been suggested by these and other sets of data considered in the course of the present research. This possibility will be discussed further with reference to the Jews and certain abstinence groups in later chapters. More general problems of religious integration and drinking pathologies are currently being investigated by the writer and others on the staff of the Yale Center of Alcohol Studies. It may also be noted, in passing, that differentials in religious participation and integration may be closely related to sex differences in, and cultural variations in the sex ratios of, drinking pathologies. This latter problem is also being considered in current research.

[35] Regular church attendance may, of course, have an effect of curtailing drinking among these students.

Irish Catholic student is apparently about as likely to become intoxicated as his less active coreligionist.

By contrast, there is a decided difference in extent of intoxication among the most religiously active Jewish students and all other Jewish students. This is especially true at higher frequencies of drinking. Also, there is apparently somewhat more intoxication among those Jewish students who seldom or never participate in religious activities and those who participate from five times a year to twice a month.[36] But in general, the slopes of the lines for Jewish students, other than the most frequent religious participants, are quite similar, and much like the slopes for Irish Catholic students of different degrees of religious participation. This cannot be said of the regularly observant Jewish students who are differentiated from all the categories shown in Figure 2 by a negligible association between frequencies of drinking and intoxication. Since these Jewish students are preponderantly Orthodox, it would appear that there are sanctions inherent in Orthodox Judaism which may currently distinguish this religion from Roman Catholicism by the greater probability of sobriety among participant members who drink alcoholic beverages.[37]

2. Nominal Membership and Participation in Orthodox Activities

Actually, data have yet to be presented which isolate the significance for Jewish sobriety of participation in Orthodox religious activities in contrast to nominal Orthodox membership. Among New Haven Jewish men, the more ritually observant were seen to be the soberest, but the nominal religious affiliation of these men was not taken into account. It has also been shown that the most religiously active Jewish students are much soberer than the less religiously active. However, more than three-quarters of the most frequent religious participants among Jewish students are nominally Orthodox. May it not be, then, that nominal membership in the Orthodox

[36] This difference may reflect vestiges of ceremonial drinking on the part of the more observant of these two categories; it may reflect greater continuity with Orthodox norms, ideas and sentiments which limit intoxication or it may reflect more effective social sanctions on intoxication as a consequence of closer integration in the religious community.

[37] Obviously, considerable additional research will be needed to establish the generality of these points. Even for the data presented above, the problem of the "compulsory" or "voluntary" character of participation may limit the significance of the conclusion reached (many of the Irish Catholics attend colleges where religious participation is required quite apart from individual student interest).

community is the important factor in Jewish sobriety, while specific participation in religious activities contributes little or nothing?

Theoretically it would be expected that while nominal membership is important as a sign of continuing identification with the Orthodox religious community, actual participation in Orthodox religious activities is fundamental. Two closely related ideas need brief reiteration and development at this point. The first is Bales' concept that Orthodox drinking customs require an "acting out" of the ideal drinking norms which counter hedonistic drinking, and that the repeated translation of these norms into behavior reinforces their connection with the sacred and controlling ideas and sentiments in the personality. However, the effectiveness of these symbolic and emotional connections in regulating drinking is presumed to depend in part upon "continued effective solidarity or community of feeling" with the members of the Orthodox religious community. This conception shades into the second and broader idea of the importance to Jewish sobriety of what Cheinisse (18) spoke of as the "force of cohesion and concentration of the religious community."[38] The question, of course, is what gives cohesion and solidarity to the Orthodox religious community. Admittedly this is a highly complex problem, intimately bound up with basic religious beliefs and the relations of Jews to the larger society. In the present context, priority is assumed for participation in Orthodox religious ritual and ceremonial, although elaboration of this point will be deferred until Chapter 5. The ritually observant Jew simply cannot, in Bales' view, drink alcoholic beverages without activating, consciously or unconsciously, the entire network of sacred ideas and feelings involving the sentiments of respect for moral authority and solidarity with family and group.[39] But it may be assumed that it is precisely participation in Orthodox ceremonial and ritual which in large part defines and intensifies these broader Jewish ideas and sentiments. The acting out of ceremonial and ritual not only reinforces a ritual attitude toward drinking, it also affirms and intensifies the connections between the central Jewish religious symbols and the sentiments of solidarity and moral authority. These, in turn, ultimately

[38] Translation mine.

[39] This applies also to the sentiments of disgust and repugnance at the idea of loss of self-control through excessive drinking, on which more will be said in Chapter 5. (Attitudes of disgust, scorn, intolerance, etc., toward drunkenness in others were shown in Chapter 2 to be most prevalent among the religiously most Orthodox.)

TABLE 24.—*Frequency of Intoxication of Nominally Orthodox Jewish Students by Regularity of Religious Participation*

	Drunk		Tight	
Religious Participation	*Less than Twice*	*Twice or More*	*Five Times or Less*	*More than Five Times*
Regular (about once a week or more)	51	3	64	4
Irregular (less than once a week)	16	4	13	7
	Chi-square = 2.07, P = .15		Chi-square = 9.06, P = .003	

give to the interrelated norms and ideas about drinking the emotional power to regulate drinking behavior.[40]

It may be derived from these premises that nominally Orthodox Jewish students who participate most frequently in religious activities will be more sober than Orthodox students who are less regular in religious participation. These expectations are partly supported by the data in Table 24. In the milder form of intoxication, the regular participants among the Orthodox are significantly soberer than irregular participants. The difference between these Orthodox categories in respect to drunkenness does not achieve statistical significance but is in the expected direction. Hence there seems to be some justification for giving priority to religious participation over and above nominal Orthodox membership.

Further evidence of the probable importance to Jewish sobriety of actual participation in Orthodox religious practices, and particularly drinking practices, may be derived by comparing the extent of intoxication among Orthodox students who rank "wine in the family" as their most important drinking situation and among those for whom other combinations of beverages and companions are most important. Data showing significantly less frequent mild intoxication

[40] This assigns a more dynamic role to ceremonial and ritual than is suggested by Thorner (101), who apparently views these phenomena as rather passive outer forms and expressions for those social ideas and sentiments which are perhaps primary in Jewish sobriety. Certainly the rituals are forms of expression, and alternative forms are possible, but they also give organization to the social sentiments, generally as well as in relation to drinking, reinforcing them and facilitating their transmission. In this connection attention may be called again (*1*) to the evidence in Chapter 2 for the residue of sacred ideas and sentiments, stemming for their early ritual drinking experiences, associated with drinking in the minds of many Jews who are far from Orthodox in current religious practice, and (*2*) to the data in the present chapter showing increased intoxication among men who have abandoned the rituals, but especially among those with little or no socialization experience of the rituals.

TABLE 25.—*Frequency of Mild Intoxication (Tight) of Orthodox Jewish Students, by Most Frequently Used Beverage and Companions*

	Five Times or Less	More Than Five Times
Wine in the family	34	1
Other combination	26	10
	Chi-square = 6.31, P < .05	

among the familial wine drinkers are presented in Table 25.[41] In respect to more extreme intoxication, not one of the 34 Orthodox students reporting on drunkenness and naming wine in the family as the most frequent beverage and companions has ever been drunk. By contrast, 6 out of 31 Orthodox students reporting on drunkenness and giving precedence to some other combination of beverage and companions have been drunk more than twice. Moreover, these differences cannot be ascribed to less frequent drinking by the familial wine drinkers. The fact is that Orthodox students who assign first-rank importance to drinking wine in the family are actually more frequent drinkers than those for whom other combinations of beverage and context are most important.[42] Thus the sobriety of the familial wine drinkers is not attributable to relatively infrequent drinking.[43]

Considered jointly, these findings on the relative sobriety of regularly observant Orthodox students and those who give precedence to wine in the family in their drinking highlight the importance

[41] "Most frequently used beverage and companions" has the same meaning as given in Chapter 2.

[42] The data are detailed in Snyder (90).

[43] Lacking specification of the religious or other character of student drinking, it cannot be said definitely that the difference in intoxication between Orthodox students for whom familial wine drinking is relatively important or unimportant (Table 25) is attributable to differential participation in Orthodox Jewish ceremonials and rituals, and especially ceremonials and rituals involving drinking. However, two facts favor this conclusion. On the one hand, the suggestion of less frequent drinking by Orthodox students who do not give precedence to familial wine drinking points to irregular participation in religious drinking practices, since strict Sabbath observance would require weekly ceremonial wine drinking. On the other hand, we have seen that nominally Orthodox students who are irregular in religious participation tend to be somewhat more often intoxicated than regular participants (Table 24). While further research would be required to establish the point with certainty, it seems more than likely that the Orthodox students who are irregular religious participants, and less consistently sober, are also the Orthodox students who give precedence in their drinking to combinations of beverages and companions other than wine in the family.

of religious participation and practice, over and above nominal Orthodox membership, in sustaining sobriety among Jews.

In brief and tentative conclusion, Orthodox Judaism, as a normative or cultural system, appears to have a distinctly sobering influence on its members. But this effect may depend in the long run upon the continuing participation of Jews in the ceremonial and ritual activities of the traditional religious community. In order to establish this conclusion more firmly, however, it will be necessary to consider the relative influences of religion, nationality, generation and class. This will be done in the next chapter.

Chapter 4

REGIONAL BACKGROUND, GENERATION AND CLASS

RELATIONSHIPS between the sobriety of Jews and their membership, participation and socialization in the traditional religious community were shown in Chapter 3. As religious Orthodoxy declined, a tendency was seen for intoxication to increase in both incidence and frequency, converging in extent with norms of the wider society. Furthermore, the more observant Jews were seen to be characteristically sober despite widespread and frequent use of alcoholic beverages, especially wine and spirits. But evidence of a correlation between religious Orthodoxy and uniformly temperate drinking is insufficient to establish an intrinsic connection between these patterns or constituent elements of them. The apparent association may simply mirror variation with other factors which are actually decisive. Thus the possible influence on Jewish sobriety of such basic sociocultural factors as regional background, generation in this country, and position in the class structure cannot be discounted without further investigation.

This is especially true in respect to the Jewish group since there has been a gross clustering of those cultural traits suggested by eastern European origin, recency of immigration, relatively lower class status, and the religious Orthodoxy which seems linked with very temperate drinking. Western European background, long residence in this country, movement in the class system and modifications of religion have tended to go hand in hand, and these in turn with changing drinking patterns.[1] But these are gross configurations, and tendencies for changes in one aspect of culture to ramify to others are often matters of degree. The Orthodox religious practices, for instance, although declining among successive generations of Jews with their ascent in the class system, persist nonetheless in attenuated form. Moreover, some Orthodox Jewish families have been American for several generations, some stem from Western Europe, and some command high status in the American class structure. As a consequence, the way is open for study of the

[1] Documentation and further evidence of some of these changes will be presented in notes supplementary to this chapter.

importance to Jewish sobriety of membership in particular regional origin, generation and class categories as compared to religious Orthodoxy. For if there is an intrinsic connection between the sobriety of the Jews and the values and practices of Orthodox Judaism, then correlations between sobriety and specific regional, generation or class categories must be demonstrably subordinate to this more basic relationship.

In terms of data available from the present research, this problem takes the form of three questions: (*1*) Can it be shown that systematic differences in sobriety and intoxication exist between more and less Orthodox Jews within any particular category of regional origin, generation or class? (*2*) Can it be shown that in regional groups, generations or classes where intoxication is most in evidence Orthodoxy is in relative decline? (*3*) Can it be shown that the pattern of sobriety is relatively constant for Orthodox Jews as between any particular categories of regional origin, generation or class?

The present chapter is devoted to the presentation and interpretation of data bearing on these questions. This should help to isolate more clearly the significance of religious Orthodoxy for Jewish sobriety, as well as the influence of other sociocultural factors. It should be emphasized, in anticipation of affirmative answers to these questions, that to assign priority to religious Orthodoxy is not to imply that regional origin, generation or class are of no consequence. Analysis will suggest, however, that the influence of these factors is less direct and decisive than is membership in the traditional religious community. The influence of particular national–cultural and stratification systems on patterns of sobriety and intoxication among Jews can perhaps best be seen in terms of the extent to which these systems affect adherence to the traditional religion. This point, however, will be further clarified as data are presented on the relations between patterns of sobriety and intoxication, religion, region, generation and class.

Region and Cultural Area

The history of the Jews in Europe for the past three centuries reveals striking cultural differences between the Jews of eastern and western Europe. The Jewish emancipation of the nineteenth century, characterized by the breakdown of the involuntary ghetto, the shedding of distinctive cultural traits, secularization and social mobility, was primarily a western European phenomenon. Jewish life there lost much of its distinctive flavor as that part of the continent rapidly became industrialized. Ethnic loyalties and traditions gave way considerably to broader national and class loyalties and ancient religious beliefs were often abandoned in favor of new secular and universalistic ideologies. Western European Jews were to be found in the vanguard of revolutionary political movements, in the emergent stratum of international capitalists, in the great centers of secular education and in other crucial positions in the larger society. But the bulk of German and other western European Jewry became committed to a middle class way of life which made them hardly distinguishable from their Gentile neighbors. In Germany, Reform Judaism, in the pattern of Protestant denominationalism, emerged as a social movement of first-rank importance. By contrast, eastern European Jewry became the stronghold of religious Orthodoxy and traditional ghetto life. Signs of imminent social change and revolution are indeed discernible from descriptions of eastern European life in the 19th century. But the Slavic countries of eastern Europe became the heart of Jewish national and religious traditionalism, and remained so until recent times.[2] The predominantly eastern European origin of American Jews has been noted previously.

On the basis of these historical considerations there is reason to suppose that differences in the regional backgrounds of American Jews might be reflected in different patterns of intoxication. As previously noted, other writers, with some factual backing, have suggested such differences and the evidence in Table 26 is partially supportive.[3] These data, based on college students' preception of

[2] General features of the emancipation in western Europe are succinctly described by Wirth (108). Developments since 1648 are treated in more detail by C. Roth, "The Jews of western Europe (from 1648)," in Finkelstein (26). Differences in socio-economic conditions of eastern and western European Jews at the turn of the century are ably surveyed by Fishberg (27). The cultural inertia of the eastern European masses during the 19th century is noted by Dubnow (22), who also treats of radical and assimilationist tendencies among the intellectuals. Eastern Jewry's traditionalism and religiosity are abundantly clear from Zborowski and Herzog's (110) portrait of the *shtetl* of the late 19th century and the early 20th. The permeation of these communities with religious values is equally evident in Samuel's (82) description as seen through the eyes of the great writer Sholom Aleichem, who also acutely perceived and portrayed imminent changes through a variety of fictional social types. Cf. Sholom Aleichem (87).

[3] For other findings and comments on this question see Chapter 3. We speak of our data (Table 26) as partially supportive since the difference in drunken behavior does not quite attain statistical significance.

TABLE 26.—*Frequency of Intoxication among Jewish Students, by Regional Background of Both Parents (in Per Cent)*

	Drunk Twice or More	Number Reporting	Tight More Than Five Times	Number Reporting
Polish	18	(28)	21	(34)
Russian	36	(92)	44	(99)
German	42	(19)	53	(19)
	Chi-square = 3.95, P = .14		Chi-square = 7.09, P = .03	

their parents' "dominant nationality" background, indicate that Jewish students recognizing a German background have been the most often intoxicated, followed in turn by students recognizing Russian and Polish origins.[4] The important question, however, is whether these differences in intoxication by regional origin directly mirror (*1*) the continuing influence of specific regional traditions or (*2*) the differing vitality of religious Orthodoxy among the regional groups. In the latter case, the primacy of the religious influence should be evident in differences in (*a*) intoxication along religious lines within any of the regional groups (Polish, Russian or German), (*b*) the sobriety of the Orthodox irrespective of nationality, and (*c*) the preponderance of the Orthodox among those of Polish origin.[5]

The data in Table 27, showing the relative sobriety of the more Orthodox students recognizing Russian background only, favor the second of these interpretations. A similar test could not be made for Jewish students of German and Polish backgrounds because the numbers of such students identified by religious affiliation were too small for analysis.[6] Nonetheless, the trend of differences in intoxication along religious lines among the few students of German back-

[4] The survey from which the student sample is drawn was discussed in Chapter 1. Table 26 includes students reporting the "dominant nationality" of both parents as Polish, as Russian, or as German. These three were the only European "nationalities" sampled in sufficient numbers for statistical treatment.

[5] For the college students, the nominal divisions Orthodox, Conservative, Reform and Secular approximate a gradient of diminishing religious Orthodoxy suitable for expressing differences along religious lines.

[6] It should be recalled that less than half the Jewish students included in the Survey sample were questioned on details of religious affiliation (cf. Chapter 2). Because of this situation and the resulting small numbers in certain Tables, such as Table 27, the Orthodox and Conservative are often combined into one category, and the Reformed and Secular into another, for purposes of statistical testing. Substantively this division seems perfectly reasonable in the light of the discussion in previous chapters of religious content, participation and drinking among these categories.

TABLE 27.—*Frequency of Intoxication among Jewish Students of Russian Background, by Nominal Religious Affiliation*

	Drunk		Tight	
	Less than Twice	*Twice or More*	*Five Times or Less*	*More than Five Times*
Orthodox and Conservative	13	2	12	3
Reform and Secular	15	15	14	18
	Chi-square = 3.06, P = .08		Chi-square = 5.11, P = .03	

TABLE 28.—*Frequency of Intoxication among Jewish Students of German Background, by Nominal Religious Affiliation*

	Drunk		Tight	
	Less than Twice	*Twice or More*	*Five Times or Less*	*More than Five Times*
Orthodox	3	0	3	0
Conservative	2	0	1	1
Reform	4	2	3	3
Secular	1	2	1	2

ground is sufficiently striking to merit presentation (Table 28). Among Jewish students recognizing Polish origins there are simply too few Reform and Secular to suggest trends according to religious affiliation.[7] However, the very fact that these students are preponderantly of the Orthodox affiliation is important. This is entirely consistent with the view that the infrequent intoxication of Jewish students of Polish origin is attributable to the relatively powerful impact of Orthodox religious tradition. Nearly three fourths of the Jewish students of Polish background are Orthodox but only about one fifth of the Russian and German categories.[8] Because of the sampling limitations discussed earlier, these data cannot be taken as an accurate reflection of the proportions of the Orthodox among American Jews of Polish, Russian and German origins, respectively (although there is no doubt that the Orthodox are more numerous among those of Polish than of German background). But this does not diminish the importance of the fact that the Orthodox are proportionately most in evidence in this sample precisely in the regional origin category where intoxication is least in evidence. Moreover, the Orthodox students of Polish background are apparently quite as sober as the Orthodox of Russian and German origin. Among the

[7] Two report Reform affiliation, one Secular.

[8] These proportions are based on totals in each regional group reporting on religious affiliation and the milder forms of intoxication.

former, only one student out of 19 reported ever having been drunk in the course of his life. Finally, it is pertinent to note that Jewish students recognizing heterogeneous regional backgrounds show a systematic increase in intoxication along religious lines.[9]

If now we substitute for particular regions a broader classification according to eastern and western European cultural areas, intoxication increases among Jewish students as their origins shift from east to west.[10] Only 29 per cent of the students of eastern European background have been drunk more than twice, compared to 41 per cent of those of western European origin. Consistently, students of mixed origins fall between these two homogeneous groups in experience of intoxication.[11] And an analogous pattern of differences appears in the milder forms of intoxication.[12] But once again, as with particular regional groups, behind the apparent differences are systematic differences in intoxication along religious lines. In Table 29 data on extent of intoxication by nominal religious affiliation are shown for Jewish students of eastern European background and the differences according to nominal religious affiliation are readily apparent. A parallel pattern of difference in intoxication by religious affiliation for students of western European background is shown in Table 30, where Orthodox and Conservative, and Reform and Secular students have again been combined because of the small

[9] Cf. Snyder (90).

[10] The eastern European category is composed of Jewish students reporting the dominant "nationality background" of each parent in one or another of the following categories: Hungarian, Polish, Rumanian, Russian, and (in two cases) Slavic. Lithuanian, Latvian, Estonian and other categories which might be classed as eastern European were not specifically coded in the College Drinking Survey and were therefore eliminated here, reducing the size of this sample. The western European category is composed of Jewish students reporting the dominant "nationality background" of each parent in one or another of the following categories: Austrian, British, Czech, Dutch, French, German, Irish, Portuguese and Scotch. Students reporting parental background as Austrian might have been classed as eastern rather than western European, since Galicia and other important territories inhabited by eastern European Jews were once a part of the Austro-Hungarian Empire. Thus, a student whose parents came from Galicia might class himself as of Austrian rather than Polish background. On the other hand, Jews of Viennese origin would almost certainly class themselves as Austrian, and since Viennese Jews were in the foreground of the emancipation, we have chosen to class Austrian Jews as western European. Czech Jews present an analogous problem but there is only one student involved here and he has been classed, albeit arbitrarily, as western European.

[11] This refers to students who report one parent's background in nationalities classed as eastern and the other's in nationalities classed as western. Detailed data are presented in Snyder (90).

[12] Data are given in Snyder (90).

TABLE 29.—*Frequency of Intoxication among Jewish Students of Eastern European Background, by Nominal Religious Affiliation (in Per Cent)*

	Drunk Twice or More	Number Reporting	Tight More than Five Times	Number Reporting
Orthodox	6	(32)	12	(41)
Conservative	19	(21)	14	(21)
Reform	48	(21)	42	(24)
Secular	44	(27)	44	(27)

TABLE 30.—*Frequency of Intoxication among Jewish Students of Western European Background, by Nominal Religious Affiliation*

	Drunk		Tight	
	Less than Twice	*Twice or More*	*Five Times or Less*	*More than Five Times*
Orthodox and Conservative	6	0	5	1
Reform and Secular	5	9	5	9

numbers. Statistical tests applied to the data in these tables indicate significant differences in intoxication along religious lines,[13] while the background factor appears unimportant.

These findings, together with the facts that the more Orthodox are in considerably greater proportion among students of eastern than of western background and appear quite sober whether of eastern or western European origin, support the view that differences in intoxication are traceable to the relative vitality of the Orthodox religious tradition in these cultural areas.[14] Collectively, the data on region of origin, religious affiliation, and their relations to Jewish patterns of intoxication indicate that religious Orthodoxy is more decisive for sobriety than the continuing influence of these other factors. The statistical findings suggest that the thread of Orthodox life may be woven into many regional culture fabrics without losing its sobering influence upon Jews. However, particular regional and broader sociocultural influences evidently condition adherence to the sobriety norm insofar as they stimulate Jews to intensify or abandon the traditional religion. Thus they must be considered as contributing to the comparative Orthodoxy and sobriety of the Jews from eastern Europe.

[13] Chi-square for the differences in drunkenness along religious lines, holding background constant, is 19.62, P (at 2 degrees of freedom) is less than .001. Chi-square for the analogous difference in milder intoxication is 23.11, P is less than .001. In making these tests, the four religious divisions shown in Table 29 were collapsed into two categories as in Table 30.

[14] More than half the students of eastern European background are Orthodox and Conservative but only a third of those of western European background.

The Influence of Generation

A convenient basis for ordering data in studies of immigration and acculturation is by generation. Members of immigrant ethnic groups have been socialized in cultural traditions alien to the host society and these traditions are transplanted to the new situation and transmitted in greater or lesser degree to children and grandchildren. Ordering data by generation provides useful points of reference for studying processes of change, rates of sociocultural integration and reactions to the cultural impact of the host society. Classification by generation is also useful for determining differential rates of change in components of a particular ethnic culture. Through analyses by generation, sociologists have discovered uniformities in order, direction and processes of sociocultural change.[15]

In our opinion, however, generation is often misused as an explanatory concept together with the concepts of acculturation and assimilation. Pertinent here is the idea that, through time, successive generations of Jews in America become more "acculturated" or "assimilated." The "younger generation" Jews are more like other Americans and consequently are more often intoxicated than their forebears. By this line of reasoning, which has time and again come to our attention in the literature and in lectures and discussions on Jewish drinking patterns, presumed increases in intoxication among American Jews are thought to be explained.[16] There is indeed descriptive truth in this argument, and evidence will soon be presented showing striking increases in intoxication with the succession of Jewish generations resident in this country. But the argument is lacking in explanatory value because it fails to come to grips with the question of why the Jews were sober in the first place. Failure to answer or even to see this question has serious consequences. First, nothing is added to our understanding of the relative absence

[15] Good examples of the use of classification by generation for purposes of sociological analysis and generalization are to be found in Warner and Srole (105) who also use generation to advantage as a structural category in analyzing the Jewish "community crisis of age-grade movement" in Yankee City.

[16] Thus Fishberg [in Bernheimer (11)] noting that Jews in "their old home" abhor drunkards, asserts with no seeming need for further explanation that "here, alcoholism is increasing, particularly among the young generation, who are adopting the habits and customs of life of their Gentile neighbors—their virtues as well as their vices." Similarly, Myerson (70) refers to the traditional Jewish reaction to the excessive use of alcohol and suggests that "as the Jew becomes Americanized" the attitude toward alcohol will change and that "Jews will drink in the same measure as other races," without further specification as to how or why or as to what part of the Americanization process is most relevant in modifying this particular attitude.

of alcohol problems among Jews in spite of their widespread use of alcoholic beverages. There is no illumination of those features of traditional Jewish life and culture which bear most directly on sobriety. Second, analysis of the kinds of changes which must be wrought in Jewish life before the traditional patterns of moderate drinking and sobriety begin to disintegrate is obscured. Isolation of cultural factors conducive to either sobriety or intoxication is not facilitated by lumping together as "acculturative influences" diverse phenomena whose relative importance to drinking behavior is unknown and then assuming that in some unspecified way these influences progressively alter the drinking behavior of successive generations of Jews.

Prerequisite to understanding the influences in American life which may be undermining continued sobriety among Jews is some idea of those aspects of Jewish culture which have been conducive to sobriety for many centuries despite prolonged and extensive contact of Jews with surrounding Gentile groups and their adoption of a variety of Gentile customs. With such a conception—albeit as a first approximation—the kinds of influences and features of American life which are apparently affecting the traditional sobriety of Jews can be more intelligently assessed. Recognition of the changes in intoxication behavior in an acculturation context where institutions and cultural values are competing, and ordering these changes by generation is a useful first step, however, in isolating variables which have explanatory value. It is in this perspective that data on the intoxication patterns of different generation of American Jews will be considered here.

Table 31 shows that intoxication increases when Jewish men in our New Haven sample concerning whom this information is available are ordered by generations resident in this country. However, the view that Jewish sobriety is primarily associated with Orthodox patterns of religious observance implies differences in extent of intoxication by degree of Orthodoxy within any of the generations, while differences between the generations should correspond to changes in the proportion of Orthodox Jews with successive generations in America. Moreover, the Orthodox Jews ought to be consistently sober regardless of generation. To test these implications, the sample of Jewish men from New Haven was classified by intoxication experience and generation, and each of these groups was divided according to the degree of ceremonial Orthodoxy (Table 32). Although the numbers in the several cells of Table 32 are very small,

TABLE 31.—*Intoxication Experience among New Haven Jewish Men, by Generations in America*

	Five Times or Less	More than Five Times
I. Foreign born of foreign parents	23	4
II. American born of foreign parents	27	8
III. American born, one or both parents American	5	6

Chi-square = 6.95, P < .05

TABLE 32.—*Intoxication Experience of New Haven Jewish Men of Different Generations, by Degree of Ceremonial Orthodoxy*

Intoxication Experience	Most Orthodox	Intermediate	Least Orthodox
Generation I			
5 or less	6	13	2
over 5	1	2	1
Generation II			
5 or less	5	14	8
over 5	0	3	4
Generation III			
5 or less	1	1	4
over 5	0	0	5

the pattern of the data is, with one exception, in accord with our expectations. True, the Intermediate men in the first generation are proportionately slightly less often intoxicated than the Most Orthodox, but it is noteworthy that this discrepancy appears in the first generation. Otherwise, it may be said that the more Orthodox appear quite sober in each generation and that the increase in intoxication through the generations corresponds to the growing proportions of Jews who are neither ritually observant nor socialized in this tradition.[17]

Confirmation of the theoretical position partially supported by data from the New Haven Jewish men is obtained from reports of Jewish students included in the College Drinking Survey. The data in Table 33 show increases in intoxication among Jewish students with successive generations in this country. As might be anticipated from studies of time differentials in social mobility, a greater proportion of Jewish college students are of mixed or American

[17] The Least Orthodox constitute only 12 per cent of the first generation, 35 per cent of the second and 85 per cent of the third. Although the numbers are too small to permit extrapolation to American Jews at large, or perhaps even to the New Haven Jewish population, there is little doubt that the decline in Orthodox ceremonial observance apparent in these data mirrors the larger American scene. Further evidence of this trend will be noted later in this Chapter.

TABLE 33.—*Frequency of Intoxication among Jewish Students, by Generations in America (in Per Cent)*

	Drunk Twice or More	Number Reporting	Tight More than Five Times	Number Reporting
Foreign born of foreign parents	18	(27)	23	(31)
American born of foreign parents	25	(181)	24	(193)
American born of mixed parents	32	(114)	30	(115)
American born of American parents	38	(173)	42	(113)
	Chi-square = 8.69, P < .05		Chi-square = 12.66, P < .01	

parentage, as opposed to foreign parentage, than is the case for the sample of Jewish men from the New Haven community.[18] Hence, in Table 33, Jewish college students have been divided into four generation categories rather than the three-fold classification used for New Haven Jewish men. This different classification scheme in no way alters the relation of progressive increase in extent of intoxication with successive Jewish generations in this country. The findings from the samples of Jewish college students and New Haven men are consistent and mutually supportive in this respect.

In accordance with our hypothesis, however, there should be differences in extent of intoxication within any particular generation according to the nominal religious divisions, Orthodox, Conservative, Reform and Secular. Data confirming this expectation are presented in Table 34 for Jewish students of foreign-born parentage, and in Table 35 for students with one or both parents American born.[19] Holding generation constant, tests indicate that intoxication experience differs significantly along religious lines.[20] Percentagewise, there is a tendency for intoxication to increase within the various religious divisions among the students with one or both parents American born, as compared to those of foreign parentage; the most noticeable instance being the increase among

[18] For an extended discussion of time factors involved in ethnic mobility in various social systems, see Myers (69).

[19] To increase the total numbers in each religious division the categories "foreign born of foreign parents" and "foreign born of American parents" have been combined in Table 34 as "foreign-born parentage." For the same reason, the categories "American born of mixed parents" and "American born of American parents" have been similarly combined in Table 35.

[20] Chi-square for the drunkenness distribution is 19.36, P (at 6 degrees of freedom) is less than .004. For the milder forms of intoxication chi-square is 18.17, P is less than .007.

TABLE 34.—*Frequency of Intoxication among Jewish Students of Foreign-Born Parentage, by Nominal Religious Affiliation (in Per Cent)*

	Drunk Twice or More	Number Reporting	Tight More than Five Times	Number Reporting
Orthodox	9	(56)	11	(66)
Conservative	14	(21)	14	(29)
Reform	31	(16)	38	(16)
Secular	38	(24)	41	(27)

TABLE 35.—*Frequency of Intoxication among Jewish Students with One or Both Parents American Born, by Nominal Religious Affiliation (in Per Cent)*

	Drunk Twice or More	Number Reporting	Tight More than Five Times	Number Reporting
Orthodox	12	(17)	21	(19)
Conservative	27	(30)	32	(38)
Reform	43	(42)	37	(43)
Secular	46	(28)	46	(28)

Conservative students. This latter difference may be attributable to the greater proximity to Orthodox traditions of the Conservatives of foreign parentage, in comparison with Conservative students of American parentage, a point which will be discussed later on in another connection. However, when religious affiliation is held constant the apparent differences by generation (Tables 34 and 35) do not prove to be statistically significant.[21] Of equal importance is the fact that the Orthodox students show surprising stability in the percentage who got drunk above the criterion. The difference in milder intoxication is larger but even this might disappear if Orthodoxy were defined by religious practice as well as nominally.

Once more, as for the sample of New Haven Jewish men, Orthodox Jews are proportionately fewer with successive generations in this country. Of the Jewish students of foreign parentage shown in Table 34, 48 per cent are Orthodox, while only 15 per cent of those with at least one parent American born are Orthodox (Table 35). In conjunction with the relative sobriety of Orthodox students within and between each generation category, these facts strongly suggest that increases in intoxication with successive generations result from the declining adherence of American Jews to Orthodox

[21] Chi-square for drunkenness is 2.31, P (at 4 degrees of freedom) is .67. Chi-square for the milder intoxication is 4.48, P is .39.

religious practices. Conversely, the facts suggest that where Orthodox religious practices are continued Jews will be relatively sober no matter how many generations resident in this country.

In general, the findings in this section support the position that the notable sobriety of the Jews is intrinsically connected with the Orthodox religious life. Whatever influences tend to undermine adherence to Orthodox religious practices apparently also tend to undermine the pattern of Jewish sobriety. Of course, these influences operate through time upon successive generations, but generation, as such, is insignificant.

The Influence of Class

A most important factor to be considered in relation to patterns of sobriety and intoxication among Jews is class position. The existing literature on this subject is contradictory and inconclusive. For instance, Glad (31) asserts emphatically that the "low rates of inebriety" among Jews do not apply to any particular classes of Jews. In support of this assertion he cites Malzberg's (66) data from New York State, which suggest no differences along socioeconomic lines, together with the other European and American statistics whose ambiguities have been discussed previously in another connection.[22] In contrast to Glad, Bales (7) specifically associates Jewish sobriety with the Orthodox Jewish immigrants from eastern Europe who are of "lower class" position in America. Fishberg (27) identifies sobriety as especially characteristic of ghetto Jews of Europe who were far from the upper reaches of the class system.

Aside from the immediate questions of fact posed by these conflicting views, there are subtler theoretical problems to be settled which pivot on class patterns of intoxication. As an outstanding example, Kant's (48) theory can be interpreted to imply changes from patterns of moderate drinking and sobriety among Jews corresponding with changes in their class position. The extended argument would run like this: The traditional sobriety of the Jews derives principally from their weak civic position. Being defined as outcasts, constituting a numerical minority with small access to

[22] The Malzberg findings to which Glad refers are based on hospital admissions for alcoholic psychoses and are probably neither comprehensive nor refined enough to permit detection of differences in inebriety among Jews along class lines. The numerous other statistical studies cited by Glad do not systematically differentiate classes or socioeconomic strata. Other limitations of these studies were noted in Chapter 3.

power and prestige and little security, vulnerable to censure and persecution, the Jews found sobriety not only prudent but imperative for individual and group survival. But in open-class societies which tolerate cultural diversity, as in America, Jews have realistic alternatives. In the measure that power, prestige and influence is achieved, the caution associated with weak civic position may be relaxed. Thus, in more secure social circumstances, Jews who continue to drink should be neither more nor less sober than their Gentile neighbors of equivalent class position. On these premises, the range of variation in sobriety and intoxication might be expected to be distributed roughly along class lines—sobriety being more characteristic of lower class Jews who have recently emigrated from European ghettos, intoxication more prevalent among those who have achieved and consolidated higher positions in the American class structure.[23]

Further illustrations of theoretical problems whose solution hinges on class patterns of intoxication are to be found in the logical implications of theories which associate Jewish sobriety with religious Orthodoxy.[24] On the one hand, these theories lead to the prediction of differences along class lines similar to the prediction drawn from the above-described extension of Kant's theory. These

[23] There is, of course, a counterargument that Jews who have consolidated higher class positions may be or may feel no safer from censure and persecution than the more recently arrived ghetto Jews who are lower in the system of stratification. As long as a structural difference between groups is recognized, the anti-Semite perhaps believes that "a Jew is a Jew" whether he be rich or poor, ignorant or educated, weak or powerful, with a corresponding feeling of insecurity by all Jews. Certainly there are many examples in Jewish history to justify the view that surface indications of security are no guarantee that the underlying hostility of the larger society has abated. If it is conceded, however, that Jews of all classes define the larger society as censorious and dangerous, the implications from Kant's basic premises are clear: there would be no relaxation of caution and sobriety among Jews who have consolidated higher class positions in America. But if it is granted that class differentiation among Jews is accompanied by changes in the definition or perception of the Jewish situation and a more relaxed attitude toward society, then the implications are equally clear: other things being equal, intoxication would be more common among Jews in higher as contrasted to Jews in lower class positions. [The tendency of society to treat the Jew first as a Jew and only secondarily as a citizen of the larger national society is well analyzed by Kennedy who, as a consequence of this and certain other features of the Jewish situation, considered the Jews to be a "quasi caste." See R. Kennedy, "The position and future of the Jews in America," in Graeber and Britt (36). A strong case against assimilation as a solution to the "Jewish problem" is made by Steinberg (92) on the basis of the tragic historical experiences of the Jews in countries where assimilation apparently progressed quite far.]

[24] Our reference is to the theories of Bales (6, 7) and Cheinisse (18).

theories imply more frequent intoxication among Jews in the higher classes insofar as mobility in the class structure is correlated with the abandonment of Orthodox religious practices. On the other hand, the same theories contain further and different implications for class patterns of intoxication. In the first place, there should be systematic differences in intoxication along religious lines within any particular class. Theoretically, intoxication should vary inversely with Orthodoxy, if class is held constant. Secondly, Orthodox Jews should be quite consistently sober at any class level. Finally, differences in extent of intoxication between classes should vary directly with the proportions of Orthodox Jews in the classes considered. If Orthodox practices decline among Jews in the higher classes, increases in intoxication must be anticipated moving from lower to higher classes. While additional inferences might be drawn from these and other theories, the preceding ones should suffice to indicate that data on class patterns of intoxication may be of value in disclosing the principal sociocultural factors involved in the sobriety of Jews.

Before presenting such data, competing conceptions of the nature of class and the character of the American class system must be acknowledged. There are differences of opinion among authorities as to what constitutes class, and how and where class lines are to be drawn. Differences of opinion exist also concerning the degree to which classes in America are becoming more open or closed. Authorities hold divergent views as to the emergence of new classes. There are, furthermore, differences of opinion as to the prevalence of class consciousness and the extent to which classes compose a system of sociocultural integration or are pitted against one another.[25] For the present purpose, however, it is sufficient, as authorities agree, that a system of stratification is a reality of American life and that individuals and groups, including the Jews, have been mobile in this system. Hence the term class, as used here, does not necessarily refer to clearly demarcated groups which have a recognized class consciousness, an identity of interests or a homogeneous style of life. "Social level" or "stratum" or "socioeconomic status" might be substituted for "class" without serious misrepresentation of our intent. Nevertheless, the choice of eclecticism as to criteria of class, class boundaries and trends in the class system imposes responsi-

[25] An excellent summary of the problems and controversies in the field of research on social stratification together with a bibliography of current literature is contained in Pfautz (74). See also Goldschmidt (34).

bilities. Indices must be used which tolerably reflect differences in high or low social evaluation, prestige, wealth, power, influence, life chances, access to cultural values, and other ponderables to which stratification theorists refer. Thus several conventional indices will be used, both singly and in combination, lest proponents of particular class theories conclude that class differences cannot be reflected in our measures.

1. Social Class

In view of these considerations, Jewish men from New Haven were assigned social class positions according to a procedure developed by Hollingshead.[26] This method yields a composite rating of three factors empirically found to be related significantly to public evaluations of social position. These factors are occupation, education and residential area. The procedure involves separate scaling or scoring of the specific occupation, educational attainment, and area of residence of each man. Scores are then weighted according to the order of importance determined from independent evidence on evaluations of social position. Specifically, the occupation score is multiplied by eight, the education score by six and the residence score by five. Summation of the resulting products yields an index which permits assignment to one of five social classes. The distribution of the 73 Jewish men in our New Haven sample according to these classes is as follows: 5 in Class I (upper), 9 in Class II, 38 in Class III, 19 in Class IV, and none in Class V (lowest).[27] Since intoxication tends to increase, moving from the lower to the upper classes,[28] the crucial questions center on whether or not social class differences in intoxication simply reflect changes in Orthodox religious practices which, in turn, are more basically related to Jewish sobriety. Are the more Orthodox men in each social class relatively sober? As between social classes, are the Orthodox consistently sober? Do the evident differences in intoxication along

[26] We are especially indebted to Professor A. B. Hollingshead for his help in classifying the sample of New Haven Jewish men according to social classes. The rationale behind the specific procedure used here has yet to be published. Essentially it is an objective procedure, but the weighting of factors refers back to the kind of subjective evaluations of community members described and analyzed by Hollingshead (41) in "Elmtown." "Social class" is used at this juncture in accordance with Hollingshead's terminology.

[27] In two cases class position could not be determined for want of sufficient information.

[28] Data on increase in intoxication by class are given in Snyder (90). Compare Table 36, below.

TABLE 36.—*Intoxication Experience of New Haven Jewish Men, by Social Class and by Degree of Ceremonial Orthodoxy*

Intoxication Experience	Most Orthodox	Intermediate	Least Orthodox
Classes I and II			
5 or less	1	5	3
over 5	0	1	4
Class III			
5 or less	7	12	9
over 5	1	3	5
Class IV			
5 or less	3	12	1
over 5	0	1	1

social class lines result from a relative decline in Orthodoxy in the higher social classes?

To answer these questions, Jewish men in each of the social class divisions were subdivided according to degree of ceremonial Orthodoxy.[29] The extent of intoxication of men in the resulting categories is shown in Table 36. Inspection of this tabulation indicates that the direction of differences in intoxication is consistent throughout with theories which associate Jewish sobriety with religious Orthodoxy. At each class level intoxication increases with diminishing Orthodoxy, while between classes the Most Orthodox men appear to be quite consistently sober. Although the proportion of Most Orthodox men is slightly higher in Class III than in Class IV, the proportion of Least Orthodox men markedly increases moving up the class ladder. These latter differences suggest a decline in the incidence of Orthodox observance with ascent in the class system. However, a more intensive analysis was made of the data in Table 36 to determine the statistical significance of differences in intoxication between groups according to class and Orthodoxy.[30] The proportions of the total in each group were determined, an angular transformation was applied to each proportion and an analysis of variance carried out. It may be concluded from this analysis that: (*1*) the different social classes have no effect on proportions intoxicated above the criterion; (*2*) the proportions intoxicated above the criterion increase with decrease in Orthodoxy ($P < .01$). In

[29] Degree of ceremonial Orthodoxy is defined as previously in terms of ritual drinking practices. Of the 73 men in the sample, 4 are excluded from this table: 2 for want of sufficient information on social class, 2 for want of sufficient information on Orthodoxy.

[30] "Group" here refers to classification by degree of ceremonial Orthodoxy within each social class division. There are, accordingly, nine groups.

other words, as ceremonial Orthodoxy decreases intoxication increases.

The data from the College survey reinforce the conclusions drawn from interviews with New Haven men as to the nature of class and religious influences on Jewish patterns of sobriety and intoxication. However, annual family income and father's educational attainment, rather than Hollingshead's index, were used as indices of class for Jewish students.[31] While the use of different class indices decreases the comparability of the findings in the two samples, it has certain advantages. In the first place, Hollingshead's procedure is not readily applicable to college students.[32] Secondly, the use of different indices obviates dependence on a single index of class position. Of course, the fact that these students have themselves reached the college educational level implies a sample bias in favor of the upper classes. Nonetheless, there is considerable diversity in the class position of these students as measured by family income and father's educational achievement.

2. Economic Level

When Jewish students who drink alcoholic beverages were classified into arbitrary income divisions ranging from lower to higher according to the College Survey categories there appeared to be no systematic increase of intoxication with income but a noticeable differentation at the extremes. Those of lowest family income were the most sober, those of highest incomes surpassed the others in intoxication.[33] These differences are consistent with the previously suggested extension of Kant's theory. But they are also consistent with theories which attribute Jewish sobriety to religious Orthodoxy, with the following provisos: there must be (*a*) differences in intoxication along religious lines within each income class, (*b*) a smaller percentage of the Orthodox in the highest than in the lowest income classes, and (*c*) a constant pattern of sobriety of the Orthodox within the various income classes.

Tests of the fulfillment of these latter conditions required a reclassification of Jewish students into only two family income

[31] A few students in the sample are married and have independent family incomes Our index refers, however, only to the income of the parental family.

[32] The difficulties in application are two: first, residential classification is impossible for students drawn from diverse communities which have not been studied ecologically; second, educational classification is hampered by the fact that these students have not yet completed their formal education.

[33] Detailed data are presented in Snyder (90).

TABLE 37.—*Frequency of Intoxication among Jewish Students in the Lower Family Income Class, by Nominal Religious Affiliation (in Per Cent)*

	Drunk Twice or More	Number Reporting	Tight More than Five Times	Number Reporting
Orthodox	4	(51)	12	(60)
Conservative	14	(37)	14	(37)
Reform	24	(21)	25	(24)
Secular	38	(32)	38	(34)

TABLE 38.—*Frequency of Intoxication among Jewish Students in the Higher Family Income Class, by Nominal Religious Affiliation (in Per Cent)*

	Drunk Twice or More	Number Reporting	Tight More than Five Times	Number Reporting
Orthodox	18	(17)	15	(20)
Conservative	26	(27)	26	(26)
Reform	42	(35)	47	(34)
Secular	53	(17)	59	(17)

classes. Reclassification was necessary to retain fairly substantial numbers in table cells for analyzing differences in intoxication at different income levels according to nominal religious affiliation. For this purpose, a family income of $7,500 a year was chosen as the criterion for dividing Jewish students into "higher" and "lower" family income classes.[34] Using this dividing line, the extent of intoxication by religious affiliation is shown for students in the lower income class in Table 37. The percentages intoxicated above the criteria obviously increase along religious lines in the order of Orthodox, Conservative, Reform and Secular. Table 38 presents similar data for students in the higher income class and again there are increases in intoxication along religious lines analogous to the differences found in the lower income class. Holding income constant, these differences by religious affiliation are statistically highly significant.[35]

Further comparison of Tables 37 and 38 reveals that in percentage terms intoxication is more prevalent among students in the higher family income class regardless of religious affiliation. However, differences by income do not achieve significance when re-

[34] This criterion was chosen because it is the coded breaking point closest to the median in the distribution of Jewish students by family income. The terms "higher" and "lower" are, of course, relative to the sample under consideration.

[35] Chi-square for drunkenness is 24.39, P (at 6 degrees of freedom) is less than .001. For milder intoxication chi-square is 20.35, P is less than .003.

TABLE 39.—*Frequency of Intoxication among Jewish Students from the Lower Level of Education, by Nominal Religious Affiliation (in Per Cent)*

	Drunk Twice or More	Number Reporting	Tight More than Five Times	Number Reporting
Orthodox	12	(41)	17	(48)
Conservative	13	(39)	18	(40)
Reform	42	(24)	40	(25)
Secular	46	(26)	48	(29)

ligious affiliation is held constant.[36] But these differences border upon significance and will merit additional consideration subsequently. For the moment it suffices to note that Orthodox students in each of these income classes are fairly sober. Together with the facts that Orthodox students compose only about a fifth of the higher class but over a third of the lower income class, these findings suggest that such differences as exist in sobriety and intoxication between lower and higher income classes are related to the lesser vitality of religious Orthodoxy among the higher classes.

3. Educational Level

A similar picture emerges when the class position of Jewish students is established by father's educational attainment instead of family income. There is no systematic increase in intoxication among Jewish students according to finely graded levels of education of their fathers but, as with income, the highest level slightly surpasses the others in extent of intoxication.[37] A division of the sample at the approximate median for educational attainment of fathers produces two educational groups which are of suitable size for analyzing the extent of intoxication by religious affiliation. Students who report no education to some high-school education for their fathers are here designated as from the "lower level of education." Students whose father's education was recorded as completion of high school and upward are designated as from the "higher level of education." Table 39 shows that Jewish students from the lower level of education differ in intoxication along nominal religious lines, increases being apparent in the order, Orthodox, Conservative, Reform and Secular. A somewhat similar pattern of differences in intoxication by nominal religious affiliation is evident in Table 40 for students from the higher level of education. There are, however,

[36] Chi-square for drunkenness is 8.27, *P* (at 4 degrees of freedom) is .08. For milder intoxication chi-square is 6.78, *P* is .15.

[37] Cf. Snyder (90).

TABLE 40.—*Frequency of Intoxication among Jewish Students from the Higher Level of Education, by Nominal Religious Affiliation (in Per Cent)*

	Drunk Twice or More	Number Reporting	Tight More than Five Times	Number Reporting
Orthodox	7	(28)	10	(30)
Conservative	31	(26)	37	(27)
Reform	36	(33)	35	(34)
Secular	35	(23)	40	(23)

certain departures in Table 40 from the usual pattern of difference. In the first place, Reform slightly exceed Secular students in extent of drunkenness, although this irregularity has no great theoretical significance. In the second place, Conservative exceed Reform students in percentage tight above the criterion. This difference is indicative of a shift in the intoxication patterns of Conservative students, a shift which will be discussed in more detail below. Despite these irregularities, differences by religious affiliation are decidedly significant when level of education is held constant.[38] Outstanding, also, is the sobriety of Orthodox students from the higher educational level (Table 40). Indeed, Orthodox students from the higher level are more sober in percentage terms than Orthodox students from the lower level of education. Since there is a decline in the proportion of Orthodox students at the higher level of education, slight differences in intoxication according to level of education may be in part attributed to a decline in Orthodoxy among the more educated classes.[39]

These findings strongly support theoretical positions which link traditional Jewish sobriety with religious Orthodoxy. Associations between sobriety, intoxication and class position appear to be subordinate or incidental to connections with religious factors. This emphatically does not mean that class stratification exerts no influence upon patterns of sobriety and intoxication, but, in analytic terms, class influences are felt indirectly. Class differentiation and mobility influence Jewish sobriety insofar as they affect retention or rejection of Orthodox religious patterns. Orthodox religious practices appear, however, to be primarily responsible for the noteworthy sobriety of the Jews.

[38] Chi-square for drunkenness is 24.50, P (at 6 degrees of freedom) is less than .001. For milder intoxication chi-square is 18.17, P is .006.

[39] "More educated" here denotes formal and preponderantly secular education. It is believed by some that the average Orthodox Jew is better educated in the traditional subjects of religious Jewish education.

Having established this with greater certitude we may turn in Chapter 5 to a consideration of further aspects of the traditional religion and the minority situation of the Jews as these bear on patterns of sobriety and intoxication. Before doing this, however, it will be useful to note a few supplementary considerations against the background of our discussion of social class.

Supplementary Notes on Class and Religion

1. Class Differences among Conservative and Reform

Certain differences along class lines in patterns of intoxication among Jewish students need to be examined in more detail. There is a substantial percentage increase in intoxication among Conservative students in the higher classes, as measured by family income and level of education of fathers. Reform students, too, show a noticeable increase in intoxication in the higher income class, although this trend is reversed by a slight decline among Reform students from the higher level of education. The general tendency, however, seems to be for Conservative students in the higher classes to differentiate from the Orthodox and approach the Reform students in their patterns of intoxication, and for the Reform to become somewhat more like Secular students in this respect. The Conservative and Reform students, taken jointly, were therefore divided into two classes, using combined income and educational criteria, and differences in intoxication along these class lines were found to border upon significance.[40]

At first glance this finding seems to upset previous conclusions as to the relative influence of religion and class on Jewish sobriety. Perhaps patterns of intoxication differ among non-Orthodox Jews as a sole consequence of changes and differences in class position. But the requirements of theories which associate Jewish sobriety with religious Orthodoxy can reasonably be met if it can be shown that lower class Conservative and Reform students are closer to Orthodox values and practices—in the sense of continuity in the transmission of culture—than are such students of the higher class. In the College Drinking Survey there is no sure and direct measure of continuity with Orthodox religious values and practices. Some insights may be gained from students' reports of the nominal religious affiliation of their fathers.[41] Our data on this point indicate that fathers of lower class Conservative and Reform students are significantly more often Orthodox than fathers of such students in the higher class.

Additional facts on the nativity of parents and the cultural background of fathers strengthen the impression that lower class Conservative and Reform students are closer to Orthodox traditions. The data show that

[40] Data and procedures are presented in Snyder (90).

[41] Jewish fathers, as well as student sons, may be shifting their own religious affiliation. Hence, the religious affiliation of fathers of Conservative and Reform students is only a clue to continuity with Orthodox traditions.

parents of Conservative and Reform students in the lower class are preponderantly foreign born, while parents of such students in the higher class are more often American born. Finally, when cultural area of origin is considered, fathers of lower class Conservative and Reform students are overwhelmingly of eastern European origin, while fathers of the higher class students are more often western European or American.[42] In sum, our findings on religious affiliation and cultural background of fathers, and nativity of parents, support the view that lower class Conservative and Reform students are closer to Orthodox traditions than are their coreligionists in the higher class. These students may perhaps be fruitfully compared to the bulk of New Haven Jewish men previously designated as "Intermediate" in respect to ceremonial Orthodoxy, that is, men who had largely discontinued Orthodox practices although they had been brought up in observant Orthodox homes. In extent of intoxication these men were between the Most Orthodox and the Least Orthodox.[43] Very likely lower class Conservative and Reform students are in a phase of transition in which many Orthodox practices have fallen into disuse but Orthodox attitudes toward drinking and intoxication persist as a consequence of socialization in more traditionally religious homes. If this interpretation is sound, there is no reason to abandon theories which associate the noteworthy sobriety of the Jews primarily with the values and practices of Orthodox Judaism.

2. Class Mobility and Orthodox Decline

It was asserted at the outset of this chapter that with the mobility of successive generations of Jews in the American class system, Orthodox religious practices tend to be modified or abandoned. Subsequently, evidence was presented at various points suggesting a decline in the proportion of Orthodox to non-Orthodox Jews in the higher classes. Our evidence from the sample of New Haven Jewish men certainly points to a decline in ceremonial observance correlative with ascent in the class system. These findings are in general agreement with those of investigators in other communities; Wirth (108) in Chicago, Koenig (56) in Stamford, Gordon (35) in Minneapolis, Warner and Srole (105) in Yankee City. However, data from the College Drinking Survey provide an opportunity for further confirmation of this trend and a chance to assess the changes in nominal affiliation which accompany the modification and discontinuation of Orthodox practices.[44]

[42] Data on these points are presented in detail in Snyder (90). In all three instances chi-square tests yield P values less than .001.

[43] The Least Orthodox are those who were not reared in and do not now observe the Orthodox traditions.

[44] The very striking decline of participation in organized religious activities, moving through the nominal religious divisions, Orthodox, Conservative, Reform and Secular, by Jewish college students has already been amply demonstrated. We may be reasonably sure, therefore, that the nominal changes analyzed here do in fact accompany discontinuation or decreasing observance of traditional religious practices.

The general theory of the trend is that the open-class society fosters social mobility which creates strains motivating the abandonment of the traditional religious practices. Strains are engendered by the incompatibility between adherence to the practices of Orthodox Judaism, considered as an organized behavior system, and the organization of behavior required by the new class patterns. Referring to the outcome of this situation for the Jews in Yankee City, Warner and Srole (105) summarize the matter this way: ". . . rising in the class system demands conformity with the standards and modes at the system's various levels. Given the choice of conforming with the behavioral modes prescribed by the sacred Law or with those demanded by the Yankee City class system, only the . . . [Jewish] elders have accepted the former." Of course, some Orthodox practices can be continued with comparative ease, and, as we have seen, some Jews carry on many of the time-honored traditions even though they have achieved relatively high status in the economic, educational, residential and other systems. Moreover, compromise between the conflicting demands of Orthodoxy and class mobility is possible. As noted in Chapter 3, Conservative Judaism represents an attempt to synthesize elements of Orthodox tradition which do not conflict too openly with wider societal integration, while Reform Judaism represents a more radical effort to resolve the incompatibilities between traditional Judaic and contemporary institutions.[45] Reform Judaism is, in addition, socially and historically identified primarily with the German Jews who emigrated to America earlier than the majority of Jews from eastern Europe. When the great waves of Jewish immigrants from eastern Europe arrived, Reform German Jews were already well established in many American communities and comprised an élite toward whom the later immigrants from eastern Europe who aspired to achieve social status were oriented. Reform Judaism thus tends to be a sign of status and the transition of many Orthodox Jews to Conservative and Reform Judaism may in itself symbolize a change in class position as well as an adjustment of expediency consequent upon wider participation in American life.

As evidence of these changes in religious affiliation along class lines, Table 41 shows significant differences in the distribution of Orthodox, Conservative and Reform students according to family income classes. Because of the nature of the student sample, it is impossible to estimate accurately proportions which each religious division constitutes in each income class in the American Jewish population at large. Nevertheless, these data are indicative of the relative distribution of income classes in these religious divisions. Scanning the percentages from left to right in the lowest income class in Table 41, it is clear that the proportion of students

[45] There is no intention of denying that wider cultural tendencies toward secularization and the rationalization of life (and a corresponding laxity in religious observance) may also have played an important role in motivating the abandonment of Orthodox practices among Jews. Quite possibly a reversal of these tendencies would be accompanied by an "Orthodox renaissance." However, admission of the possible role of these factors does not vitiate the importance of the kinds of institutional incompatibilities to which we refer.

TABLE 41.—*Nominal Religious Affiliation of Affiliated Jewish Students, by Family Income Classes (in Per Cent)*

Family Income (in dollars)	Orthodox	Conservative	Reform	Number Reporting
Under 2,500	16	5	2	(20)
2,500–4,999	36	37	33	(84)
5,000–9,999	35	33	15	(69)
Over 10,000	13	25	50	(64)
Totals	*100*	*100*	*100*	*(237)*

Chi-square = 41.48, P < .001

in each religious division diminishes in the order, Orthodox, Conservative, Reform. In the middle income classes, this trend begins to reverse. In the highest income class, the proportion of students in each religious division increases in the order, Orthodox, Conservative, Reform. Moreover, data on generation status suggest the roles played by historical order of arrival and the factor of time in the stratification of the American Jewish population. In this latter connection, it is noteworthy that the proportion of foreign-born students in each religious division declines in the order, Orthodox, Conservative, Reform, while the proportion of American-born students of American-born parents mounts in the same order. Finally, an analogous pattern appears in respect to fathers' education, although educational differences are not so marked as in the cases of income and generation—a consequence, perhaps, of the extraordinary emphasis upon learning in the Orthodox tradition itself.[46]

The significance of these findings for the present research lies in the elucidation of the part played by class mobility and stratification in modifying Jewish patterns of moderate drinking and sobriety. Insofar as Orthodox practices are continued, sobriety is common no matter what the class level. But new class patterns compete with Orthodox institutions for the individual's time and loyalty, and, as Jews move in the class system, Orthodox practices tend to fall into disuse. Since the norms, ideas and sentiments most conducive to uniformly temperate drinking are integral with the traditional religion, the net effect of class mobility is a reduction in their vitality, preparation for the adoption of new modes of drinking and convergence with wider societal patterns of intoxication.

3. Sample Limitations and Class Differences

The evident movement away from Orthodox Judaism in the higher classes necessarily poses this question, if it is borne in mind that intoxication increases as Orthodoxy declines: Why are there not more pronounced differences in intoxication along class lines in our sample of Jewish college students? Part of the answer lies in the fact that this sample of students, for the reasons noted in Chapter 1, included Orthodox and, to a lesser ex-

[46] Detailed data on nominal religious affiliation by father's educational level and by generation are presented in Snyder (90).

tent, Conservative students in greater numbers than their probable proportions in the population. By virtue of being in college these students almost certainly overrepresent the "well-to-do" strata of Orthodox and Conservative Jews. But being Orthodox and Conservative they tend to be comparatively sober. Thus, their disproportionate representation tends to offset systematic increases in intoxication from lower to higher classes in the student sample.

This tendency is enhanced by the class distribution of the Secular students in the sample. As previously noted, the Secular exceed all categories of religiously affiliated Jewish students in extent of intoxication and additional data in this chapter have indicated their relatively frequent intoxication in both the lower and higher classes, as defined above.[47] However, the Secular students do not increase proportionately in the higher classes, as do the Reform, but are about equally distributed in the higher and lower classes.[48] If it were not for these students, differences in intoxication along class lines would be more readily apparent in the student sample corresponding to changes from Orthodox to Conservative to Reform Judaism. To what extent the class distribution of Secular students in this sample reflects the actual distribution of Secular Jews among Jewish college students or the American Jewish population is a question which cannot be finally answered from data gathered in the present research.

4. Secularization

In their general social characteristics, Secular Jewish students are more akin to Conservative than to Orthodox and Reform students. There is a close correspondence between Secular and Conservative students in income, education and generation characteristics, suggesting that these are similarly mobile strata tending toward wider participation in American life.[49] But given close correspondence in these basic characteristics, why are the Secular so much more often intoxicated than the Conservatives? There is the obvious religious difference, but this begs the question of the concrete social and psychological factors differentiating the Secular students from those who remain religiously affiliated, particularly the Conservatives whom they otherwise resemble in important characteristics. It seems reasonable to assume that many Secular students are in a process of cultural transition which involves profound inner conflict and outright rejection of traditional Jewish values, while Conservative students are making, or have made, an adjustment of expediency which entails more continuity and less rejection

[47] Cf. Chapter 3. Actually, the degree of association between frequency of drinking and frequency of intoxication in Reform and Secular students, respectively, is much alike. The difference in extent of intoxication between these categories was therefore attributed in part to higher frequencies of drinking among the latter rather than to more effective constraints in the drinking situation among the former. Nevertheless, Secular students ranked highest of all Jewish students in extent of intoxication.

[48] Details are given in Snyder (90).

[49] Details are tabulated in Snyder (90).

TABLE 42.—*Frequency of Intoxication among Jewish Students Reporting Father's Religious Affiliation as Orthodox, Self as Conservative or Irreligious*

	Drunk		Tight	
	Less than Twice	*Twice or More*	*Five Times or Less*	*More than Five Times*
Student Conservative	7	2	7	2
Student Irreligious	1	6	1	6
	Chi-square = 4.06 $P < .05$		Chi-square = 4.06 $P < .05$	

of Orthodox values. Frequent and perhaps excessive drinking among Secular Jewish students could be interpreted as an expression of agression and hostility toward comparatively Orthodox parents and other symbols of traditional Jewish authority, or as a radical technique of assimilation. Moreover, acknowledgement by Conservative students of some religious affiliation suggests emotional involvement in a definite normative system or moral framework, while open espousal of irreligiosity by Secular students hints at the kind of loss of normative orientation, with confusion and self-preoccupation, which Durkheim (24) called "anomie." In certain instances frequent intoxication by Secular students may signify developing alcoholism in which a traditionally "un-Jewish" means of adjustment is being used to alleviate tensions perceived individualistically and magnified by the loss of "sense of direction."

The question of alcoholism among Jews will be discussed briefly in Chapter 6. However, the relation of radical cultural transition and secularization to high frequencies of intoxication among Jews can be determined here in a tentative way.[50] For this purpose, some additional assumptions are necessary. First, it will be assumed that students who designate themselves as in one category of religious affiliation (including Secular) but report their fathers in a more Orthodox category are in some measure rejecting traditional authority and values. It will be further assumed that the rejection of these values is more pronounced among Secular students who report their fathers as Orthodox than among students who report their fathers as Orthodox but themselves as Conservative. It then follows that the sons of Orthodox fathers who express irreligious attitudes should be intoxicated more often than those who identify themselves with Conservative Judaism. The data presented in Table 42 support these suppositions.[51]

Of course, increasing intoxication need not be an inevitable consequence

[50] More generally, Horton (43) has shown a high correlation between rapid acculturation and inebriety among "primitive" peoples.

[51] The numbers in Table 42 are very small for two principal reasons. First, the vast majority of Jewish students reported religious affiliations the same as their fathers and are therefore not included. Second, the "Irreligious" category has been pared down to exclude students heretofore designated as Secular who simply failed to list a specific religious affiliation or reported themselves as unaffiliated.

of secularization per se.[52] But the fact that secular ideas and attitudes are so conspicuously related to relatively frequent intoxication among Jewish students is made more comprehensible by considering the larger societal context. Without indiscriminately characterizing our society as secular, it is fair to say that secular ideas and attitudes are prominent and acceptable in American culture. In conjunction with the relatively open class system, the prominence of these ideas and attitudes has great significance for certain types of Jews. To the Jew who aspires to higher social status and full assimilation, secularization represents a legitimate mode of dissociating from things Jewish and identifying with broader cultural values short of outright apostasy and conversion. To the rebellious Jew the adoption of secular ideas and attitudes provides a socially acceptable rationale for escape from traditional familial and communal controls. Seen in this perspective, the secularization of many Jews not only signifies the dissolution of traditional cultural and social controls but is indicative of the ongoing processes of shifting group loyalties and readiness to accept new attitudes and modes of behavior, including drinking behavior. We may speculate that the associated patterns of secularization and intoxication which deviate from traditional Judaic norms would have been rare in an earlier European society integrated by religious institutions antagonistic toward Judaism and characterized by rigidity of class boundaries.

[52] Where nominal change entails the substitution of a new secular orthodoxy (e.g., political Zionism) for the older religious Orthodoxy, without seriously disrupting Jewish social ties, sobriety may persist. We assume that intoxication will be more likely where secularization reflects (*a*) deep intrafamilial conflicts or discontinuities in the socialization process, and (*b*) strong assimilationist motives.

Chapter 5

INGROUP–OUTGROUP RELATIONS

THE THEORIES of Kant (48), Fishberg (27)[1] and others emphasize the ingroup–outgroup situation as decisive for Jewish sobriety.[2] Certain logical and empirical inadequacies in these theories were pointed out in the discussion in Chapter 1. Nevertheless it would be negligent to dismiss the minority status of Jews in a Gentile world as of no importance for Jewish sobriety. Nearly all students of Jewish drinking behavior have attributed significance to this situation in one way or another. Even Bales (7) suggests that the fear of retaliation from dominant groups may provide reinforcement to a norm of sobriety which he thinks derives ultimately from religious beliefs and practices. A survey of the literature on the influence of the ingroup–outgroup situation on Jewish drinking behavior, however, makes it especially clear that speculation has far outrun the accumulation of supporting evidence. By and large there has been cavalier indifference to the need for basing theories on firm factual foundations. Only Glad (31) attempted direct verification of Kant's type of theory which explains Jewish sobriety as a minority sect reaction to fear of censure from powerful majorities.[3] Glad interprets his own evidence as nonsupportive of the theory, but for reasons discussed elsewhere (90) Glad's findings are inconclusive.

There is some further indirect evidence bearing on this problem.

[1] Fishberg's views as relevant here are best expressed in Bernheimer (11).

[2] The Jewish group is designated as an "ingroup" so as to suggest consciousness of group identity vis-à-vis the larger Gentile society (the outgroup), and in recognition of a cultural tradition which embodies in many ways an ethnocentric view. However, these terms are intended only as ideal types. By no means do all nominal Jews experience an equivalent sense of "ingroupness," and distinctions in this respect have an important bearing on Jewish drinking behavior. For elaboration of these concepts see Sumner (98).

[3] Kant wrote (48): "Women, ministers, and Jews do not get drunk, as a rule, at least they carefully avoid all appearance of it, because their civic position is weak and they need to be reserved. Their outward worth is based merely on the belief of others of their chastity, piousness and separatistic lore. All separatists, that is, those who subject themselves not only to the general laws of the country but also to a special sectarian law, are exposed through their eccentricity and alleged chosenness to the attention and criticism of the community, and thus cannot relax their self-control, for intoxication, which deprives one of cautiousness, would be a scandal for them."

Bales (7) made a painstaking analysis of what he calls the empirical adequacy of Kant's argument and, like Glad, concluded that the facts do not support the theory. However, the facts upon which Bales based his rejection of Kant's theory are not facts concerning ingroup–outgroup influences on Jewish drinking behavior. The facts which in Bales' opinion challenge the empirical adequacy of Kant's explanation are drawn from histories of alcoholics. Bales reasons that, in the last analysis, Kant's theory attributes sobriety and the absence of alcoholism among Jews to the operation of the cognitive faculties—that is, the Jews, although they drink frequently, avoid excess and addiction by rationally assessing the consequences. This presumed rational assessment is made in the context of the actual or potential censure to which members of the disadvantaged Jewish minority are exposed. But experience with alcoholics does not support an assumption that knowledge of the dangers and undesirable consequences of excessive drinking enables the exercise of good judgment or "will power" sufficient to prevent alcoholism. Accordingly, Bales concluded that Kant's explanation and the analogous explanations of others are empirically inadequate.

Bales' criticism of the "rationalist fallacy" in these arguments is astute and suggestive. It highlights the naiveté of trying to explain the consistent sobriety of the Jews without some disciplined understanding of the nature of alcoholism. The critique also points to a body of facts which must be accounted for, at least by implication, in any adequate explanation of Jewish sobriety. Bales' reasoning, however, tends to obscure the need for a thorough analysis of the influence of the ingroup–outgroup situation on Jewish drinking behavior. This results from the implicit assumption that the nature of that influence is of the sort which Bales imputes to Kant's brief description and that the Jewish response is actually a purely rational one. This assumption, however, has no systematic evidence to support it. In Bales' argument this assumption is connected by a chain of inferences to facts on the etiology of alcoholism, and Kant's type of theory is accordingly found wanting. But Bales' readmission of Kant's explanation as a secondary factor in Jewish sobriety testifies to his own reluctance to dismiss ingroup–outgroup relations as of no consequence for the sober response of Jews to beverage alcohol.[4] We must therefore question whether the assumption of a rational response to imminent censure or danger exhausts the significance of

[4] See also Bales (6).

the ingroup–outgroup situation for Jewish sobriety. It seems that the resolution of the problems engendered by Bales' criticism of Kant's theory lies in further factual investigation of the influences on Jewish drinking of the Jewish ingroup, the Gentile outgroup and the relations between Jews and Gentiles.

Yet another facet of the ingroup–outgroup situation remains to be considered. The outgroup has been held by some observers to exercise a demoralizing influence on Jews in their use of alcoholic beverages. Fishberg (27) and Myerson (70), for instance, assert that the assimilating Jew who has increasing contacts with Gentiles is more prone to drunkenness and alcoholism than his compatriot of the ghetto.[5] The implications are clear: relations with the outgroup, which have been seen by Kant, Fishberg and others as a major cause of Jewish sobriety, are seen also in an entirely different light as the source of increasing intoxication and alcoholism among Jews. The evidence supporting this latter view is sketchy. It consists largely of clinical impressions and a few statistics which suggest greater inebriety among relatively assimilated Jews. But little or nothing has been revealed of the conditions under which changes are induced in Jewish drinking behavior and attitude, or the actual role of ingroup–outgroup relations in the process.

It is apparent that several questions of fact must be answered before a general evaluation of the impact of the ingroup–outgroup situation on Jewish drinking behavior can be made. For example, can immediate social pressures from the outgroup be inferred from a difference in Jewish drinking behavior in ingroup and outgroup contexts? Are these pressures handled differently by various categories of Jews and, if so, why? Do Jews perceive social pressures re-

[5] The demoralizing influence of outsiders and the identification of hedonistic drinking with assimilation (more accurately, with idolatry) is not a new idea or simply an observation of modern theorists but one that has long standing in Jewish culture, as the following tradition indicates: "'And they called the people unto the sacrifices of their gods: and the people did eat and bowed down to their gods [Numbers 25:2].' They [the Midianites] followed his [Balaam's] advice. . . . They put up shops for them and placed therein prostitutes and in their hands were all manner of attractive things. . . . And a young woman issued forth bedecked and perfumed and lured him and said, Why do we love you and you hate us? . . . Thereupon she gave him the wine to drink, and Satan burned in him. . . . When he asked her for sexual intercourse she said, I will not submit until you slaughter this to Peor and bow down to him. And he replied, I will not bow down to an idol. She said to him, You are only uncovering yourself. And he was mad with passion for her and did so." This tradition, with variations and amplifications, occurs in numerous ancient Talmudic and Midrashic sources, cited in Snyder (90).

garding drinking in terms of ingroup and outgroup? Are these perceptions related to stereotypes of Jews and Gentiles which are part of the Jewish cultural tradition? If so, what is the nature of these stereotypes and what functions do they serve? Does the vitality of these stereotypes depend upon strong group identification and participation in other aspects of Jewish culture? Can the findings on these various points be woven together with those in earlier chapters which show such a decided difference in the relative sobriety of Orthodox and non-Orthodox Jews? How then, is the significance of the ingroup–outgroup situation for Jewish drinking behavior to be assessed? These are the kind of questions which the present chapter will attempt to answer, if only in a preliminary way.

Intoxication in Ingroup and Outgroup Contexts

The question has been raised whether or not there is a difference in response to alcohol when Jews drink with members of the ingroup or in outgroup contexts. A behavioral difference in this respect should be indicative of the nature of ingroup and outgroup influences on Jewish sobriety. Suggestive evidence is to be found in the reports of our sample of New Haven Jewish men on the social contexts in which episodes of intoxication occurred. Of course, pinning down all these contexts is an impossible task when respondents have been intoxicated frequently. Descriptions were actually obtained for only 40 per cent of the instances of intoxication reported by men in this sample. Of these instances, however, 60 per cent took place either in military service or in college, with military service predominating. It is not certain that the social composition of the drinking group was preponderantly Gentile in all instances of intoxication in the service or in college. But the answers of several men questioned on this point indicate that the companions were frequently non-Jewish. Moreover, of the 17 in this group who had been intoxicated more than 5 times in their lives, 12 experienced some or all of the episodes of intoxication in the service or in college.[6] When it is borne in mind that drinking actually occurs more often in ingroup than outgroup contexts, the fact that a substantial proportion of intoxications oc-

[6] In the case of a thirteenth man it could not be ascertained whether intoxication occurred during this period. Actually, our data on experience in military service are not as satisfactory as they might have been because specific and detailed questions on service experiences were not included in the interview schedule. After the first interview, however, the interviewer made it a point to probe possible connections between intoxication and service experience.

curs in outgroup contexts assumes considerable significance. Without obscuring occasional instances of intoxication in Jewish settings, as at a Bar Mitzvah or wedding, the evidence points to the influence of the larger Gentile society in modifying Jewish patterns of moderate drinking and sobriety.

Because many of the Jewish students in the College Drinking Survey (96) sample attended colleges where a plurality or substantial minority of the student body are Jews, military service probably represents a more extreme outgroup situation than does college for these students. Consequently, a comparison of the patterns of drinking and sobriety in veterans and nonveterans among the Jewish students should be indicative of ingroup–outgroup influence. A reflection of these influences is to be found in the fact that of those Jewish veterans who reported on the regularity or irregularity of their drinking patterns in military service, 65 per cent had had an irregular pattern as against 35 per cent with a regular pattern. Of course regularity or irregularity may mean many things and there is no assurance from these data that Jewish students were more prone to intoxication while in the service. Subsequent questions on differences between current civilian drinking and practices while in the service revealed that 49 per cent of the veterans now drink less, 37 per cent about the same, and only 14 per cent more than while in the service. Still there is possible ambiguity in statements concerning "drinking more" or "drinking less," which may refer to frequency of drinking rather than to quantities consumed. But from what is known of Jewish interpretations of "drinking more" or "drinking less" there is little doubt that quantity was foremost in the minds of these students. Hence, a substantial proportion of Jewish veterans who reported drinking more in the service were almost certainly expressing an increase in the quantities of alcoholic beverages consumed in particular drinking situations and not just an increase in frequency of drinking.

The soundness of this interpretation is indicated by the fact that Jewish student veterans reported substantially higher frequencies of intoxication than nonveterans. On the one hand, only about a fourth of the nonveterans reported having been drunk twice or more or tight more than five times. On the other hand, about half the veterans had exceeded these limits. Uncritical reliance on gross differences in intoxication between veterans and nonveterans, however, may be misleading. Veterans in college tend to be older than non-

TABLE 43.—*Frequency of Mild Intoxication (Tight More than Five Times) in Veterans and Nonveterans among Jewish Students, by Age Classes (in Per Cent)*

Age	Veterans	Number Reporting	Nonveterans	Number Reporting
21 or less	49	(29)	25	(336)
Over 21	54	(101)	24	(45)

veterans and consequently have had more time to accumulate experiences of intoxication.[7] Age differences must therefore be taken into account before differences in intoxication among the Jewish students can be attributed to the service situation. To determine the effects of age differences, veterans and nonveterans were divided into two age classes (according to whether or not they were above or below the mean age for the sample of Jewish students) and were further classified by extent of intoxication. The resulting distribution is shown in Table 43 and it is clear that veterans in both age classes exceed nonveterans while differences by age are inconsequential.[8]

The difference in extent of intoxication between the veterans and nonveterans is particularly noteworthy because it does not apply to college students as a whole. On the basis of their general study of drinking among college students, Straus and Bacon (96) concluded that there are no significant differences in intoxication between veterans and nonveterans when age differences are taken into account. This is not the case with Jewish students. Apparently military service is related to greater experience of intoxication while age difference is insignificant within the narrow age range of these students.

SOCIAL PRESSURES

More direct evidence of the differential influences of social environments on Jewish patterns of drinking and intoxication is contained in sections of the New Haven interviews. The 73 Jewish men in the New Haven sample were asked whether they had been criticized for their drinking practices, either for "not drinking enough" or for "drinking too much." In reply, 41 said they had felt criticism for not drinking enough, while only 16 reported criticism for drinking too much. Forty-seven respondents identified the sources of these

[7] On this point, see Straus and Bacon (96).

[8] Chi-square of the difference by veteran status is 18.54, P (at 2 degrees of freedom) is less than .001. To simplify presentation, only data on milder intoxication are shown in Table 43. Data on more severe intoxication, showing an analogous difference by veteran status, are presented in Snyder (90).

TABLE 44.—*Sources of Social Pressures on New Haven Jewish Men to Drink More or Less*

Pressure	Jewish	Mixed	Non-Jewish
To drink more	2	11	18
To drink less	15	1	0

Chi-square = 35, P < .01

pressures. Analysis of the results (Table 44) indicates that Jewish men perceive the Jewish group as exerting pressures in the direction of moderate drinking and sobriety, while the non-Jewish milieu is perceived as the primary source of pressures to drink to excess.

The content and sources of the pressures summarized in Table 44 deserve further attention. With the exception of one case which is equivocal, all Jewish men who had been criticized for drinking too much reported the source of criticism as specifically Jewish and familial. "The folks used to think I drank a little too much," or "My wife doesn't like me to drink at all," were typical comments. By contrast, criticism for not drinking enough was confined almost exclusively to the categories of friends, acquaintances and business associates. Also, several men who reported criticism from mixed sources for not drinking enough added qualifications such as "mostly non-Jewish." Of the two men who reported exclusively Jewish criticism for not drinking enough, one said he was teased on Passover for just touching the wine to his lips, whereas the traditional rule calls for drinking the better part of four cups. The other indicated a jocular form of criticism from relatives—"We need lots of schnapps 'cause old X is here," hardly to be interpreted as an expectation that the respondent should actually drink larger amounts. Reactions to this kind of ingroup criticism are essentially humorous. But outgroup criticism of not drinking enough may evoke responses of moral indignation, resentment and resistance. Typical are reactions such as these: "They call me a sissy, but I don't care." "They try to get me to take more, but I never do." "It's just none of their business!"

These data are sufficiently unambiguous to permit some important inferences. In the first place, twice as much felt pressure to drink more was reported than to drink less. This suggests the covert nature of the social pressures on adults within the Jewish group and the implicit acceptance of the sobriety norm. But should overt social pressure be brought to bear on the individual by other Jews, it will more than likely be in the direction of moderate drinking and sobriety. This does not mean that Jewish men never find themselves in the position of refusing a drink offered by a Jewish host. However, such a situation would not ordinarily generate sufficient tension to leave an emotional residue which would be expressed as a feeling of social criticism. In the second place, a substantial number of Jewish men feel that the social milieu does bring pressure on them to drink more than they ordinarily drink. But these pressures are perceived as emanating primarily from the outgroup. In sharp contrast, the outgroup is seldom or never perceived as exerting explicit pressure toward moderate drinking and sobriety.

Variations in Response to Outgroup Pressures

In the light of the facts on the social sources of pressures to drink less moderately, the more frequent intoxication among Jews in military service and college can perhaps be understood as a response to outgroup pressures. Our New Haven data, however, indicate a decided absence of intoxication in the course of daily contacts with non-Jews within the community. This raises the question as to why Jewish men often yield to outgroup pressures in the service and in college, but only rarely in the course of ordinary events. Certainly intracommunity contacts between Jewish men and Gentiles are frequent and there is evidence in our interviews that drinking is sometimes involved in these situations. The interview materials also confirm that in these latter situations social pressures are often brought to bear on Jewish men to drink beyond the limits to which they are accustomed. Our view is that the solution of this problem hinges on the different types of socially structured situations and relations which arise between Jews and non-Jews within the community, in military service and in college.

1. Sobriety in Intracommunity Relationships

While supporting data cannot be presented in quantitative form, there is reason to believe that role and situation are more often instrumentally defined by Jewish men during intracommunity contacts with non-Jews than during military service or in college. There is also reason to believe that an instrumental definition of the situation helps to constrain the drinker from intoxication. If these assumptions are valid, constraints should be at a maximum where social pressures to drink more are experienced by Jews in the course of daily intracommunity relations with Gentiles.

The idea that an instrumental orientation exerts constraints in the drinking situation stems in part from Glad's (31) suggestions based on his comparative study of Jewish, Irish Catholic and Protestant attitudes toward drinking. As set forth in Chapter 1, Glad proposed that Jews tend to be oriented toward long-range goals in contrast to the Irish who are more concerned with proximate goals. Among Jews, recognition, achievement and understanding take precedence over proximate goals like warmth, friendliness, and concern for how people feel, which Glad believes are more valued by the Irish. Glad therefore suggested that in most situations Jews drink as an incidental means to the achievement of the long-range goals, and that heightened concern with those goals necessitates constraint in the drinking situation. But lacking more refined measures of value emphases in these two cultures, such generalizations seem hazardous. Also, in Glad's construction there is some implication of indifference on the part of Jews to proximate goals such as warmth, friendliness and concern for the feelings of others, for which there is no factual basis. There would seem, however, to be factual justification for asserting a cleavage in Jewish life whereby the satisfaction of proximate goals is confined to relations with Jews, while the satisfaction of goals giving rise to an instrumental orientation is more characteristic of relations with Gentiles. Certainly in the eastern Europe of a few generations ago the expressive and affective life of Jews was of necessity, as well as voluntarily, restricted to family, ghetto and ethnic community. Relationships with Gentiles were largely defined by the Jews' precarious "middleman" role between nobility and peasant masses.[9] Concern with economic survival daily forced Jews out of the emotionally satisfying and protective ghetto, but in the capacity of "economic man." There was little approach to the cultivation of primary-group ties on the part of either Jews or Gentiles. Moreover, ethnic cleavage tends to persist in the modern American community, although in attenuated form.[10] In daily community life the affective and expressive relations of Jews are still to a large extent confined within the boundaries of family and ethnic group. Our New Haven data suggest that, by contrast, relations with non-Jews tend to be instrumentally defined; in intracommunity contacts with

[9] In describing contacts between Jews and non-Jews in the eastern European *shtetl*, Zborowski and Herzog (110) have this to say: "The market represents the chief contact between the Jew and the non-Jew, who for the *shtetl* is primarily the peasant. Aside from the market and scattered business negotiations, they inhabit different worlds. . . . The seeds of all their relations are in this market place contact." On the middleman role of the Jews in eastern Europe, see Dubnow (22).

[10] For a brief description and documentation of the persistence of ethnic cleavage between Jews and Gentiles in America, see Snyder and Landman (91).

non-Jews, New Haven Jewish men are typically in business roles (sales and service and professional roles) characterized by functional specificity and affective neutrality. The situational goals are the contract, the sale, making a good impression, and the larger goals of money, recognition and status which these imply. In these situations, cognitive interests are given primacy. It is imperative "to be on one's toes" and "keep one's wits about one" in order to manipulate objects and persons in the situation to the desired end. Consequently, an element of renunciation and discipline is introduced; the individual feels pressure not to "give in" to modes of gratification like intoxication which disrupt cognitive processes and interfere with the achievement of larger objectives.[11]

Evidence of an instrumental structuring of relations with non-Jews and the constraints which this definition exerts on drinking was spontaneously given in the course of interviews with New Haven Jewish men. The following interview excerpts illustrate these points quite explicitly:

> [Mr. X, a salesman, 50 years old:] "I sell. I'm out on the road. I could get a drink in every home I go in. They're [non-Jews] always offering but I usually give them an excuse. I tell them I'm on doctor's orders not to drink. In that way I don't insult anyone. [At a later point in the interview:] I don't get to know my customers that well. You can't get too familiar with them or they start to take advantage of you. They want to treat you like one of the family but you have to draw the line." [30]
>
> [Mr. Y, 47 years old, an executive in the transportation field in a capacity which brings him into personal contact with a wide range of the firm's customers, largely non-Jewish:] "When I do drink nowadays it's a question of entertaining business-wise, and 'occasions.' . . . When I'm entertaining [in business connections] I feel you've got to keep a certain amount of decorum. You're talking to people. After all, you're doing it for a purpose!" [19]
>
> [Mr. Z, 60 years old, owner of a small building firm, states that he does a good deal of his drinking in "business" and with "business associates" who are predominantly non-Jewish. Under these circumstances, he says:] "I'll do what the rest are doing. If they're having high-balls, I'll sit in and hold on to that glass for sociability. . . . A man shouldn't

[11] For a general definition and discussion of an instrumental orientation and the constraints arising therefrom, see Parsons (72). In discussing various possible modes of orientation of an actor to a situation Parsons warns that the cognitive, cathectic and evaluative modes are present in every situation, but adds that there is a "relative primacy of the different modes." What is important for our purpose is that if the actor's orientation is instrumental, cognitive interests have primacy and expressive or gratificatory interests which might disrupt the cognitive process are subordinated.

> drink, but there are times a man has to have a drink. But the less you drink, the better. People shouldn't take more than two drinks on any occasion. Two drinks should be the limit. . . . I entertain a lot but that's not any personal expense. We buy liquor at Christmas and other times but that's business, not personal. With business associates, I'll go wherever they take me. I try to make them feel as pleasant as possible." [32]

It would be erroneous to suppose that the instrumental orientation expressed in these excerpts is something distinctively Jewish. Obviously this attitude is required by many roles in society, occupied by Jews and non-Jews alike. It would be equally erroneous to imply that all intracommunity relations between Jews and Gentiles are instrumentally defined by Jews. In the modern American community, social contacts frequently arise between Jews and Gentiles which fall within the range of primary-group relations. However, in choosing intimate non-Jewish friends, Jews may avoid those who drink excessively and who might put pressure on them to do likewise. The following excerpt illustrates this process of selection where friendship alternatives are open:

> "My closest friends are Jewish [but] . . . my friendships have spread out in recent years to include many non-Jews. [He lives in a very mixed neighborhood. But he adds:] None of my friends are excessive drinkers!" [43]

What is important, however, is that an instrumental orientation may exert a constraining influence on intoxication among Jews at precisely the point where they are likely to be urged and pressed to drink in a hedonistic fashion, namely, in contact with Gentiles. It is also important that, while anxiety about the loss of cognitive orientation is evidently a deterrent to intoxication in these situations, the cognitive emphasis is in the nature of a means to other ends rather than an end in itself. There is no obvious relation between this emphasis and the general valuation of mental faculties deriving from the Jewish tradition of learning and study briefly discussed in Snyder and Landman (91).

In considering Jewish resistance to pressures to drink excessively in the course of intracommunity contacts with non-Jews, the proximity of the Jewish family and Jewish community should not be forgotten. These, presumably, act as negative sanctions on intoxication. Stable relations with family and ethnic community may also strengthen the Jewish man's personal sense of Jewishness with which. as we shall try to show later, the concept of sobriety is intertwined.

Indeed, as long as family and community sanctions are imminent and the sense of ethnic identification strong, outgroup pressures to drink more may intensify adherence to the sobriety norm. A stubborn feeling that "they [Gentiles] cannot break me" seems to be reflected in the remarks of several respondents, and an instrumentally structured role relationship would simply reinforce this resistance. Changes from norms of moderate drinking and sobriety should occur where emotional investment is shifted to the non-Jewish outgroup, where ingroup sanctions are no longer imminent and where an instrumental orientation no longer constrains. In circumstances of this kind, resistance to outgroup pressures may be expected to weaken. Anticipated is a tendency toward conformity with patterns of drinking or intoxication characteristic of the particular group or stratum with which the individual identifies.

2. Intoxication in Military Service

These conditions for change are closely approximated in military service and to a lesser extent in college and the facts suggest that Jews actually are more prone to intoxication in these contexts. However, data on the contexts of intoxication need to be supplemented by qualitative impressions before the impact on Jewish drinking behavior of situations like military service can be fully appreciated. In the service Jews are severed from the intimate milieus of family and community which support patterns of moderate drinking and sobriety. They are impelled by circumstances to make primary-group identification with non-Jews whose drinking patterns are at variance with their own. Conformity to norms of relatively heavy drinking is evidently often a condition of acceptance into these intimate, tightly knit primary groups which studies of army life (86) suggest are essential for the maintenance of individual morale. As one New Haven man expressed it:

> "I started in the Army like a lot of others. No one in my old gang drank. I started drinking more in the Army with the attitude of trying to be one of the boys." [Actually this man drank frequently before entering the service. His reference is to hedonistic drinking.] [30]

Moreover, military service not only disrupts normal social relations and routines but apparently often undermines instrumental, goal-directed activities. This tendency is reflected time and again in the assertion by Jewish men that they drank more in the service because there was nothing else to do. The following comment is not at all atypical:

> "I drank more in the Army. There wasn't much else to do. When you were in town you went to bars with the Company. You'd sit and drink and listen to records. I usually get sick before I lose control but this completely excludes the Army. I guess I've passed out a few times, at that, in the Army." [40]

Military service, too, is a context alien to the eastern European Jewish tradition and especially the Orthodox religious tradition.[12] A perusal of the reports of the New Haven Jewish men on their military experience often gives the impression that they were "fish out of water." General discomfiture, together with the disintegration of goal-directed activities and experience of social pressure, is clearly expressed in this case:

> "I did a fair amount of drinking in the Army. Every time we'd get a week-end pass we'd drink. Why? Didn't have a hell of a lot else to do. My buddies in the Army would criticize me [for not drinking enough]. You'd want to stay sober enough to get back to the truck, and they wouldn't care. They weren't Jewish—damned uncomfortable I was in the Army!" [47]

Sometimes military service appears to be an acutely anxiety producing situation for Jewish men. Cut off from emotionally supportive relations with family and ethnic community and from the community of values which give daily routines and instrumental activities their meaning, some Jewish men become extremely anxious and confused. In isolated instances, alcohol was sought as a means of escape from an alien and distressing situation, as the following excerpt testifies:

> "Two or three times in the Army I just went out, left camp, had a few drinks—from that point I don't remember until I got up the next morning. In the Army I was depressed and homesick. I went out and got drunk. They called it psychoneurosis. Then, I snapped out [after a medical discharge]. Didn't drink any more after that." [He means that he did

[12] There is a long history of Jewish protest against military service in eastern Europe, a protest which stemmed partly from pacific religious ideals and partly from reaction to the deliberate attempts of despotic governments, such as the regime of Nicholas I of Russia, to crush Judaism and assimilate the Jews through the imposition of long and harsh terms of military service. For evidence of this situation in 19th century Russia and Poland, see Dubnow (22). The traditional rejection of temporal power as a means of maintaining Jewish "moral hegemony" is discussed by Reisman (77).

not drink hedonistically subsequent to his military experience; he currently drinks beverage alcohol about 125 times a year.] [57]

However, acute loss of orientation and accompanying anxiety may be the exception rather than the rule. Perhaps more typically Jewish men drink heavily in military service to gain acceptance into Gentile primary groups toward which it is meaningless to assume an instrumental attitude and from which basic emotional supports are sought because there is no alternative.

While the data are less detailed, the themes which New Haven Jewish men express in regard to drinking experiences while in military service are reiterated by Jewish college students. Questioned as to the regularity of their drinking patterns and whether they drank more or less while in the service, many Jewish students who reported that they drank more appended comments such as these:

"As the boys went, I went."

"I went along with the crowd at times."

"I found it necessary for social reasons, I had to get along with the men I was living with."

"Pass the time."

"Disgust with environment [combat], and not being able to get home."

3. Response of Different Religious Categories

Is there a marked difference among Jews of different religious affiliation in response to the situational pressures to drink immoderately which arise in military service? Different responses to the same situational pressures might indicate varying intensities of inner sentiments supporting Jewish norms of moderate drinking and sobriety. Similarities, while not vitiating the role of inner attitudes, would certainly point to the importance of the social environment in sustaining or modifying these norms. Unfortunately our New Haven data are insufficient to permit refined conclusions on these points and the small number of Orthodox veterans in the student sample seriously limits the possibilities of generalization. Clues are nonetheless forthcoming from the data in Table 45 on the extent of intoxication of veterans and nonveterans among the Conservative and Orthodox, combined in a single category, and the Reform and Secular, likewise combined. Although significant differences appear between these religious categories irrespective of veteran status, there is also significantly more intoxication among veterans when

TABLE 45.—*Frequency of Intoxication (Drunk Twice or More) in Veterans and Nonveterans among Jewish Students, by Nominal Religious Affiliation (in Per Cent)*

	Veterans	Number Reporting	Non-veterans	Number Reporting
Orthodox and Conservative	33	(15)	12	(125)
Reform and Secular	62	(21)	35	(89)

religion is held constant.[13] While insufficient to nullify differences between more and less Orthodox Jews, the service situation evidently exerts a powerful influence towards heavier drinking which is responded to by all the religious categories.

The burden of the evidence appears to be that the internalization of norms and ideas antithetical to hedonistic drinking is often insufficient to sustain patterns of moderate drinking and sobriety in the face of strong situational counterpressures, such as those which arise in military service. Evidently, conscience alone cannot guarantee conformity to behavioral patterns which are at variance with primary-group norms. The moral consensus of the primary group appears to be a potent factor determining the character of the individual's drinking behavior. The obverse implication of an increase in intoxication in the service is, of course, the overwhelming importance to Jewish sobriety of regular participation in a Jewish milieu which supports norms of moderate drinking and sobriety. Where the sober dictates of individual conscience and primary-group consensus are in harmony, as in the Orthodox religious community, the likelihood of continued sobriety would appear to be greatest despite extensive drinking.

4. Insulation of Orthodox Jews from Outgroup Pressures

The data in this section also point to an important latent function of the broader religious complex in sustaining Jewish norms of moderate drinking and sobriety. Orthodox norms circumscribe the social life of observant Jews so as to minimize the emergence of close, primary-group relations with Gentiles. This is readily apparent in the prohibition on intermarriage, in dietary restrictions, and the

[13] Chi-square of the difference in drunkenness along religious lines, holding veteran status constant, is 19.28, P (at 2 degrees of freedom) is less than .001. Chi-square of the difference by veteran status is 10.18, P (at 2 degrees of freedom) is less than .01. Analogous data on milder intoxication have been omitted here but are presented in Snyder (90).

like. But no less important is the totality of norms which channel the Jew's emotional and expressive life within the confines of the Jewish community.[14] By curtailing the development of primary-group ties with non-Jews, Orthodox Judaism insulates its adherents from outgroup pressures to drink immoderately. Orthodoxy does not do away entirely with social contacts between Jews and Gentiles. Thus mere social contact with Gentiles is hardly a cause of intoxication among Jews. But Orthodox Judaism tends to narrow the bases of Jews' contacts with outsiders largely to the economic area where instrumental attitudes predominate. The effects of this circumscription are twofold. On the one hand, the potential influence of primary-group relations with non-Jews in modifying drinking behavior is mitigated. On the other hand, the structure of the permitted role relationship may itself induce additional constraints in the drinking situation.

The observant Jew is thus doubly protected from outside pressures to drink hedonistically, while within the confines of the Orthodox community consensus supports sobriety and the act of drinking is ritually controlled. With the continuation of ethnic cleavage but a decline in religious motives for drinking, the instrumental drinking described by Glad (31) is perhaps becoming more important to Jews. Accordingly, continued separatism and the value complex from which instrumental attitudes derive may represent a second line of defense against intoxication. But where the insulating function of Judaism disintegrates and instrumental orientation is disrupted, moderate drinking and sobriety apparently often give way to convivial and hedonistic drinking.

Ethnocentrism and Jewish Sobriety

That strong moral condemnation of intoxication is prevalent among the more Orthodox Jews was shown early in this work; and in the present chapter, it was seen that Jews connect social pressures for moderate drinking with the ingroup and for "more" drinking with the outgroup. Actually, these ideas and sentiments are indicative of underlying cultural stereotypes of sober Jew and drunken Gentile and of the incorporation of sobriety in the ethnocentrism of the Jewish group.[15]

[14] The insulating character of Orthodox Judaism has been discussed in the recent sociological literature by Warner and Srole (105).

[15] The structuring of these stereotypes in the religious tradition has already been indicated in the discussion of the Purim festival in Chapter 2.

1. Stereotypes of Sober Jew and Drunken Gentile

The elucidation of Jewish stereotypes can be started by considering the responses of Jewish men to questions pertaining to beliefs about Jewish and Gentile drinking practices. In the New Haven interviews, the Jewish respondents were directly asked whether they thought Jews drink more, less or about the same as Gentiles. On the basis of responses to these questions, it may be concluded that the prevailing belief is that Jews drink less than non-Jews. Of the sample of 73 men, 54 asserted this to be the case. Not a single man asserted that Jews drink more than non-Jews and only 7 felt that Jews and non-Jews drink about the same, while the remaining 12 refused to offer a definite opinion on this point. In questioning respondents, no attempt was made to specify whether "more" or "less" referred to the incidence of drinking, frequency of drinking or amounts consumed. Where respondents made assertions about the simple incidence and frequency of drinking among Jews and Gentiles, these were usually consistent with their beliefs about drinking to excess. In other words, it was implied that the incidence and frequency of drinking among non-Jews is greater than among Jews, which is by no means necessarily the case.

It must be observed at once that questions about drinking among Jews and non-Jews induced considerable conflict in respect to particularistic and universalistic values. A few excerpts from the interview records will illustrate the nature of the competing values:

"Definitely [Jews drink less], but I can't think in those terms." [3]

"I don't see any reason why they [the Jews] should be any different from anyone else." [44]

"I think everybody should drink less than they do." [41]

"I didn't study it. I'm not looking into it. There are all kinds of fish in the sea." [38]

"Give me half a minute to think. I'm an authority? Jews are a minority. There are fewer Jews. I think they're about the same. I think the Irish drink more than Italians. Poles drink. Jews are human. Jewish peddlers used to drink when they were cold. Jews shouldn't be an exception. They're no chosen people." [37]

"That may be just prejudice. I don't like to make general statements." [35]

"I'd hate to say. Most of my friends, Jews and non-Jews, drink about like I do." [28]

"Hard to tell, it's up to the individual." [26]

"There's an old saying among Jews of my class—my father has an old theory that Jews drink less than Christians. It's hard to say. It might be so. I don't mean this with a racial bias, it just might be that Jews drink less." [46]

"That's something I wouldn't say, I couldn't say, but I think they do [drink] less. There are very few drunkards among the Jewish race." [57]

"I don't think it has anything to do with nationality. I don't want to bring it in. If Christians were raised in a non-drinking environment they wouldn't either." [12]

"Well, I don't think necessarily less—they—I think you can base it on occupation, on per cent. There's more Gentiles patronizing taverns, grilles, etc., than Jews." [16]

These examples are sufficient to show that, while the prevailing Jewish belief is that excessive drinking is a Gentile characteristic, there are strong competing values which make it difficult for many Jews to admit discussion of the matter in these terms. The conflict between universalism and particularism is nothing new in Jewish culture. It has been the fundamental paradox of normative Judaism since ancient times.[16] In all probability the protracted minority status of the Jews has sensitized them to this value conflict and current democratic ideologies have reinforced the universalistic side of the coin. Time and again the themes that "we're all human," and "it's up to the individual," and "these things are not racial or nationality matters" are to be found alongside statements of a highly particularistic and ethnocentric nature in the interviews.

In the historical experience of the Jews in Europe, there was probably considerable objective basis for Jewish beliefs about excessive drinking among Gentiles. At least historians of Jewish life in eastern Europe, such as Dubnow (22), relate that the Gentile peasantry became intoxicated with tiresome regularity. In America, where there are many millions of abstainers, the objectivity of these Jewish beliefs is open to some question, although abstinence sentiment is most apparent in rural areas while American Jews are predominantly urban.[17] What is sociologically significant, however, is not the objective truth or falsehood of these beliefs but whether or not they are believed. As Thomas and Thomas (100) observed, "If men define situations as real, they are real in their consequences." Of further significance is the question as to whether or not Jewish beliefs about drinking among Jews and Gentiles are linked with basic moral ideas and sentiments. The problem is whether or not these beliefs reflect

[16] Cf. Moore (68).

[17] For evidence of the concentration of abstinence sentiment in rural areas see, e.g., Jellinek (51).

concepts of ethnic virtue whose emotional importance is magnified by reference to opposite characteristics in outsiders.

In an effort to probe deeper into this problem, the New Haven Jewish men were asked whether they had the idea in childhood that sobriety was a Jewish virtue, drunkenness a Gentile vice.[18] In response to this question, 27 of the 73 men answered yes, 38 answered no, and 8 said they did not remember or could not answer. Taken at face value, these findings seem partially to contradict the results and inferences from the more matter-of-fact question as to whether Jews drink more or less than non-Jews. But in the face of further evidence the apparent contradiction fades away. Later in the interview, Jewish men were asked whether or not they were familiar in childhood with stories, songs, poems or saying which suggested sobriety as a Jewish virtue, drunkenness as a Gentile vice. As an example, the little ditty "Shikker iz a Goy" (Drunken is a Gentile) was frequently cited. Despite the logical inconsistency, responses to this question reversed the trend of answers to the previous question on sobriety as a Jewish virtue, drunkenness as a Gentile vice. A majority of 48 men answered that they were familiar as children with such folk beliefs, only 17 replied that they were not, while 8 said either that they did not remember or could not answer.

The increase in affirmative answers to the second of these two questions is associated with the relinquishment by some Jewish men of universalistic attitudes in the interview situation. This turnabout accompanied the respondent's recognition that the interviewer knew the prevailing folk beliefs and that it was therefore no longer necessary to conceal ethnocentric ideas behind a universalistic front. This process of relaxation in the interview situation may be illustrated by some examples. One elderly man who said that Jews and Gentiles drink "about the same" asserted later that drunkenness is "more a Gentile characteristic," although he felt obliged to qualify this by the phrase, "in a way." When the interviewer subsequently inquired whether he knew "Shikker iz a Goy," he was surprised and delighted, and insisted on singing the entire song, as well as some other ditties of similar import, for the interviewer's benefit. In another case the respondent tenaciously denied awareness of any differences between Jews and Gentiles. At the mention of the song

[18] It was hoped that referring the question to childhood would remove some of the guilt felt for entertaining such an idea and thus allow freer discussion. Moreover, we wished to know whether or not these were beliefs of long standing.

"Shikker iz a Goy," however, he exclaimed, "Say, you must have really studied this!" and went on to say that he had long been familiar with these notions. Nevertheless, some Jewish men were either reluctant or refused to give up their universalistic attitude. Moreover, the insistent qualification that "they [the folk beliefs] didn't leave any impression on me" was often heard. In one interview, a relative of the respondent happened to be present when the interviewer mentioned "Shikker iz a Goy." The respondent, who had answered in the negative to the preceding question on the imputation of drunkenness to Gentiles, just shook his head: "Never heard of it!" At this his relative remarked, in amused astonishment, "Aw, come on—everybody knows that! Why, mother used to sing me to sleep with it when I was a baby!" The respondent smiled a bit sheepishly but continued shaking his head, indicating with a wave of his hand that he was ready for the next question.[19]

The qualitative import of Jewish stereotypes could easily be lost among statistics and anecdotes. Thus it may be well to give the content of the little song, "Shikker iz a Goy," which has been translated from the Yiddish as follows:

> The Gentile goes into the saloon, the saloon,
> And drinks there a small glass of wine; he tosses it off—his glass of
> wine.
> Oh—the Gentile is a Drunkard—a drunkard he is,
> Drink he must,
> Because he is a Gentile!
>
> The Gentile comes into our alley, our little street,
> And breaks the windows of us poor Jews;
> our windowpanes are broken out,
> For—the Gentile is a Drunkard—a drunkard he is,
> Drink he must,
> Because he is a Gentile!
>
> The Jew hurries into the place of prayer;
> An evening prayer, a short benediction he says,
> and a prayer for his dead.

[19] It is pertinent to note here that ceremonially Orthodox Jewish men are readier to acknowledge familiarity in childhood with folklore imputing sobriety to Jews as an ethnic virtue, drunkenness to Gentiles as a characteristic vice. Data on this point are presented in Snyder (90). These data, however, must be interpreted with caution. They do not inevitably mean that Jewish men who claim to be unfamiliar with these stereotypes are not in fact familiar with them. But there is a possibility that these beliefs are diffused more widely among the Orthodox.

For—the Jew is a sober man—sober is he,
Pray he must,
Because he is a Jew.[20]

It would be an exaggeration to impute great historical or educational significance to this song itself. It evidently originated in the Russian ghettos and is unquestionably not known to many Jews. However, the linkage of sobriety with Jewish identity, drunkenness with Gentile identity is so explicit that it seems doubtful that such a ditty could gain much currency unless it were congruent with generally held Jewish concepts and values. Moreover, the ideas expressed in "Shikker iz a Goy" are quite consistent with Clark's (19) recent satirical "Portrait of the Mythical Gentile," an attempt to depict the essence of current Jewish stereotypes of Gentiles. As his opening remark, under the heading "Gentile Appetites," Clark characterizes prevailing Jewish beliefs as follows:

> "All Gentiles are drunkards. They have not only debauched themselves, but have made drunkards of many Jews. The Gentile drinks enormously, but without savor, being insensitive to vintage and admixture."

The substance of these findings is that sobriety has been incorporated into the ethnocentrism of the Jewish group. In his classic discussion Sumner (98) pointed out that the principal function of ethnocentrism is the clarification and intensification of a group's norms and sentiments through the magnification of their opposites as characteristic of disliked or hated outsiders. Following Sumner's reasoning, stereotypes among Jews of sobriety and drunkenness in terms of Jew and Gentile clarify sobriety as "our way" and intensify the emotional sentiments supporting it with broader feelings for things Jewish as opposed to things which are not.

Sumner, however, referred in his discussion of ethnocentrism to a relatively undifferentiated "primitive society" and probably presupposed a solidarity which cannot be taken for granted in the heterogeneous nominal Jewish group of today. The influence of Jewish stereotypes as a deterrent to intoxication may well depend upon the vitality of a larger network of ethnocentric ideas and sentiments

[20] Translated by Bales (7). While Bales cited this song and the "stigmatization of the Goyim as drunkards," he did not develop the possible reinforcing effects which this stereotyping may have on Jewish sobriety. Rather, he turned to a consideration of the menace which the drunken peasants constituted to the Jewish town dwellers in Czarist Russia, and to the question whether Jewish sobriety was a response to this situation.

which are not equally distributed among nominal Jews. In the minds of many Jews beliefs that Gentiles drink more than Jews may be propositions which have little or no relevance apart from their objective status as true or false.[21] Before such beliefs can regulate drinking behavior through the dictates of conscience and social sanction they must be imbued with emotional value and moral significance. Whether or not reinforcement for a norm of sobriety stems from Jewish stereotypes would seem to depend on the kinds of ideas and sentiments which are more generally mobilized by the symbols of ingroup and outgroup—Jew and Gentile. To touch on the implications of this problem requires more extended discussion of the probable role of ceremonial Judaism in giving definition and emotional support to Jewish group symbols, ethnocentric norms and ideas.

2. Significance of the Orthodox Definition of the Jewish Situation

The ceremonial observances of Orthodox Judaism are interlaced with a system of basic religious ideas which, while universal in much of their ethical import, are nevertheless ethnocentric in character. It is the basic ethnocentric ideas of traditional Judaism which in large measure define the situation of the religious Jew in society at large. These premises define the Orthodox Jew's position vis-à-vis the criticism and hostility of the wider society, which have been referred to extensively in the literature on Jewish drinking behavior, as well as toward its attractions. Our supposition is that stereotypes of sober Jew and drunken Gentile take on emotional connotations which reinforce a pattern of sobriety through association with these broader ethnocentric ideas and supporting sentiments.

While Orthodox Judaism has no monopoly on ethnocentrism, the ethnocentric concepts of traditional Judaism are not to be understood solely as a defensive reaction to discrimination and rejection by society. Orthodox Judaism has made capital of the ingroup–outgroup situation. As was noted earlier, the Orthodox view presupposes a special and sacred covenant of the Jews with God. Much of the message of the Scriptures is devoted to the ideas that the Jews are chosen, separate and sacred, with a special mission and purpose in this world. Orthodox injunctions set apart and in-

[21] In fact, the writer has observed situations where references to the characteristic sobriety of Jews apparently motivated nominal Jews to drink immoderately.

sulate Jews from profane contact with outsiders. Tradition exhorts the pious Jew to exemplify the superiority of Judaism and belief in the one true God by strict conformity to the Law (the Torah). Orthodox Jews know that there will be censure and retaliation from outsiders and catastrophe in this life. This is interpreted, in accordance with Biblical concepts, as the instrument of God's judgment for failure to live up to the dictates of the religion.[22] The traditional Jewish point of view, together with its general social implications, is well expressed by Moore (68) as follows:

> "God 'hallows his Name' (makes it holy), therefore, by doing things that lead or constrain men to acknowledge Him as God. And as it is God's supreme end that all mankind shall ultimately own and serve him as the true God, so it is the chief end of Israel, to whom he has in a unique manner revealed himself, to hallow His name by living so that men shall see that the God of Israel is the true God. This is the meaning of the kiddush-ha-shem, the hallowing of the Name . . . The opposite of the hallowing of the Name is the profanation of the Name (ḥillul-ha-shem). It includes every act or word of a Jew which disgraces his religion and so reflects dishonor upon God. The world judges religions by the lives of those who profess them—the tree by its fruits. It was thus that the Jews judged other religions; the vices of the heathen prove the nullity of the religions which tolerated such behavior, and even encouraged it by the examples of their gods. A favorite topic of Jewish apologetic was the superiority of Jewish morals, not merely in precept but in practice, and they argued from it the superiority of their religion, thus inviting a retaliation which the heathen world let them experience in full measure. Individuals, sects, religions, which profess to be better than others must always expect to have their conduct observed with peculiar scrutiny and censured with peculiar severity."

The sociological significance of this passage is that in the total context of ingroup–outgroup relations the pious Jew feels a generalized pressure or motivation to live in accordance with the dictates of his religion—a pressure which arises in part from his own ethnocentric assumptions.

In some respects, Moore's conclusions as to the principle motive to moral conduct in Judaism parallel Kant's explanation of Jewish

[22] God's punishments for disobedience as well as the rewards for conformity to the Law are stated in no uncertain terms in Leviticus, and the role of outgroups in this process is very clear: "Ye shall be slain before your enemies: they that hate you shall reign over you" (26:17); "And I will bring a sword upon you, that shall avenge the quarrel of my covenant" (26:25); "And I will scatter you among the heathen, and will draw out a sword after you: and your land shall be desolate" (26:33); "And ye shall perish among the heathen, and the land of your enemies shall eat you up" (26:38).

motives for sobriety. As between these eminent thinkers, however, there is a difference in emphasis which is pertinent here. Kant mentions the idea of "chosenness" but he stresses the "outward worth" of the Jew, based on the belief of others in his "separatistic lore."[23] He seems to imply that it is simply a concern for status or worth in the eyes of outsiders which motivates Jews to reserve. Then Kant's argument takes an ambiguous turn. He writes of the Jews' fear of "intoxication which deprives one of caution" in apposition with outgroup censure and criticism. Kant's remarks thus become open to two kinds of dubious interpretation.

The first doubtful line of reasoning is that the individual Jew or the Jewish group has experienced, and consequently eschews (or, on the basis of experience realistically anticipates and therefore eschews) direct criticism, censure or retaliation from Gentiles while in a state of intoxication or for achieving such a state.[24] The evidence that has been presented here on the character and sources of direct ingroup and outgroup pressures in respect to drinking, as well as on Jewish responses to and perception of these pressures, makes it difficult to sustain such an interpretation.

[23] The relevant passage from Kant was cited at the beginning of this chapter (footnote 3). Moore, incidentally, does not treat of the question of Jewish sobriety.

[24] This first line of reasoning is quite clearly exemplified by Fishberg in Bernheimer (11). At one point Glazer (32) also seems to favor this kind of argument, although he modifies it somewhat by saying: "It is not consciousness of the siege that prevents any individual Jew from taking one more drink—motivation is more complicated than that. But it is the consequences of the siege, passed down from generation to generation. . . ." The case of the American Negro is particularly instructive as a test of the theory that simple avoidance of retaliation or censure can motivate the sobriety of relatively defenseless minorities. Authorities agree that the Negro in America, occupying an inferior social position, has been the butt of criticism from whites and often the object of persecution. Individually and collectively Negroes are vulnerable to punitive caste controls and occasional outrages against person and property. Yet, as Dollard (21) points out in his discussion of the psychic compensations or "gains" which accrue to Negro lower class and caste status, the behavior of lower class Negroes in "Southern Town" is quite permissive in respect to the expression of aggression and sexuality and, apparently, drunkenness. Dollard cites Johnson (53) as follows: "The frolics and 'parties' held on Saturday nights were mentioned by practically all the younger members of the community. The Churches inveighed against them. . . . They are held from house to house; there is usually an abundance of corn whiskey. . . ." Moreover, Skolnick (89) found that, in New Haven, Negroes exceeded all other ethnic and racial groups in rates of arrest for "drunkenness." (The Jewish rates were the lowest.) Berezin (10) cited statistics to the effect that Negroes in large northern cities "constitute a large, if not the single largest, market for the sale of alcoholic beverages." There is indication from a recent study by Jellinek and Keller (52) that Negro alcoholism rates are somewhat lower than white rates for the nation as a whole, but these rates may be affected by underre-

The second and subtler line of reasoning appears in the writings of Haggard and Jellinek (38) as follows:

> "The most reasonable of these explanations [of Jewish sobriety] seems to be the one given by Kant, who thought that the Jews, forming isolated groups within other nations and being exposed to constant censure, must avoid, in the interests of racial welfare, anything that would make them conspicuous. Their temperate use of alcohol is an unconscious defense against the censure of their race."

How the avoidance of conspicuousness in the eyes of others could be a criterion for the selection and perpetuation of Jewish norms, including the temperate use of alcohol, is difficult to see. The bulk of orthodox Jewish observances are conspicuous to many Gentiles. Indeed to staunch anti-Semites the totality of Judaism is conspicuous, and it is to be doubted that the devout Jew who observes his Sabbath is blissfully unaware of the situation. As for the standard of "interests of racial welfare" to which Haggard and Jellinek allude, if this refers to individual or group wisdom of an essentially prudential character or to a standard *ex post facto* imposed upon the group by an observer, it is of doubtful value in explaining Jewish sobriety. But if it means that ideas of welfare are associated with temperance in drinking among Jews, we can only agree, with the proviso that they are probably associated also with the "intemperate" use of alcohol by certain other groups. The attachment of the idea of group welfare to particular ways is, of course, exactly what Sumner (98) considered to be the common or defining characteristic of the mores. However, what is or is not imbued with the idea of welfare by Orthodox Jews is not determined by the avoidance of conspicuousness.[25] Jews might indeed have appeared less conspicuous to many Gentiles had they been more prone to drunkenness, their very sobriety being a point of differentiation, at least in their own

porting of the medical conditions on which they are based. On the whole, the evidence at least indicates that in urban areas, where Jews are also concentrated, intoxication is quite common among Negroes and that subordinate minority status is of itself insufficient to induce a pattern of sobriety. It is possible, however, that where the more ascetic forms of Protestantism have gained strong adherence among Negroes, and where there is striving among them to differentiate from the lower classes and emulate white middle-class "respectability," pressures to sobriety will be intense and enhanced by consciousness of race difference.

[25] For situationally or permanently assimilating Jews, however, what is or is not conspicuous in terms of wider societal norms may be of the utmost importance to perceived welfare and in determining behavior.

eyes.[26] Nor does the fact that hedonistic drinking and intoxication are officially censured in Christianity, as well as in Judaism, mean that a striving to live up to Christian norms is the motive for Jewish sobriety. Adherence to traditional Judaism is certainly intimately bound up with ideas of group welfare, and in the Orthodox view welfare in turn is indicated by the status of relations with outsiders. But what is welfare to Orthodox Jews—that is, what ways of behavior are imbued with the element of welfare—is primarily determined by the Law and the criterion of conformity to the Law, whose norms are defined as fixed and immutable, revealed by God and embodied in tradition.[27] Acts which are believed to threaten welfare are above all acts which deviate from and negate the ingroup religious code, the more so if they do so conspicuously in the eyes of both Jews and Gentiles. The importance of this emphasis, as opposed to a general Jewish need to avoid conspicuousness in the

[26] The evidence on Jewish stereotypes suggests that this is very much the case. The thesis can even be entertained that non-Jewish criticism, far from being actually or potentially directed at intoxication and ensuing behavior, was directed at the uncompromising sobriety of the Jews. A recent comment by Glazer (32) is suggestive: "Something happened and it's hard to say whether it was that the Jews began drinking less or the rest of the world began drinking more. . . . In any case, sobriety, was added to the catalogue of traits that annoyed the Gentiles." The tacit assumption of this statement is quite the opposite of Kant's. It implies that Jews might have been less the butt of criticism had they seen fit to "let their hair down" and get drunk now and then, although the "damned if you do, damned if you don't" principle might well have prevailed. That the Jews early distinguished themselves and were distinguished by their sobriety among surrounding peoples is suggested by a variety of facts. For instance, the Hellenic society and culture which enveloped Judaism for centuries after the Macedonian conquest hardly looked on intoxication with disfavor, as McKinlay (63, 64) has demonstrated. Evidence on drunkenness among such peoples as the Persians, the Babylonians and certain Semitic peoples in the Mediterranean region has also been compiled by McKinlay (62). Of greater significance is historical evidence of excessive drinking in more recent times by European peoples among whom large numbers of Jews have lived in comparative sobriety. For example, according to Sebastian Franck (47), inebriety was common to both sexes and among all classes in 16th century Germany, the prevailing attitude being one of indifference. Franck even noted the contrasting sobriety of the Jews and attributed their wealth to their "abstinence." The drunkenness of the eastern European Gentile peasantry has already been noted. Apparently, drunkenness often accompanied the most violent expressions of anti-Semitism in those countries, and it is constantly noted in this connection and derided by Jewish historians such as Dubnow (22).

[27] It is not intended to imply that Judaic norms have in no way been subject to modification, reinterpretation and alteration, and that realistic adjustment to changing life conditions has had no role in this process. Our point is simply that the Orthodox emphasize the immutability of the religious system and associate individual and group welfare therewith.

interests of racial welfare, is that it leads to different predictions as to the behavior of religious and irreligious Jews in the face of outgroup censure and criticism.

These considerations lead, then, to a third interpretation latent in Kant's argument, which becomes clear in conjunction with the passage from Moore, cited above. Moore in no way detracts from the importance of outsiders as a source and reference for the Jew's moral judgments of behavior and as a stimulus to conformity with ingroup norms. But where Kant fails to be explicit, Moore emphasizes the basic idea of moral superiority in Judaism which gives the pious Jew a sense of inner worth or dignity in being Jewish. The principles of the hallowing and profaning of the Name derive their power to motivate moral conduct among Jews in a hostile environment from the initial premise of moral superiority. Theoretically, the enhanced motivation to conformity with Jewish norms is a resultant of the interaction of the fundamental ethnocentric idea together with the censure and hostility of outsiders. In this view, the Jew who is deeply committed to the premise of Jewish moral superiority simply intensifies conformity to his own distinctive cultural norms in the face of outgroup pressure and criticism. He intensifies also his scrutiny of the moral conduct of fellow-Jews in the light of Jewish norms. In association with these ethnocentric ideas and relations of hostility with outsiders, cultural definitions of sobriety as a Jewish virtue, drunkenness as a Gentile vice, should enhance motivation to conform to Jewish norms of moderate drinking and sobriety.[28]

3. Ceremonial Participation and the Mobilization of Sentiments in Support of Group Symbols and Ethnocentric Ideas

The character of Jewish response to outgroup censure would seem, however, to be determined by the intensity of sentiments supporting basic ethnocentric ideas. Lacking belief and emotional conviction as to their own moral worth in being Jewish, many Jews may tend more toward conformity with wider societal norms when faced with outgroup criticism and censure. Evidently this is what Sartre (83) means when he says: "What stamps the *inauthentic* Jew

[28] Probably it was in this sense that two of the New Haven Jewish men asserted in an "off the record" manner, at the conclusion of their interviews, that the need to "keep up a good front" and "save face" before Gentiles was a basic motive in Jewish sobriety. These men do not, of course, go on to point out that what constitutes "good front" or "face" is determined by the values of the ingroup.

is precisely this perpetual oscillation between pride and a sense of inferiority, between the voluntary and passionate negation of the traits of his race and the mystic and carnal participation in the Jewish reality." But given the sense of inner worth and value in Jewishness, Jews may simply emphasize those aspects of behavior, including sobriety, which are culturally defined as distinctively Jewish. A basic problem is thus how the symbols of Jewishness come to command the moral sentiments so as to sustain the sense of inner worth and motivate conformity to Jewish ideals.

It is our own hypothesis that, more than any other feature of Jewish life, participation in the ceremonials and rituals of Orthodox Judaism fosters the sense of inner worth together with ethnocentric ideas and moral sentiments. Theoretically, ceremonial and ritual are especially effective because of the particularly strong internalization of group symbols, norms and ideas which takes place through this kind of activity. As Durkheim (23) observed, the social functions of ceremonial and ritual have to do primarily with the maintenance of group solidarity and the integration of group symbols, norms and ideas with supporting emotions or sentiments.[29] According to Durkheim, ceremonial and ritual are everywhere accompanied by sacred as opposed to utilitarian attitudes, and characteristic sentiments of reverence and respect. Durkheim ultimately identified these sentiments with veneration for the authority of society itself rather than with the intrinsic properties of the sacred symbols, objects or states of nature they are assumed to represent, as had earlier writers. He perceived, however, that the connection of norms and ideas with supporting sentiments of solidarity and moral authority is achieved through the use of collective symbols (and particularly the major symbols of the authority of the group itself) in the context of ceremonial activity. In Orthodox Jewish ceremonial and ritual the sacred symbols of God are endlessly reiterated and so also are the various symbols of the Jewish group itself. Through ceremonial participation Jews reenact their solidarity with the group and renew their contact with the overwhelming symbols of its moral authority. The familistic character of many ceremonies also dramatizes and reinforces the system of authority in the family, integrating "concrete" or "real" authority with the "abstract" symbolism of the moral community. There is no need

[29] A good summary of Durkheim's ideas, as they are pertinent here, is contained in Parsons (73).

here for a detailed exposition of this symbolism. What is pertinent is simply that the symbols of the moral community are prominent and that the internalization of these symbols (that is, their connection with the sentiments of solidarity and moral authority) is enhanced through ceremonial and ritual activity. From this point of view Jewish ceremonial and ritual patterns are conceived of as more than forms for the expression of religious ideas and sentiments. They are also a mechanism which transmits and sustains basic Jewish cultural values. Presumably ceremonial observance strengthens the value of Jewishness, as well as the moral sentiments which group symbols command. We believe, too, that ceremonial participation, or socialization within this tradition, facilitates the internalization of the Orthodox definition of the Jewish situation in relation to the larger society. Theoretically, then, stereotypes of sober Jew and drunken Gentile should elicit the most powerful moral sentiments supporting a norm of sobriety among more observant Jews, while participation in ceremonial and ritual should enhance motivation to conform to this norm in the context of tense ingroup–outgroup relations.

4. Effects of Ceremonial Participation on the Intensity of Sentiments Supporting Ethnocentric Marriage Norms

There are no data by which to test directly the extent to which stereotypes of sober Jew and drunken Gentile activate sentiments which support norms of moderate drinking and sobriety among Jews. Nor can the precise relationships between ceremonial observance and the mobilization of these sentiments be determined. Actually, all the evidence on reduced condemnation of drunkenness and increased intoxication with declining Orthodoxy are consistent with the point of view set forth above. The problem is that declining Orthodoxy also correlates with changes in other aspects of Jewish culture—such as ceremonial drinking—aspects which may independently contribute emotional support to norms of moderate drinking and sobriety. Hence, it is exceedingly difficult to isolate the specific contribution of ethnocentric ideas and sentiments.

A partial resolution of this dilemma lies in the demonstration that sentiments supporting ethnocentric ideas are strongest among the more ceremonially Orthodox in respect to behaviors unrelated to drinking and intoxication. In this connection, data on marriage preferences from our New Haven study are highly suggestive. The intensity of sentiments opposing marriage between Jews and Gentiles is probably an especially good index of commitment to broader ethnocentric ideas because intermarriage so obviously threatens the integrity of the Jewish moral community.[30] Ordinarily, students of acculturation and assimilation pay particular attention to ethnic behaviors and attitudes regarding intermarriage on the assumption that these data reflect the continued solidarity or dissolution of the group. Available statistics (8) indicate a high rate of inmarriage among Jews, although the rate of intermarriage has fluctuated widely in different times and places, reaching a recent peak in pre-Nazi Germany, where Orthodox Judaism was in relative decline. Statistics gathered in New Haven (54) suggest that intermarriages are less than 10 percent of all Jewish marriages. The data from the New Haven interviews show also that Jewish men, irrespective of ceremonial observance, share the belief that Jews should marry Jews rather than Gentiles. Our immediate concern, however, is not with intermarriage rates as such. It is rather with the strength or intensity of sentiments supporting the belief that inmarriage is desirable, as these may relate to ceremonial observance. Our hypothesis is simply that the intensity of sentiments supporting this ethnocentric belief among Jews diminishes with declining ceremonial observance.

In the New Haven interviews a series of questions put before the Jewish men were designed to elicit the relative intensity of sentiments supporting the inmarriage norm. The respondents were first asked to assume that they had a son of marriageable age who had met a congenial girl with whom he had common interest. They were then presented with five hypothetical situations and requested to indicate the degree of their preference for a girl of either Jewish or Protestant origin (although not necessarily religiously observant in either case). In each situation a value conflict was introduced by associating the Jewish girl with an undesirable personal or social characteristic while the Protestant girl was described as socially and personally desirable. Preferences in each situation were recorded on a four-point check list of intensity, as follows:

1. I would much prefer her to be Jewish even if she . . . (the particular undesirable characteristic).

2. I probably would prefer her to be Jewish even if she . . . (the particular undesirable characteristic).

[30] Unless there is conversion to Judaism.

3. I probably would prefer she not . . . (have the undesirable characteristic) than that she be Jewish.

4. I would much prefer she not . . . (have the undesirable characteristic) than that she be Jewish.

Responses to each question were scored 1, 2, 3 or 4 (a score of 1 being the strongest preference for Jewishness) and the scores on the five questions were summed into an index of intensity of sentiments.[31] The minimum score of five, therefore, indicates the strongest preference for Jewishness. A maximum score of 20 would indicate strongest preference for a Protestant girl in the face of the undesirable characteristics associated with the Jewish girl. The mean and median scores of the 58 men who gave adequate information on all five questions were 8.2 and 8.0, respectively. Theoretically, a neutral score would be 12.5. Thus the central tendency of the sample is in favor of marriage with the Jewish girl despite her undesirable characteristics.

The hypothesis that ethnocentric sentiments are strongest among the ceremonially more observant was tested by constructing two categories of strong and weak sentiments and comparing the distribution of the Jewish men in these categories according to degree of ceremonial Orthodoxy.[32] Men with index scores of 8 or less (i.e., below the mean) are considered to have "strong sentiments" favoring inmarriage, while those with scores above 8 are considered to have "weak sentiments" in support of this norm. It is clear from Table 46 that the intensity of sentiments supporting an ethnocentric marriage norm progressively weakens with declining ceremonial observance.[33] Moreover, a further analysis of men concerning whom social class information is available suggests that the factor of ceremonial observance intensifies ethnocentric sentiments at different social class levels (Table 47).[34] There is deviation from theoretical expectations in Class IV (the lowest class) because the one Least Orthodox man in this class who answered the questions on marriage preferences was strongly in favor of inmarriage. Also, the Most

[31] This index is not, properly speaking, a scale of intensity of sentiments. The supposition was that a simple summation of scores would sufficiently differentiate extremes of strong and weak sentiment. Confirmation of the present findings through the use of refined scale techniques is greatly to be desired. The writer is indebted to Dr. Jackson Toby, of Rutgers University, for the design of these questions.

[32] Defined, as before, in terms of ritual drinking experience.

[33] P is less than .01.

[34] Social classes are here defined by Hollingshead's procedure, as outlined in Chapter 4.

TABLE 46.—*Intensity of Sentiments Supporting Ethnocentric Marriage Norms among New Haven Jewish Men, by Degree of Ceremonial Orthodoxy*

	Strong Sentiments	Weak Sentiments
Most Orthodox	9	3
Intermediate	18	11
Least Orthodox	3	12

TABLE 47.—*Intensity of Sentiments Supporting Ethnocentric Marriage Norms among New Haven Jewish Men of Different Social Class Levels, by Degree of Ceremonial Orthodoxy*

	Most Orthodox	Intermediate	Least Orthodox
Classes I & II			
Strong sentiments	1	3	0
Weak sentiments	0	2	5
Class III			
Strong sentiments	5	9	2
Weak sentiments	2	6	7
Class IV			
Strong sentiments	2	6	1
Weak sentiments	1	3	0

Orthodox and Intermediate categories in Class IV are not differentiated. But in Classes I and II and and in Class III, where the numbers are more substantial, ethnocentric sentiments systematically weaken with declining ceremonial observance.

There is not a one to one correspondence between relatively high frequencies of intoxication and high scores on the index (indicating weak ethnocentric sentiment). Some Jewish men with high scores have seldom or never been intoxicated. However, of the men reporting on marriage preferences who had been intoxicated more than five times in their lives, seven had scores of 10 or more on the index while only four had scores below 10. These findings suggest that a weakening of ethnocentric sentiments, although not in itself productive of intoxication, may be among the necessary conditions for increasing intoxication among Jews.

More generally, the findings suggest that the relative value of Jewishness is enhanced by ceremonial observance and that the sentiments supporting ethnocentric ideas are stronger among ceremonially Orthodox Jews. It is plausible to infer from these facts that the imagery of sobriety as a Jewish virtue, drunkenness as a Gentile vice, elicits strong moral sentiments in support of norms of moderate drinking and sobriety through association with a broader network of ethnocentric ideas and sentiments which are deeply internalized in the personalities of the more Orthodox Jews. As ceremonial observance wanes, however, stereotypes of sober Jew and drunken Gentile may lose their power to mobilize and reinforce emotions supporting these norms because the symbols of Jewishness lose the inner emotional significance achieved through ceremonial participation. Just as the sentiments supporting ethnocentric Jewish ideas about marriage lose their intensity, so, we suggest, do sentiments elicited by stereotypes of sober Jew and drunken Gentile, and for essentially the same reasons.

5. Evaluation of the Role of Group Stereotypes

With these concepts in mind, we may essay a more general evaluation of the role which stereotypes of sober Jew and drunken Gentile may play in Jewish sobriety in conjunction with the Orthodox definition of the situation and relations of hostility with outsiders.

To the religious Jew sobriety is a Jewish virtue. It is a measure of the Jew's worth, not directly in the eyes of Gentiles, who are reputedly prone to drunkenness, but in his own eyes and in the eyes of members of his group. Sobriety is a standard, among others, by which the degree of fulfillment of obligations to God and to the Jewish religious community may be determined. To the pious Jew intoxication is antithetical to the dictates of his religion. It is incompatible with the performance of daily rituals which demand consciousness, caution, self-control and discipline lest the Name be profaned. The religiously observant Jew has ritualized the use of beverage alcohol; he has brought drinking within the sphere of the most powerful social controls and moral sentiments. As Kant suggested, intoxication does deprive one of caution and it is linked in the mind of the devout Jew with loss of self-control and the commission of any number of acts which may be profane, unclean, aggressive, sexual, and otherwise improper in nature.[35] For the

[35] One of the most explicit statements of these consequences of immoderate drinking is contained in the Apocryphal writing known as 3 Baruch 4, 16–17: "Know therefore, O Baruch, that as Adam through this very tree obtained condemnation and was divested of the glory of God, so also the men who now drink insatiably the wine which is begotten of it, transgress worse than Adam and are far from the glory of God, and are surrendering themselves to the eternal fire. For no good comes of it. For those who drink it to surfeit do these things: neither does a brother pity his brother, nor a father his son, nor children their parents, but from the drinking of wine come all evils, such as murders, adulteries, fornications, perjuries, thefts, and such like." The cultural relativity of some of these ideas about the consequences of

religious Jew retaliation from the outgroup is inseparably connected, symbolically, with all relaxation of moral standards and religious discipline. Tensions between ingroup and outgroup therefore provide a tremendous rationale and motive for applying negative social sanctions to intoxication and for creating an atmosphere in which sobriety is expected of all.[36]

Beyond this, to the Jew who takes pride in his religion, intoxication and the drunkard are symbols of outgroup moral degeneracy and targets for scorn and derision. In the imagery of the group, to be a drunkard is to profane oneself, to become like the irresponsible Gentile. The hypothetical sanction is extirpation. Among the strictly observant, Jews who outmarry are considered dead. Funeral ceremonies are held and future contacts with the defectors are taboo. Similarly, in the symbolism of the group, intoxication and the drunkard are identified with ceasing to be a Jew. In this context the implications of a well-known Jewish folk saying become clear: "A Yid a Shikker, zoll geharget veren!" [A Jew who's a drunkard, may he get killed!] It is not just that the Jewish drunkard may expect to be or will be killed by a hostile outgroup; he deserves death!

---

heavy drinking is suggested by Mangin's study of the Vicosinos Indians of Peru. In the recurrent fiestas of this group, drinking to the point of intoxication is normal but overt expression of aggression is infrequent. Nor is intoxication apparently related to criminal behaviors. There is some increase in sexual activity during the fiestas, but this appears to be primarily related to increased opportunities for intercourse resulting from a relaxation of the system of chaperonage rather than from drinking itself. (William P. Mangin, personal communication.) We may note also that Bales (7) has called attention to the importance of drinking as a sexual substitute in rural Irish culture. The sexually suspect male is he who fails to drink of an evening with "the boys." The folklore is that such a man is "likely to prowl around in the streets, getting girls into trouble and destroying their characters."

[36] There is some question as to whether or not beliefs about retaliation and catastrophe as instruments of God's judgment for Israel's failures actually gained a real foothold among the Jewish people until the powerlessness of the group was concretely experienced by several generations in the Diaspora. This is intimated in Moore (68). Thorner (101) suggests, however, that even prior to the Diaspora "Their [the Jews'] strategic position in the Fertile Crescent invited attack from the great warring empires, another situation which intensified the group solidarity and alertness to Yahweh and his Commandments. . . . Thus both prior to and during the Diaspora a gradually internalized value-system with its demand for a rationally controlled impulse-life subordinate to what were considered higher ends came under constant threat of attack and was thereby consolidated." The further working out of this aspect of Orthodox ideology so as to motivate and rationalize the solidarity of the Jews as God's chosen people in the Diaspora is alluded to by Reisman (77): "Occasionally, the group's 'nerve of failure' was supported by the notion that its very powerlessness proved the Jews to be in fact the Chosen of God. In this way, defeat itself could strengthen the faith of the 'saving remnant' of Jews."

The imagery of sobriety as a Jewish virtue, in sharp contrast to the sinful drunkenness of Gentiles, has further implications once the Orthodox Jewish definition of outgroup retaliation as punishment for the relaxation of religious discipline is taken into account. Through this system of ideas hedonistic drinking and intoxication become connected with all the realistic and imaginary anxieties and fears of extreme punishment from Gentiles which are so manifestly present in the Jewish group. Acute intoxication may thus symbolize more dramatically than other modes of deviant behavior a state of helplessness and vulnerability which cannot be offset through the exercise of that self-control and moral discipline which Judaism enjoins. The obverse of this situation is the fear of releasing all the aggressive and retaliatory impulses which are relentlessly checked by the Orthodox religion and the exigencies of a powerless minority status. Consequently, the counteranxieties elicited by the very idea of intoxication may be extraordinarily powerful.

It may be suggested, however, that with declining ceremonial and ritual observance the sentiments associated with beliefs about sober Jews and drunken Gentiles tend to wane. Powerful group symbols lose emotional support. The "outer" moral authority of Jewishness and its correlate of inner worth lose significance, while anxieties about retaliation and the expression of aggression are lessened along with the relaxation of Jewish moral standards and religious discipline.[37] To individual Jews the cognitive and emotional meaning of these ideas derives from a broader context of identification with Judaism. It is worth reemphasizing that this identification is most clearly expressed, sustained and transmitted through Orthodox religious ritual and ceremonial.

[37] With regard to anxieties over the expression of aggression, Wikler (107) in the course of his discussion of a case of experimental readdiction to morphine offers an interpretation similar to that given here. Having noted cultural differences in attiudes toward the expression of aggression, Wikler comments: "Similar differences in attitudes may be found in the case of Jews who have been reared in traditional orthodox Jewish environments and those who have been 'assimilated.' As Samuel points out, the overt expression of aggression has always been condemned in the traditional Jewish culture, while the impact of 'assimilation' has tended to alter such attitudes. In the experience of the author, as well as that of others, the incidence of chronic alcoholism is low among Jews of orthodox background, compared to the incidence of opiate addiction. The reverse seems to be true in Jews of 'Reform' or non-religious background. It is of interest that the subject of the present investigation, who was of orthodox Jewish background, disliked alcohol because 'it made me drunk and got me into fights'."

6. Persistence of Group Stereotypes beyond Religious Boundaries

There is, of course, an ethnic cleavage which persists beyond the boundaries of religion. In the process of socialization many Jewish children internalize and carry on traditional Jewish attitudes which parents still share despite the abandonment of ceremonial observances. Moreover, anti-Semites incessantly manage to discover or conjure up characteristics which set apart even secular Jews from their fellow citizens. Among Jews themselves there is recognition of a common descent and of an ethnic heritage, although many Jews are evidently in doubt as to the nature of this heritage.[38] Of late, considerable fanfare has been sounded over Jewish nationalism with the ascendance of the State of Israel to legitimate political status among the nations. For the more secular in the American Jewish community, philanthropic and political activities, in contrast to specifically religious activities, enhance the sense of Jewish group membership. In this connection it is pertinent to note that acknowledgment of stereotypes of Jewish and Gentile drinking appears to be related to continued sobriety despite the abandonment of most ritual observances.[39] But suggestive as these facts may be of the influence of ethnic stereotypes on Jewish sobriety beyond the traditional community of religious participation, they should not obscure the likelihood that these stereotypes are most pervasive and powerful within the religious community. It is in terms of cultural continuity with the Orthodox religious tradition that these beliefs and their normative influence can be best understood.

General Effects of the Ingroup–Outgroup Situation

The tentative general conclusions to be drawn from the present research with respect to the influence of the ingroup–outgroup situation on Jewish drinking behavior and sobriety are these: It is not direct censure for intoxication from outsiders, or the realistic possibility of censure or retaliation while in a state of intoxication, which is most significant for Jewish sobriety. In the American cultural setting, direct social pressures from outsiders concerning drinking apparently work in the opposite direction. They tend to induce con-

[38] The confused state of conceptions of the Jewish cultural heritage is mirrored in Infield's (45) effort to define contemporary Jewish culture. Virtually the only substantive feature which Infield finds common to contemporary Jews is "the odium of defection," although he proposes some questions whose answers might yield more abstract common denominators.

[39] Data are presented in Snyder (90).

vivial and hedonistic drinking among Jews, rather than moderate drinking and sobriety. Jews actually conform to these outgroup pressures precisely where relations of solidarity with the Jewish community are situationally disrupted or permanently attenuated. By contrast, it is the Jewish group which exerts direct social pressures inducing moderate drinking and sobriety. The effectiveness of these ingroup pressures apparently varies directly with the solidarity of Jews with the Orthodox religious community.

But none of these effects can be divorced from the more general context of tensions which exist between Jews and Gentiles in society as a whole. Intergroup tension may intensify Jewish ethnocentrism and heighten conformity to traditional norms among more religious Jews. When refracted through Orthodox ideology, the threat of conflict and anxieties about retaliation probably stimulate ingroup moral discipline. Acute intergroup tension may also reduce Jewish participation in Gentile society and motivate a return to the ingroup and a renaissance of traditionalism among the less religious, more assimilated Jews. As one New Haven Jewish respondent put it:

> "When times are good the Jew forgets his religion, but then the Goyim gets his fur up and it's back to the old ways." [31]

Consequently, sobriety having the status of a Jewish virtue, adherence to this norm may be affected by the vicissitudes of tension and antagonism between the Jewish ingroup and the Gentile outgroup in society at large. It is our belief that in these terms Kant's explanation of Jewish sobriety makes sense. To be stressed, however, is the fact that the basic ideas and ceremonials of traditional Judaism have a certain autonomy or vitality which is not immediately contingent on ingroup–outgroup tension and it is with these ideas and practices that Jewish sobriety is most intimately associated. Before the response of Jews to the ingroup–outgroup situation can be understood in respect to the drinking of alcoholic beverages and other behaviors, the incidence and impact among Jews of these cultural patterns must be taken into account.

These tentative conclusions are compatible with broader sociological conceptions of the nature and consequences of relations between status groups in society at large. In their recent general discussion of this subject, Stone and Form (93) call attention to the fact that a group's self-respect is not always commensurate with the social honor which it is accorded by society. They reiterate Max Weber's observation that the sense of dignity experienced by a group may bear no correspondence to its objective position in the actual status hierarchy. As Weber says: "Even pariah peoples who are most despised are usually apt to continue cultivating in some manner that which is equally peculiar to ethnic and status communities: the belief in their own social honor."[40] Following Weber's thought, Stone and Form go on to observe:

> "The sense of dignity that transcends the negatively privileged position of a status group is anchored in the future, often contingent upon the fulfillment of a mission. . . . When the characteristic sense of dignity or personal worth of members of status groups and aggregates is examined with reference to their objective status, and gross intransigencies are disclosed, the conditions for what Hughes has termed 'status protest' have been established. Where there are great disparities between dignity and objective status, a group may reject existing status arrangements and establish itself as a status group outside the ongoing status structure of the community."[41]

The historical condition of the Jews in Western civilization might be characterized as one of chronic status protest in this sense. However, the disparity between inner worth or dignity and objective status (which is the condition for status protest) is not solely a consequence of the hostility and contempt of society. It is also a function of the ethnocentric ideas of the Jews themselves. These ideas are most clearly embodied and transmitted in the Orthodox religious tradition and internalized most effectively through Orthodox Jewish ceremonial and ritual observance. It is also possible that through the elaboration of ceremonial and ritual Jews have given expression to the need to reject existing status arrangements and to establish themselves in large measure outside the ongoing status structure of the wider society. Adherence to Jewish norms of moderate drinking and sobriety is, as we have shown, intricately bound up with Orthodox ceremonial and ritual observances. Deviation from these norms may thus also be broadly conceived as a complex function of the vitality of ceremonial Judaism considered together with the objective position and subjective evaluation accorded to Jews by society.

Clarification of the Roles of Ritual Drinking and Other Factors

The analysis in the present chapter would be seriously misleading if the imagery of sobriety as a Jewish virtue, together with broader

[40] Cited in Gerth and Mills (30).

[41] The concept of "status protest" is developed by Hughes (44).

ethnocentric ideas and sentiments and the pressures arising from ingroup–outgroup relations, were conceived of as causing the sobriety and virtual absence of drinking pathologies among Jews in some ultimate or final sense. No such thought is intended. Under certain conditions these factors are assumed to provide strong motivation and reinforcement to a norm of sobriety and, accordingly, constitute part of a complex of sociocultural variables which must be considered. But other features of Jewish culture may certainly contribute to the effective social regulation of the use of beverage alcohol. In this connection we share Bales' belief that the extensive ritualization of drinking in Jewish religious ceremonial is of the utmost importance, and nothing in this chapter precludes this possibility.[42] Especially to be noted is the fact that traditional Jewish religious symbolism quite explicitly links the major ethnocentric idea with the ritual drinking situation. Thus the Sabbath Kiddush concludes with these words (75): "For Thou hast chosen us and sanctified us above all nations, and in love and favor hast given us the holy Sabbath as our inheritance. Blessed art Thou, O Lord, who hallowest the Sabbath." Yet in focusing attention on ritual drinking there is a tendency to lose sight of other factors. It might easily be concluded from Bales' discussion that ritual drinking by itself creates all the powerful ideas and sentiments in traditional Jewish culture which are opposed to intoxication and hedonistic drinking. And at times Bales himself seems to advocate this narrow conception. However, he does mention secondary factors in Jewish sobriety and refers to the "underlying ideas and sentiments" associated with the ritual use of wine as providing the "primary emotional impetus" to the hatred of intoxication and barriers to the formation of addictive motives among Jews.

Actually, there is a twofold significance to ritual drinking in Bales' argument which is not always clear. On the one hand, ritual drinking may be conceived as giving form and expression to religious ideas and sentiments integral with a larger pattern of ceremonial and ritual observance. Because of his involvement in a wider pattern of ceremonial and ritual observances, the pious Jew approaches alcoholic beverages with a generalized ritual attitude. On the other hand, insofar as ritual drinking is experienced early and practiced continuously in life, this specific mode of drinking has the effect of re-

[42] Our reference here and in the ensuing discussion is to Bales' ideas as set forth in his dissertation (7) and reiterated in summary form (6).

inforcing in the personality the ideational and emotional connections between the act of drinking and the most powerful sentiments and symbols of social control in the Jewish group. In short, the traditional prescriptions to drink ceremonially reinforce the connections between the ideas and sentiments associated with the generalized ritual attitude and the act of drinking itself. A stable attitude toward the drinking of alcoholic beverages is consequently molded which does not leave the outcome of drinking to chance, individual experiment, fear or ignorance.

But there is still the knotty problem of the generalization of a controlled attitude toward drinking. This problem is most broadly illustrated by the fact that human behavior is so flexible that patterns of ceremonial drinking can alternate with patterns of convivial and hedonistic drinking within the same cultural framework. The Tarahumara of Central America aptly exemplify such an alternation: At certain culturally appropriate times and places alcoholic beverages are consecrated and used for religious purposes, while at other times the same beverages are used in semiorgiastic fashion apparently devoid of sacred significance. Norms, ideas and sentiments do not seem to carry over from the one context to the other.[43] Why, then, has there been no such alternation or dualism in Orthodox Jewish life?

Part of the solution to this problem probably lies in the fundamental idea of Orthodox Judaism as a "total way of life" through which all man's activities are to be sanctified. Orthodox Judaism presses for integration, for the permeation of all facets of life with sacred symbolism. The possibility of this kind of integration appears to be bound up with a pattern of close communal living. The hostility and discrimination of outsiders has contributed to this integration by forcing Jews to live under the compact social conditions congenial to it. The tendency toward permeation of all activities with religious values is clearly evident in the Orthodox requirement that the Jew must pronounce a benediction before drinking any beverage in any circumstance. This custom obviously facilitates the extension to the drinking situation of ideas and sentiments of reverence and respect and the larger moral meanings associated with being a religious Jew, even though the situation is not otherwise of an essentially religious character. But reinforcing the tendency toward a controlled use of alcoholic beverages, which is immanent

[43] Dr. Jacob Freed, personal communication.

in the extension of a ritual attitude, are the ethnocentric ideas and sentiments and pressures arising from the ingroup–outgroup situation. Through the network of ethnocentric symbolism and sentiments the idea of sobriety becomes integrated with the feeling of moral superiority in being Jewish. Orthodox Jews have claimed legitimacy for their religion and defended Judaism through the cultivation of and adherence to what they conceived to be a morally superior discipline. In this perspective, stereotypes of sober Jew and drunken Gentile define intoxication among Jews as a threat to the basic claims and defenses of Judaism and as a threat to the particular personalities whose self-esteem and integration derive from the religion. It seems likely that, in association with collective stereotypes, the inner meaning of intoxication for the Jew himself is the degradation of Jewishness. For the Jew to become intoxicated symbolizes the futility of the Jewish moral struggle in a society which holds Jewishness in disesteem. Perhaps, then, these additional factors help to explain the apparent sobriety of ghetto Jews who used alcoholic beverages in convivial situations, as wedding celebrations, in which drinking might have taken a hedonistic turn. Very likely some Jews were not so pious in these circumstances as always to bless the beverages prior to drinking. But to become intoxicated under these conditions would have been "un-Jewish."[44] Evidently, the inner and outer social pressures "not to let down" on this *point d'honneur* were and still are very strong for Jews who are solidary with the Jewish community.

The complex reinforcing factors conducive to Jewish sobriety may persist, of course, even where the ceremonial use of alcohol is in decline. Obviously, ritual drinking directly depends upon the vitality of the larger religious and ceremonial pattern. Beyond this, ceremonial and ritual evidently are also a powerful mechanism for giving Jewishness and ethnocentric ideas strong inner emotional meaning, while Orthodox beliefs provide a definition of the situation which motivates sobriety in the context of tense ingroup–outgroup relations. Consequently, we suspect that these additional factors lose their power to motivate sobriety among less Orthodox Jews whose identification with traditional Judaism is weak or who situationally identify with Gentiles on a primary-group basis, as in military service or in college. It may be suggested, however, that these additional factors helped to preclude the extensive development of pat-

[44] On this point, see Zborowski and Herzog (110).

terns of convivial or hedonistic drinking in alternation with the ceremonial and religious use of beverage alcohol in the closely knit Jewish community.

It is important to note that, theoretically, the effectiveness of norms, ideas and sentiments in regulating intoxication depends upon their internalization in the personality. They must be anticipated in the drinking situation itself. Social sanctions from members of the group after the individual has reached a state of intoxication or developed a pattern of inebriety are not of primary significance. To be effective, the regulatory norms, ideas and sentiments must be elicited immediately in the drinking situation and be supported by the consensus or social expectancies of the surrounding milieu. In fact, Bales stresses the specific act of ritual drinking precisely because he believes that the internalization of a controlled attitude toward drinking is facilitated by the overt and repeated practice of drinking in a religious context, and in our opinion this is correct. However, the internalization of the reinforcing ideas and sentiments to which we have alluded need not necessarily depend upon the experience of intoxication or even the experience of drinking. The broader process of socialization is sufficient to structure these elements in the personality. Through the internalization of ideas and sentiments associated with Jewishness and the Jewish situation, and ideas of sobriety as a Jewish virtue, drunkenness as a Gentile vice, Jews bring to the drinking situation powerful moral sentiments and anxieties counter to intoxication. That these factors do not derive from the specific experience of drinking does not preclude their being a part of the normative orientation toward the act of drinking itself. We might say, then, that through the ceremonial use of beverage alcohol religious Jews learn how to drink in a controlled manner; but through constant reference to the hedonism of outsiders, in association with a broader pattern of religious and ethnocentric ideas and sentiments, Jews also learn how not to drink.

Chapter 6

SIGNS OF ALCOHOLISM

ALCOHOLISM and other extreme drinking pathologies have been mentioned in this study only in passing comment. The chief concern thus far has been the description of certain aspects of Jewish drinking patterns and variations in these patterns as related to other sociocultural factors, primarily religious. The occurrence of intoxication has been described within this context. As noted in Chapter 3, however, measures of intoxication cannot be indiscriminately equated with indices of alcoholism or other extreme drinking pathologies. The remarkable sobriety of Orthodox Jews in particular, considering their extensive drinking, certainly implies an absence of alcoholism, and the various sociocultural factors contributing to this situation must play a role in minimizing alcoholism. But the converse idea, tacitly assumed by most writers on Jewish drinking, that alcoholism tends to increase with intoxication, does not necessarily follow. High rates of alcoholism are not invariably associated with frequent intoxication, as will be indicated below. There are reasons for believing, however, that increased alcoholism does accompany more frequent experience of intoxication by those American Jews who deviate from traditional religious patterns. To suggest why this should be so requires at least brief consideration of the factors which may contribute to alcoholism.

The distinguishing feature of alcoholism as described, for example, by Jellinek (46), Bacon (1), Bales (7), and McCarthy and Straus (97) is the inability of the drinker to control or regulate his drinking within the bounds of social propriety.[1] To some extent this is necessarily a relative matter. Norms of propriety vary from group to group and the degree of "loss of control" in drinking perhaps differs from alcoholic to alcoholic, shading back into borderline cases of "problem drinkers" who may or may not become alcoholics. It

[1] The term "alcoholism" as used here is synonymous with "alcohol addiction." This is to be distinguished from other concepts, such as "chronic alcoholism" in the sense of diseases associated with inebriety, as often used in the scientific literature, or "alcoholism" as used popularly in referring to inebriety or intoxication. For a review of definitions and consensus among a number of other authorities on this defining characteristic, see Jellinek (46).

seems established, however, that alcoholism is usually a progressive disease taking many years for its full development, and the characteristic loss of control over drinking takes on additional meaning in this perspective.[2] In what Jellinek calls the "crucial phase" of alcoholism "loss of control" in the drinking situation occurs. This means that drinking starts a reaction which is subjectively experienced as a deep need for alcohol and results in continued drinking to the point of being either too intoxicated or too sick to ingest more alcohol. The episode may last hours or weeks. At this juncture the drinker can apparently still regulate the situations in which he will drink, but if he starts drinking he cannot always regulate the quantity he will consume, although this inability may be immediately rationalized. Later, after the development of a series of symptoms, the crucial phase evolves into a "chronic phase" typified by generalized loss of control over drinking. Now drinking and related behaviors (e.g., intoxication and hangover) permeate a wide variety of times, places and circumstances where they are socially defined as inappropriate and seriously interfere with the performance of conventional social roles. In this stage of alcoholism the principal focus of the life pattern is drinking, and the bulk of time, energy and ingenuity is devoted to maintaining and protecting this activity. Although authorities are not sure of the degree of social integration of the alcoholic's personality in the formative stages of the disease, they suggest that alcoholism tends to be related to social isolation and in its later stages usually involves deterioration of social relationships and heightened egocentricity of the personality.[3]

To explain alcoholism, researchers have typically approached the problem with the aim of discovering some constitutional or personality type or factor, either necessary and sufficient or at least

[2] Statements on the developmental nature of alcoholism and characteristics of this development are based primarily on the detailed statistical study of 98 alcoholics by Jellinek (50). Jellinek's original research was later augmented by the administration of a questionnaire "to some 2,000 alcoholics" and his phase concepts were restated accordingly (49). Since there is no systematic presentation of data in the latter report, factual reference herein will be made to the original study, although the ideas and terminology are essentially the same in both.

[3] For indication of breakdown of social participation, see Bacon (27). The suggestion of a greater degree of social integration (or "attempting to maintain relatively stable positions in their communities") among certain categories of alcoholics (specifically those seeking clinic help) than had previously been assumed is found in Straus and Bacon (95). Extensive references to social isolation trends and personality egocentricity are to be found in Jellinek (50). Compare also our remarks and data, in Chapter 3, on early deterioration of religious participation among problem drinkers.

predisposing for the disease. These efforts, stemming from various scientific disciplines, have failed to delineate any uniform type or factor, although progress has been made, for instance, in unraveling some of the motivational and other elements involved in particular cases.[4] The suggestion to be developed here is not that "dynamic factors" are irrelevant in the etiology of alcoholism but that normative or "orienting factors" are essential components both in the development and the prevention of the disease. This implies that differences in group rates of alcoholism can be explained in part by the differing content of the normative orientations toward drinking (i.e., norms, ideas and sentiments) which are acquired by individuals from different cultural or subcultural groups through processes of socialization and social interaction.

Expressed most generally, group rates of alcoholism may be conceived as resultants or functions of three principal variables:[5]

1. The group incidence (or rates) of acute psychic tensions or severe needs for adjustment of the sort that probably play a dynamic role in alcoholism and which may differ widely both in content and origin;

2. the type of normative orientation toward drinking which is embedded in the culture of the group;

3. the availability of culturally defined alternate means of adjustment (whether positively sanctioned patterns or culturally typical deviations)—referring to modes other than drinking which permit partial or total satisfaction of the severe needs for adjustment which may enter into alcoholism.[6]

[4] See, for example, Sutherland, Schroeder and Tordella (99). Summarizing 37 reports of organized research on personality characteristics of alcoholics, these writers say: "No satisfactory evidence has been discovered that justifies a conclusion that persons of one type are more likely to become alcoholics than persons of another type. This conclusion agrees with the clinical findings of Wexberg (106) that 'there is no alcoholic personality prior to alcoholism'." For a review of etiological theories of alcoholism, see Jellinek (46).

[5] This applies where alcohol is available.

[6] This framework has been outlined by Bales (6). Further details, particularly as these factors may enter into the determination of individual cases of alcoholism, are to be found in Bales (7). In a recent paper Ullman (103), following essentially the same framework, has played down the role of acute psychic tensions apart from situational stresses relating to early drinking experiences. While Bales and the present writer would agree that the "juxtaposition of a stress situation (analogous to the electric shocking of rats) with drinking experiences in which drinking itself is important to the individual" (Ullman, p. 606) is important in fixation on alcohol as a means of adjustment, it seems premature to minimize the role of more general and acute personality problems as these may enter into the formation of the addiction initially, or in activating the addiction later on, i.e., after an interval of sobriety perhaps of many years' duration, by providing new impetus to drinking. However, these questions can only be settled by further research.

In the individual instance, alcoholism is seen as involving the conjunction, through a process of symbolic and emotional connection, of acute needs for adjustment and a particular type of normative orientation toward drinking, namely a utilitarian (or hedonistic) orientation, and, further, a "definition of the situation" on the part of the drinker which precludes the utilization of possible alternate means of adjustment to pressing emotional needs which may be more or less consciously understood. Here only normative orientations toward drinking can be treated, and only in a cursory manner, in order to suggest certain distinctions which may warrant further sociological research on alcoholism, and to suggest the conditions under which alcoholism among Jews might increase.

The essence of a utilitarian orientation is not only that intoxicating effects are sought in the act of drinking, but that these are sought for individual purposes—whether consciously perceived or simply felt as generalized needs or tensions of the personality—quite apart from or in conflict with the purposes of the moral community. In short, drinking for the more extreme effects is defined in idea and sentiment as being related to the self-regarding needs of the individual as an individual. Following Bales' (7) suggestion, alcoholism "may be conceived of as a utilitarian type of drinking which has the further feature of a compulsive, involuntary character. The compulsive character of the drinking is supposed to be due to more or less severe underlying needs for adjustment or tensions which are oriented toward drinking as a means of adjustment by a nucleus of utilitarian ideas and sentiments now beyond conscious control." Utilitarian drinking attitudes may, of course, be arrived at by individual trial and error. It seems likely, however, that they are deeply embedded in certain cultures and subcultures, transmitted and activated by communication from emotionally significant persons in the social milieu, and readily transformed into addiction proper in conjunction with acute personality distress.

Insofar as present research permits the suggestion of generalizations, Irish country culture appears to be an "ideal type" case of a deeply embedded tradition of utilitarian drinking. There is also a tradition of convivial social drinking in which drunkenness is common, but there is an extensive body of tradition which tends to orient individuals toward drinking for the effects of alcohol as a generalized means of individual adjustment.[7] In the Irish folk tradition,

[7] See Bales (7) for a fuller description of Irish drinking patterns. In Bales' opinion, the "orienting factor" of a cultural tradition of utilitarian drinking primarily ac-

drinking for the intoxicating effects of alcohol is not only regarded as appropriate in certain group contexts, but "natural" for a means of individual adjustment.[8] It is especially important to note that apparently even the convivial drinking which can be conceived of primarily as an expression of solidarity is typically an expression of the solidarity of a particular segment of the group (e.g., "the boys"), often standing in relations of hostility to other segments of the community and with drinking serving as the vehicle for the expression of aggression. Moreover, Irish drinking is entirely secular[9] apart from the ritual of the Mass during which the priest uses the wine sacramentally while the laity is excluded from partaking.[10] It is interesting to note that there has been considerable reaction to convivial and utilitarian drinking among the Irish in the form of abstinence movements, largely under the leadership of the clergy, e.g., Father Mathew. Reaction to traditional folk drinking perhaps reflects a basic institutional conflict and conflict between Irish folk and Catholic religious ideals. Certainly in Glad's study there is an abundance of material suggesting moralistic evaluations, guilt feel-

---

counts for high rates of alcoholism among the Irish as compared to the Jews. This is because differentials in the incidence of neuroses and psychoses in these two groups are far less extreme than differences in alcoholism rates. The incidence (or rates) of neuroses and psychoses are interpreted as indices of severe needs for adjustment of the sort which may enter into alcoholism. Differentials in acute needs for adjustment are invoked to explain why one Irishman becomes an alcoholic while another does not in the same cultural setting. For references to the incidence of neuroses and psychoses among the Irish and Jews, see Snyder and Landman (91). Glad (31), too, believes that an "affectivity orientation" toward drinking—which concept certainly subsumes the utilitarian—is responsible for the relatively high "rates of inebriety" among the Irish.

[8] The tradition of utilitarian drinking is clearly exemplified in the Irish folk custom of giving a man "a hair of the dog that bit him," referring to drinking on the morning after a night of indulgence so that the effects of alcohol will relieve the distressing symptoms of previous heavy drinking. This is a common practice among alcoholics. Jellinek (49) considers it characteristic of the onset of the chronic phase in alcoholism. The practice has an analogue in the recognition (affective and cognitive) of "withdrawal" symptoms and the readministration of the drug as the only "known" means of alleviating distress, which Lindsmith believes to be a *sine qua non* of drug addiction. Compare Bales (7).

[9] Even the famous Irish wake is secular in character.

[10] It is pertinent to note that priests of Irish Catholic background, who as members of Alcoholics Anonymous are confirmed alcoholics on their own admission, report that their sacramental use of wine at Mass in no wise threatens them with a loss of control in drinking. (Instances reported in personal communication by Selden D. Bacon.) Members of Alcoholics Anonymous in the Protestant Episcopal Church have also reported to the author that they have no problem of control arising from wine drinking in connection with Holy Communion.

ings, parental restrictions and ambivalence and clandestine activities in association with drinking among adolescents of Irish Catholic background.[11] The existence of such a schism intensifies conflict as well as separation between drinking and the core moral symbolism, sentiments and activities of the group. This, in turn, may have a bearing on the tendency among the Irish for the ideas and sentiments associated with drinking to get "beyond conscious control," as Bales (7) has put it.[12]

Before expanding this latter idea through brief discussion of the abstinence orientation toward drinking, the Peruvian Indian Culture recently studied by Mangin (67) may be cited as an instance of frequent drinking and drunkenness where the cultural integration of these patterns with the central rites and symbolism of the group may have the effect of minimizing alcoholism.[13] Among the Vicosinos Indians, who had a long history of drinking prior to cultural contact with Europeans, drinking to the point of intoxication is a normal feature of the recurrent fiestas. On such occasions almost everybody drinks in this way—"it is the custom"—and while drunkenness is common, neither drinking nor drunkenness are culturally defined as responses to personal needs or tensions of the individual. Drinking and drinking to get drunk are not dissociated from the rites and symbols which intensify the solidarity of the entire group and dramatize its authority; they are integral with them and customarily defined as such. Although there is at present no way of

[11] See Glad (31), pp. 435–6, 437, 439, 440. In discussing the ambivalence of Irish Catholic parents toward drinking and the restrictions which they impose on their children, Glad suggests (pp. 442–3) that excessive drinking (and related behavior) may induce restrictions, or that restrictions may induce excess, or that "part of the excess among the Irish may result from the restriction and part of the restriction may result from the excess." However, in all three cases there is presupposition of a moral conflict about drinking and an attitude which implies that drinking can only be to "excess."

[12] The extent of alcoholism in Ireland, historically and presently, is a problem which needs research. It is established that rates of alcoholism among the Irish in America have been high, although these may be converging with general American rates. High rates of alcoholism among the Irish in the earlier stages of their American immigration could be broadly interpreted as a function of the sudden dissolution of rural community patterns in which drunkenness, but not necessarily alcoholism, was prevalent. Bales' documentary research gives the impression of considerable alcoholism among the Irish in Ireland for some centuries, but needs the support of systematic research.

[13] Mangin's basic report (67) contains only limited reference to drinking. Detailed results of his field study as it pertains to drinking, which provide the basis for our present remarks, will be published in the near future. (William P. Mangin, personal communication.)

measuring in this group the factors of psychic tension and alternate means of adjustment which may bear on alcoholism, alcoholism is apparently rare among the Vicosinos Indians, who see nothing immoral or asocial about either drinking or drunkenness.

If, as Bales (7) suggests, addictive drinking is a utilitarian type of drinking of a compulsive, involuntary character, there is the further implication that "... Before the individual can become addicted, those ideas and sentiments which are associated with the act of drinking in his individual personality must either be primarily utilitarian in the first place, or, if primarily religious and moral, must somehow be reduced to impotence, transformed, or replaced by utilitarian ideas and sentiments which are isolated from or in conflict with the moral and rational controls of the personality." The case of a normative orientation for abstinence is especially interesting when viewed in this connection. Where abstinence is practiced continually there is, of course, no alcoholism. But should drinking be attempted by those raised with this orientation, the reaction can be extreme. At least this is suggested by the data in Table 47 where the frequency of intoxication of college students in three ascetic Protestant groups[14] is compared with that of Irish Catholics, Italian Catholics and apparent Jews. There is a systematic increase in frequency of intoxication, moving from the Jewish group to the Catholic groups to the Protestant groups. These data should not be construed as representing the comparative overall effectiveness of the norms of these groups in minimizing intoxication. The percentages in Table 47 are based on the numbers of students in each group who have had some experience of using alcoholic beverages. They therefore do not reflect the large numbers of abstainers, especially in the Protestant groups, who have never been intoxicated. Indeed, further computations suggest that from an over-all point of view, that is, considering both abstainers and drinkers, the two extreme groups, the Jews and Mormons, are the most effective, and the middle group of Irish Catholics the least effective, in this respect. But it should also be recognized that the pattern of the data in Table 47 is not an artifact resulting from the exclusion of abstainers from consideration, thereby obscuring a prevalence of intoxication which is essentially constant from group to group. Nor is it a reflection of a tiny minority of drinkers who

[14] "Ascetic" is used in the present context essentially as a convenient synonym for abstinence-oriented. Mormons do not regard themselves as Protestants but for convenience in expression they are grouped with the Protestant denominations.

TABLE 47.—*Intoxication among College Students of Selected Religiocultural Groups (in Per Cent of Drinkers Only)*

	Never Drunk	*Drunk Over 5 Times*	*Never Tight*	*Tight Over 5 Times*	*Number Reporting**
Jewish affiliated†	51	4	40	19	(253)
Italian Catholic‡	42	10	27	30	(210)
Irish Catholic	39	13	24	36	(708)
Methodist (white)	33	16	19	42	(752)
Baptist (white)	29	15	16	47	(564)
Mormon	21	21	11	44	(778)

* These totals, upon which percentages are based, include those giving no information on intoxication and therefore yield the most conservative estimates both of proportions never drunk or tight and proportions tight and drunk more than five times. This accounts for the lack of perfect correspondence with percentages reported elsewhere, e.g., Straus and Bacon's (96) data on intoxication among the Mormons. However, inclusion or exclusion of those giving no information does not alter the ordered relationship among the groups shown here except to even up Methodists and Baptists in percentages drunk over five times and to put Mormons higher than all others in per cent tight over five times.

† Known affiliates with one of the three religious groups: Orthodox, Conservative or Reform.

‡ Includes 2.9 per cent listed as "no affiliation" and 2.5 per cent listed as Protestants; over 90 per cent listed as Roman Catholic.

are extreme deviants among the Protestants. Actually, drinkers comprise substantial segments of these student groups of Protestants (in the range of 50 to 69 per cent) and the drinking of these students need not necessarily result in extensive intoxication apart from cultural influences of the sort we are considering. The further fact that many of the drinkers among the latter are not especially frequent drinkers, in comparison with the members of other groups—although there is considerable range of variation in this respect—renders the relatively extensive intoxication among them all the more striking. While, in accord with our discussion above, these data on intoxication cannot by themselves be taken as definite indications of differentials in "problem drinking" or incipient alcoholism, they are consistent with and suggestive of such a situation.[15]

In discussing the occurrence of intoxication in the Mormon group, Straus and Bacon (96) observed that "If drinking behavior

[15] The possibilities of determining from the College Survey materials the incidence of premonitory signs of alcoholism among Mormon students and others of ascetic Protestant background who drink were only briefly touched upon in Straus and Bacon's comprehensive report on student drinking. These problems are currently under investigation by the author and his colleagues at the Yale Center of Alcohol Studies.

is adopted, variation must be the rule since there is no norm. Extremes are likely since the behavior itself represents rejection of social rules. The models for behavior are either members of other groups or dissident members of their own group." To these observations may be added the suggestion that while there is indeed no generally practiced norm of drinking, there is nonetheless a tacit norm in the ascetic abstinence definition which creates an expectancy of extremes, namely, that drinking is necessarily utilitarian or hedonistic. Mormons and other ascetic Protestant groups divorce the act of drinking entirely from the contexts and symbolism which are primary sources of social control (e.g., family, church, and religious community). By cultural definition alcoholic beverages and drinking are driven out of the very centers of social control both in a contextual sense and in terms of the ideas and sentiments associated with drinking as these are structured in the personality. It is difficult to convey the significance of this fact as it may affect personality and bear on alcoholism rates among persons reared with an abstinence orientation. Its possible relevance can perhaps be appreciated by considering the following passage from Bales (7) in which he speaks of the alcoholic's fixation on alcohol as a means of adjustment and the gradual process of social isolation in the alcoholic:

> "As the alcoholic becomes more involved and obsessed by his addiction, he becomes more and more socially isolated, more rebellious and resentful of outer social control. The overt excuses, subterfuges, lies, evasions, retaliations and the like, into which the compulsive drinker is forced as a mode of protection from social pressure and controls can be viewed as the outer correlate of the inner wall of rationalizations, justifications, and other devices which protect the fixation factor itself from the attacks of internalized social controls—rational scrutiny and moral judgment. The outer and inner aspects are probably most accurately conceived as comprising two aspects of a circular process, each phase reinforcing the other. *Conceived structurally, the inner correlate to the outer social isolation of the fixation is an isolation of the fixation element from other inhibitory and controlling aspects of the personality structure which are derived, both genetically and contemporaneously, from a vital contact and communication with emotionally acceptable outer controls.* This structural isolation, along with the imperative nature of the dynamic factors involved, is regarded as the main explanation of the extraordinary strength and persistence of the fixation.[16]

[16] Italics added.

To recapitulate from this vantage point, in the setting of American society, where drinking is prevalent, the abstinence orientation of the more "fundamentalist" Protestant sects enhances the probability of the isolation of attitudes toward drinking from other inhibitory and controlling aspects of the personality as follows:

(*1*) By dissociating the act of drinking entirely from the contexts in which the central personality controls are learned;

(*2*) By defining drinking as utilitarian or hedonistic only and in active conflict with the purposes of the moral community;

(*3*) By necessitating that the act be learned (if it is learned) from dissident members of the group or members of other groups who may suggest and reinforce utilitarian drinking attitudes.

This is not to imply that all persons reared with an abstinence orientation who begin to drink will necessarily become alcoholics. But it does suggest that rates of alcoholism may be relatively high among persons of ascetic Protestant background who begin to drink. In such cases drinking may well occur before any total or complete breakdown of religious participation. But the complete immorality of the act, as culturally defined, may induce sufficient conflict to motivate a rapid deterioration of relationships with the religious community. In turn this may intensify the individual's isolation from emotionally significant and formerly acceptable sanctioning agents, thereby further enhancing the utilitarian significance of drinking. Whether or not religious participation deteriorates prior to drinking or after the development of alcoholism among persons of ascetic Protestant background is an interesting problem for future research.

That the drinking experiences of such persons often have characteristics of acute disorientation and stress, analogous to the shock situations in which rat behavior becomes "fixated" or stereotyped, seems probable. In this connection it is pertinent to allude once again to Ullman's (102) findings on the recollections of first drinking among "addictive" and "nonaddictive" drinkers. As indicated previously, significantly more of the addictive drinkers began drinking at a later age, recalled a greater time lapse between first and second drinking experiences, became intoxicated, and recalled drinking in places outside the home in the company of persons other than the family.[17] This suggests social contextual and psychological disso-

[17] Compare, in Chapter 2, reports of the circumstances of first drinking experiences of Jews, which are in most instances point for point opposed to the circumstances recalled by the alcoholics studied by Ullman. The children of alcoholic parents, of course, may early internalize utilitarian drinking attitudes.

ciation of drinking from the centers of moral authority early in the drinking patterns of alcoholics.

In Orthodox Judaism the ideal of sobriety and many of the negative ideas and sentiments associated with drunkenness and the drunkard are not unlike those of the ascetic Protestant sects.[18] This is not surprising in view of the shared Old Testament background of group purposes and moral conceptions and the analogous pressures for discipline which these sects, as well as the Jews, probably experienced in asserting their claims to inner worth and status, i.e., "chosenness." But where ascetic Protestantism has driven alcohol and drinking entirely from the realm of central moral ideas and sentiments and the social contexts in which these are learned and expressed, Orthodox Judaism long ago took the opposite tack. Alcohol and the act of drinking were contextually and symbolically incorporated into the spheres of moral authority, primarily through extensive use in ritual acts of religious communion and secondarily by extension of religious symbolism to other than strictly religious usages. As a consequence the Orthodox Jew cannot, as it were, split the concrete act of drinking from the controlling elements in his conscience. Religious norms, ideas and sentiments about drinking are "stamped in" (integral with a larger network of moral ideas, sentiments and ritual behaviors) in the course of socialization in the family, and take the place of utilitarian attitudes.

That the activation of these norms, ideas and sentiments depends upon integration and participation in the moral community through which they are constantly relearned and expressed is probable; and that this, in turn, depends on the vitality of the larger religious pattern follows necessarily. The possibility of replacement of the traditional cultural orientation toward drinking therefore increases as the Orthodox pattern gives way to social class and other institutional pressures, as Jews relinquish ceremonial and ritual and shift from Orthodox to Conservative, Reform or Secular, and as the social bases of contacts with outsiders are extended. There is no reason, however, to anticipate marked reaction in the direction of alcoholism among non-Orthodox American Jews, such as might be found among Mormon drinkers. This is because most Conservative

[18] See, in Chapter 2, the near identity of Mormon and Orthodox Jewish student attitudes toward drunkenness in others. Much of the militant abstinence propaganda of certain Protestant groups might be viewed as the functional counterpart of the Jewish "Shikker iz a Goy" in sustaining sobriety as an ideal. The difference is, of course, that the abstainers focus their distaste on drinking as well as on drunkenness and the drunkard, while for Jews drinking is traditionally prescribed.

and many Reform and "Secular" Jews have been socialized in the Orthodox drinking tradition. Moreover, even with the decline of Orthodox ceremonial and ritual drinking, Jews are still oriented by their culture toward moderate drinking as family and social customs. Nonetheless, increases in alcoholism are expected, especially where discontinuity with the traditional religious culture is greatest, i.e., among Reform and Secular Jews.

Substantiation of the general ideas suggested here might be attempted in various ways. Case and statistical studies of the religious background and practices of Jewish alcoholics should be revealing. Bales (7), in analyzing a few cases of Jewish alcoholics, detected either non-Orthodox backgrounds or departure from Orthodox traditions: "Although it was not possible to be sure in all cases, in seven out of the eight Jewish cases the patient was not at present living an Orthodox life, or there was definite reason to suppose he had not received any extensive Orthodox training; one of the cases may have been Orthodox, although this is not definitely stated."

No systematic study of case histories of Jewish alcoholics has yet been undertaken but in five reports of Jewish alcoholics which have come to attention there is a suggestion of departure from Orthodox traditions in the socialization experience or early in life.[19] Mention has been made previously (Chapter 3) of Malzberg's (66) statistical evidence of an increase in rates of alcoholic psychoses among Jews in America. It does not seem far-fetched to assume that this increase is related to the decline of religious orthodoxy. That changes are slow, almost infinitesimal, is indicated by the fact that Roberts and Myers (79), in a recent study of patients under psychiatric treatment in New Haven for mental illnesses, found no Jews among 89 patients undergoing treatment for alcoholism even though Jews had the highest rates of treatment for psychoneurotic disorders among the religious groups considered.[20]

[19] Descriptions from R. M. Henderson; personal communication.

[20] J. K. Myers (personal communication) states that in the category "alcohol and drug addiction" (used in Roberts and Myers' report) there were no drug addicts. This category included 89 alcoholics, 61 of whom were Catholics, 28 Protestants. In discussing the extraordinarily high rate of treatment for psychoneurotic disorders among Jews, Roberts and Myers (79) commented: "It is our opinion that the acceptance of psychiatry probably accounts for the inordinately high rate of psychoneurosis among Jews. The explanation for this must be considered in terms of the ethnic structure and the tradition of the Jewish group in addition to its religious organization. Among Jews it is generally accepted that there is no conflict between religious

Another way of determining the possible relationship of alcoholism among Jews to the dissolution of traditional religious patterns is through an examination of premonitory signs of alcoholism among Jewish college students. This method has weaknesses, which will shortly be discussed, but it also has advantages which justify its initial use in preference to case history data on Jewish alcoholics (which may later be used for confirmation). The principal advantages are these: Firstly, the method obviates the selective factors which may apply to the treatment of alcoholism in later life at medical or other centers from which case histories are ordinarily obtained. Secondly, the drinking experience of Jewish students can be directly related to data on religious affiliation and practice which may be unrecorded in alcoholic histories. Thirdly, the data on drinking and religious participation by the students can suggest the proportions of Jews with drinking experiences of a possibly alcoholic nature among different religious categories whose proportions in the larger population from which Jewish alcoholics are drawn are unknown.

A first indication of "problem drinking" and tendencies toward alcoholism can be found in reports of interference with normal social relations and functions, and experiences of formal sanctions, in connection with drinking. To measure these phenomena Straus and Bacon (96) developed a "social complications scale" which they applied to a 10 per cent sample of college students and which has been further applied in the present study to the 606 Jewish student drinkers included in the College Drinking Survey.

"Students were asked whether drinking had ever interfered with their preparation for classes or examinations, caused them to lose close friends or damaged friendships, made them miss appointments or lose a job, resulted in accident, injury or arrest, or brought them before college authorities." From these questions a Guttman type social complications scale of five categories was developed.

---

doctrine and psychoanalytic theory. This is in contrast to a partially supported opposition among Catholics. From the standpoint of community attitude, the Jews exhibit a high level of acceptance of psychoanalytic psychiatry with a minimum of disturbance of their social values. The Jewish attitude is widely divergent from the Irish as is substantiated by our finding that not a single patient of Irish birth was receiving psychotherapy for psychoneurosis. Although this explanation of the rates of psychoneurosis in terms of the acceptance of modern psychiatry appears plausible, we cannot definitely state that the actual occurrence of the illness is not higher among Jews."

Full discussion of this scale is given in Straus and Bacon's (96) report; here it is sufficient to note that:

> "The scalable characteristic (from the above questions) was that of social complications associated with drinking. At the lowest point on the social complications scale (most likely to occur without implying occurrence of other items) were the questions about failure to meet academic or social obligations (drinking had at some time interfered with preparation for classes or examinations or resulted in missing appointments). At the second scale position were the questions on loss of friends or damage to friendships attributed to drinking. Last came the questions about formal punishment or discipline because of drinking (loss of job, arrest, or coming before college authorities)."

As these scale positions are considered from lower to higher the probability of patterned experience of less extreme complications is very great (coefficient of reproducibility is .97). For example, students who have experienced loss of job, arrests (two or more), or have come before college authorities for drinking, have almost certainly had an accident or injury, lost or damaged friendships, and failed to meet academic obligations in association with drinking. In addition, there is generally a high correlation between the social complications scale and such factors as the quantity–frequency of drinking and frequency of intoxication.[21]

The interest here is not primarily in the over-all scaling of social complications in the Jewish as compared to other groups, although this is important, but in variations within the Jewish group along nominal religious lines. All the evidence thus far points to a more effective social regulation of intoxication among religiously participant and Orthodox Jews. The social complications scale, however, mirrors signs of deviation in drinking-related behavior going beyond mere departure from norms of moderate drinking and sobriety (which in itself might damage Jewish friendships). By taking account of failure to meet obligations, accident and injury to the self, and experience of formal societal sanctions, the scale suggests violation of a wider nexus of norms of propriety than is necessarily suggested by intoxication. The question is whether or not this kind of latitude in drinking-related behavior increases among Jewish students as

[21] Straus and Bacon (96). There is a cultural or group relativity to the social complications scale which somewhat limits its usefulness for comparisons. For instance, among Mormon students, who are ideally abstainers, mere drinking may result in immediate loss or damage to friendships quite aside from further complications, while among Jewish students this would not be the case since virtually everyone drinks.

TABLE 48.—*Social Complications of Drinking among Jewish Students, by Nominal Religious Affiliation*

Scale	Orthodox		Conservative		Reform		Secular	
Type	%	*Number*	%	*Number*	%	*Number*	%	*Number*
0*	96	96	93	80	90	60	77	50
1	4	4	4	3	4	3	9	6
2	0	0	2	2	4	3	8	5
3	0	0	1	1	0	0	5	3
4	0	0	0	0	2	1	2	1
Totals	*100*	*100*)	*100*	*86*	*100*	*67*	*101*	*65*

* No Complications. By convention, no response to the relevant questions on social complications is taken as "no positive response," in accord with the procedure used in the College Drinking Survey.

religious participation declines and affiliation shifts from Orthodox to Conservative, to Reform and Secular. The data in Table 48 suggest that this is indeed the case. If this distribution is divided into two categories of "no" and "some" complications, a significant difference is found along religious lines from Orthodox to Secular.[22] That there is a tendency toward convergence with wider societal statistical norms, even in these patterns of individual variation, is indicated by the fact that for male students in general the percentages from lower to higher scale types run as follows: 66, 17, 11, 4, 2.[23]

An analysis was also made of the relations between nominal religious affiliation of Jewish students and certain signs of the supposed "prodromal phase" of alcoholism, again with the expectation of a progressive increase in the incidence of such symptoms among Jewish students who are more and more peripheral to the Orthodox religious tradition. The indices of incipient alcoholism used here are based on Jellinek's (50) systematic effort to delineate sequential phases in the development of alcoholism. Prior to the crucial phase (characterized by loss of control in the drinking situation), Jellinek suggests a prodromal phase in which drinking achieves an importance which it does not have for the average individual. A question on "sneaking drinks" (thought to be indicative of the prodromal phase) was included in Jellinek's original study and of 98 alcoholics replying to that questionnaire only 7 failed to report sneaking drinks. Among the 87 alcoholics who gave further information, 41 per cent reported sneaking drinks prior to loss of control, 36 per cent at its

[22] Chi-square is 18.46, P is less than .001.

[23] This is for a 10 per cent sample. See Straus and Bacon (96), p. 159.

TABLE 49.—*Possible Signs of a Prodromal Phase of Alcoholism among Jewish Students, by Nominal Religious Affiliation*

	Surreptitious Drinking		Anticipatory Drinking		*Number*
	%	*Number*	*%*	*Number*	*Reporting**
Orthodox	1	(1)	4	(4)	(93)
Conservative	4	(3)	7	(5)	(76)
Reform	8	(5)	19	(12)	(63)
Secular	12	(7)	20	(12)	(60)
	Chi-square = 9.05, P = .03		Chi-square = 14.61, P = .002		

* Same for both items.

onset and 23 per cent after its onset. On the basis of Jellinek's concept of a prodromal phase in alcoholism, two questions were included in the College Drinking Survey pertaining to drinking "before a party or social gathering in order to be sure of getting enough" (anticipatory drinking), and "liking to be one or two drinks ahead without others knowing it" (surreptitious drinking). The responses of Jewish students to these questions are shown in Table 49. Increases along religious lines are clearly indicated.

The designers of the College Drinking Survey questionnaire believe there is ambiguity in the question on drinking before a party, and responses to this question are of doubtful value as prognosticators of alcoholism.[24] Casual observation suggests that informal drinking before a large party may be customary in certain college settings; the responses therefore cannot be taken as definite indication that alcoholic beverages have come to "mean more" to a particular individual than to his peers.[25] It is to be noted also that among Jewish students affirmative responses to this question were largely independent of affirmative answers on surreptitious drinking. The question on surreptitious drinking is open to less ambiguity, and since it is known from Jellinek's study to be a very common experience beginning early in the drinking histories of alcoholics, surreptitious drinking is probably a better prognosticator of alcoholism. To predict that about a fifth of Reform or Secular Jewish students (the anticipatory drinkers) might become alcoholics would be wild speculation. That some of the 8 to 12 per cent of Reform and Secular students who are surreptitious drinkers are manifesting signs of serious complications of an alcoholic nature in their drinking

[24] R. Straus, personal communication.

[25] In the case of Jews, however, drinking in this manner "to be sure of getting enough" is certainly suggestive of variation from traditional drinking patterns.

behavior is possible (although a single measure of this kind cannot be taken as a reliable basis for prediction). Actually, the percentages of Reform and Secular students reporting surreptitious drinking correspond closely with the percentages for Irish Catholic and British Protestant students. Among the Irish Catholics 12 per cent report surreptitious drinking, and among British Protestants 9 per cent, while in the sample of all male students 10 per cent reported drinking surreptitiously.[26]

A second behavior trait which Jellinek (50) considers a sign of the prodromal phase in alcoholism is the "blackout," which refers to amnesia, not occasioned by loss of consciousness, for behavior during part of a drinking episode. Of the 98 alcoholics in Jellinek's original study at least 90 had experienced blackouts. Among those who gave further information, 58 per cent reported experiencing blackouts before loss of control, 19 per cent at its onset and 23 per cent later on. Data on blackouts experienced by Jewish students are presented in Table 50. A progressive increase is evident through the nominal religious divisions, Orthodox, Conservative and Reform; and while fewer Secular than Reform students had experienced blackouts, their occurrence was reported more frequently by Secular than by either Orthodox or Conservative students. Especially noteworthy is the fact that not one Orthodox student had experienced a blackout. Actually an occasional experience of a blackout is perhaps not uncommon; 18 per cent of the male student drinkers in the College Drinking Survey had experienced it. It is rather repeated experience of this phenomenon which suggests incipient alcoholism.[27] It is nonetheless interesting to note once again how Reform and Secular students tend to approximate the wider collegiate norm, while Orthodox and Conservative students deviate sharply.

On the supposition that the practice of surreptitious drinking and experience of blackouts together might be a more valid measure of the incipient alcoholism than either factor alone, the responses of the 318 Jewish students who reported on nominal religious affiliation

[26] Irish Catholic and British Protestant refer to the samples specially selected for the present study. On surreptitious drinking among the 10 per cent sample of all male students, see Straus and Bacon (96).

[27] Jellinek (49) notes that the blackout " . . . may occur on rare occasions in an average drinker when he drinks intoxicating amounts in a state of physical or emotional exhaustion. Nonaddictive alcoholics, of course, also may experience 'palimpsests,' but infrequently and only following rather marked intoxication. Thus, the frequency of 'palimpsests' and their occurrence after medium alcohol intake are characteristic of the prospective alcohol addict."

TABLE 50.—*Experience of Blackouts by Jewish Students, by Nominal Religious Affiliation*

	Experienced Blackouts		Number Reporting
	%	*Number*	
Orthodox	0	0	(93)
Conservative	4	3	(75)
Reform	18	11	(62)
Secular	14	8	(59)

were examined in respect to both these traits. Only two of these Jewish students reported both surreptitious drinking and blackouts: one is Reform, the other Secular.

While data on surreptitious drinking and blackouts among Jewish students have certain advantages over alcoholic case histories and statistics in suggesting the relationship of selected sociocultural factors to the incidence of behaviors assumed to be precursors of alcoholism, they suffer from certain deficiencies. Obviously, these measures do not indicate changes in the incidence of alcoholism in fully developed form. Moreover, surreptitious drinking and blackouts are not decisive prognosticators of alcoholism. Jellinek (50) is quite explicit on the limitations of data of this kind:

> "Blackouts and sneaking drinks suggest definitely the existence of a preparatory or prodromal phase of alcoholism which probably has more characteristic and, therefore, more definitely prognostic elements than these two behaviors. Because of the importance of definite prognostic symptoms of alcoholism, this at present poorly defined preparatory phase should be explored . . . However, in order to predict more definitely the development of the basic phase as represented by loss of control, a more detailed knowledge of the preparatory phase is required."

Since Jellinek first derived these symptoms and phases, no one has systematically determined their value in predicting alcoholism by statistical study of their incidence in nonalcoholic and alcoholic populations and by follow-up studies. Nevertheless, many authorities believe that surreptitious drinking and blackouts are good prognosticators of alcoholism, and their high incidence in alcoholic populations is far more than a guess.[28]

[28] For instance, in addition to Jellinek's original and later research, R. M. Henderson (personal communication) has collected data from over 2,000 alcoholics in an effort to verify Jellinek's phase concepts. Henderson considers surreptitious drinking and blackouts as characteristic prealcoholic symptoms. If group differences in rates of alcoholism are assumed to be functions of a differential incidence of "racial" or genetic factors, then differences in prealcoholic symptoms among Jews could mirror increasing intermarriage and mixture with non-Jewish "stock" as

Alcoholism, as noted previously, cannot be equated with frequent intoxication itself—a behavior which may be "normal" in certain groups or common during specific periods in the lives of otherwise moderate drinkers. The characteristic is, rather, the initial loss of control in the drinking situation, perhaps often anticipated by or associated with the traits measured above, and the subsequent generalized inability to regulate drinking so as to avoid conflict with a very wide complex of norms of propriety. Nonetheless, the records of those Jewish students who exhibited the highest frequencies of intoxication (drunk more than 20 times and tight over 50 times) were selected for brief examination of certain other aspects of their drinking behavior and religious characteristics. Of the nine students who met these criteria seven had "passed out" (i.e., lost consciousness) two or more times, four reported blackouts, and three surreptitious drinking. Only three of these nine Jewish students were in the group who reported on nominal religious affiliation, but these three are Secular. Moreover, of these nine most frequently intoxicated Jewish students, five reported no religious participation, three reported participating one to four times a year, while one reported participating once or twice a month.

Granting the normative orientation toward drinking in Orthodox Jewish culture, these findings seem to support the generalizations made by Cheinisse (18) in France half a century ago:

> "Judaism has in general conserved up to the present time this characteristic of collective and social ties which the other churches have lost little by little, and it is precisely this force of cohesion and concentration of the religious community which has kept the great Jewish mass from alcoholism. But wherever the traditional tie is weakened, one immediately sees the alcoholic contagion open a fissure and penetrate this milieu which previously appeared absolutely refractory."

On the other hand, as one of the New Haven Jewish men expressed it:

> "It took a long time . . . for a people to be able to say 'Shikker iz a Goy,' and traditions don't die overnight." [31]

Orthodoxy declines. (This was suggested to the writer by a practicing physician.) However, Jewish students who reported surreptitious drinking also reported both parents as Jewish, except in one case where the father's origin was not determined. Uniform religious affiliation of parents is not a perfect index of "homogeneous racial" background but it suggests that sudden "race" mixture will not account for differences in possible signs of alcoholism among Jews along religious lines. (This, of course, does not rule out the possibility that genetic or constitutional factors may play a conditional role in the etiology of alcoholism among Jews or other groups.)

More generally, the findings of this study indicate that the problems of alcohol which beset American society cannot be understood apart from a consideration of the broader sociocultural matrix in which drinking occurs. Drinking itself is obviously not the exclusive cause of these problems since Orthodox Jews clearly demonstrate that virtually every member of a group can be exposed to drinking alcoholic beverages with negligible departure from a norm of sobriety and without the emergence of drinking pathologies such as alcoholism. Still more important, these findings suggest that the emergence of drinking pathologies where drinking is prevalent cannot be explained by exclusive reference to individual psychology or to a mysterious "craving" for alcohol presumed to be physiologically determined. The possible role of psychophysical processes is not denied but social and cultural phenomena, especially those related to normative or cultural traditions regarding drinking, appear to be essential for the emergence of these pathologies. Where drinking is an integral part of the socialization process, where it is interrelated with the central moral symbolism and is repeatedly practiced in the rites of a group, the phenomenon of alcoholism is conspicuous by its absence. Norms of sobriety can be effectively sustained under these circumstances even though the drinking is extensive. Where institutional conflicts disrupt traditional patterns in which drinking is integrated, where drinking is dissociated from the normal process of socialization, where drinking is relegated to social contexts which are disconnected from or in opposition to the core moral values and where it is used for individual purposes, pathologies such as alcoholism may be expected to increase.

Appendix

Sample Interview

Introductory Note

Special Interviewing Procedures.—In making initial contacts with respondents, it was necessary to give some kind of rationale for the interview. To this end, the following suggestions were usually followed: (*1*) immediate mention that the research was sponsored by Yale University; (*2*) presentation of letters of introduction from the Yale Center of Alcohol Studies, signed by Dr. Selden D. Bacon and Dr. Leon A. Greenberg; (*3*) a statement to the effect that there was little information on drinking practices and attitudes of the American people and that this was one of a series of studies to determine what these practices and attitudes are and what similarities and differences there are among various age, occupational, nationality and religious groups; (*4*) an explanation that the respondents were selected at random from the City Directory and that it was important that everyone cooperate; (*5*) an explanation that anonymity was guaranteed and that information would be used only for scientific research purposes. It was also made clear that the interview would take at least 2 hours and that privacy was desired. In addition, certain topics were systematically avoided. No references were made to "abnormal" drinking; "characteristics" of Jewish culture, e.g., low Jewish rates of drinking pathologies; or local Jewish community organizations. Also, contacts were never made or interview appointments suggested between Friday evening and Saturday evening. In regard to the actual interview situation, standardization and comprehensiveness were emphasized. The order of questions was varied and the phrasing changed when it seemed absolutely necessary; in actual fact, however, this was seldom done.

In addition to these general points, the original schedule contained a number of special reminders to the interviewer which have been omitted from the sample schedule, below, to conserve space and promote readability. These reminders were concerned with definitional conventions and areas in which much detailed information or the respondent's own terms were particularly desired. For example, at one point there was a reminder to the interviewer of the definitions of drunk, tight and high as used in the present research. At another point, where the respondent was asked to describe a person who was drunk, tight or high, there was a reminder to record the replies verbatim.

Format of the Schedule.—The questions which were asked orally by the interviewer are shown in quotation marks; those which the respondent read himself are shown in regular type. The replies are in italics, and in this sample schedule have been somewhat edited for readability and to disguise identity. The schedule included space for impressionistic comments by the interviewer. In the sample reproduced below, these comments happened to be quite extensive and are here omitted.

It will be obvious that only part of the information elicited by the schedules, of which the following is a sample, has been analyzed and used in the present research.

CASE No. 21

"The first thing we need is some general background information. If you will just fill out this sheet to the best of your ability we can go on to other questions."

1. How long have you been living in New Haven? *nearly all my life* years
2. Do you consider New Haven your home? Yes *x* No
3. Date of birth: Day *22* Month *January* Year *1901*
4. Sex: Male *x* Female
5. Height: *5* Feet *8* Inches
6. Weight: *160* Pounds
7. Place of birth:
   If in the U. S. A.: City or Town *Wilford* State *Conn.*
   If not in the U. S. A.: City or Town Country
8. Occupation (be as specific as possible): *lawyer*
9. Are you: Single Married, living with spouse *Yes*
   Widowed Separated Divorced
   Remarried, living with spouse
10. How many rooms do you have in your home? *7*
11. Do you own or rent your home? Own *x* Rent
12. How many people are living in your household (include servants): *5*
13. How many children have you? *2*
    Number of sons *1* Daughters *1*
    Ages of sons *12* Ages of daughters *8*
14. What approximately is your family's income? (Either on a weekly, monthly, or yearly basis): $ a week, month year [not answered]
15. Your formal education. Do not include religious education. Check highest point you reached.
    None Some grammar school Completed grammar school
    Some high school Completed high school
    Some college Completed college *x*
    Graduate, professional or technical school (specify): *law school*
16. To what community associations and organizations do you belong?
    Include any clubs, professional associations, religious organizations, and charities which you support regularly: *Temple Emanuel; Phi Ep.*

"The rest of the questions aren't so automatic. I'll just ask them and you give me the answers to the best of your ability. I'll jot down your answers as we go along."

17. "When and from what country did your family come to the United States?" *My father came to this country from Austria between 1880 and 1900. My mother also came over from Austria about the same time.*

18. "Are you living near any of your relatives now, and about how often do you see them?" *My father and mother lived in New Haven, but they're now deceased. I have some brothers and sisters who are living nearby. I see them about once every other week. We're a close family. It's much the same situation with my wife who comes from Westbury and has relatives in New Haven and Wilford.*

19. "Are there many Jewish people living in your neighborhood?" *Yes, they're mostly Jewish.*

20. "How much religious schooling did you have?" *One to two hours every week during the school year. I was taught Hebrew 'til the age of 13 by a private teacher.*

"How about your wife and children?" *I don't think my wife has had any religious training, but her father's a good Bible student. The children go to Sunday School—I haven't pushed them hard—but there's a tendency among Jewish people to go back to religion.*

"How much ordinary education did your wife have?" *She went to high school and then to a private finishing school.*

21. "Do you belong to any congregation now? What kind? Orthodox? Conservative? Reform?" *Yes, I belong to a Reform congregation.*

22. "Here is a list of various religious practices. Will you please take a look at them, one by one, and check those which you regularly practice today. Next to that, there is a second column. In the second column, please check all those practices which your parents regularly performed when you were a child."

	You Now	Your Parents
1. Wife going to the Mikvah	*No*	*No*
2. Laying Tefillin	*No*	*No*
3. Keeping a Kosher home	*No*	*Yes*
4. Speaking Yiddish at home	*No*	*Yes*
5. Saying Kiddush	*No*	*No*
6. Making Passover Seder	*Yes*	*Yes*
7. Writing on the Sabbath	*Yes*	*Yes*
8. Cooking on the Sabbath	*Yes*	*Yes*
9. Lighting Chanukah Lights	*Yes*	*Yes*
10. Eating only matzos on Passover	*No*	*Yes*
11. Having sons circumcised	*Yes*	*Yes*
12. Buying meat from Kosher butchers	*No*	*Yes*
13. Fasting on Yom Kippur	*No*	*Yes*
14. Bar-Mitzvah for a son	*Yes*	*Yes*
15. Daily attendance at synagogue	*No*	*No*
16. Fairly regular Sabbath attendance	*No*	*No*
17. Going to synagogue only on high holy days	*Yes*	*Yes*
18. Saying Kaddish	*Yes*	*Yes*

Comments:

23. "How much, do you think, is spent for food in your household on a weekly or a monthly basis?" *I would estimate that from $10 to $15 is spent every day in the week, including guests, but not including eating out and money spent on alcohol.*

"How much money do you spend on alcohol per week or month?" *For personal use, it's negligible—one, two or, say, four bottles a year—about $20. That's not including what I give away as presents.*

24. "Before we start these questions about your practices with respect to drinking alcoholic beverages: Do you ever drink any of them?" *Yes.*

"What would you include under the term alcoholic beverages?" *Anything that's intoxicating is an alcohol beverage: if it has any alcoholic content at all.*

25. "About how often do you drink beer?" *I drink a glass once or twice a year.*

"Wine?" *About 15 glasses a year.*

"Hard Liquor?" *About twice a month. It's occasional, nothing steady. I won't drink at all unless there's some company or it is connected with some social event.*

"Did you include drinking wine in ritual or festive situations, such as at Kiddush or at Bar Mitzvahs, in this estimate?" *Yes, I drink ritual wine on Passover and holy days. It goes in cycles—I don't have any at all in my home.*

26. "About how much do you usually drink at a sitting of Beer? Wine? Hard Liquor?" *I occasionally have a glass or two of beer. Of wine, I have a little glass which is no more than a double whisky glass and never more than two of these. When I drink hard liquor, I only have two or three highballs—if I've had two or three highballs I've had plenty.*

27. "Do you like them? Beer? Wine? Hard Liquor?" *Yes, I like hard liquor, wine and beer in that order. In the case of hard liquors, there have been cycles in my preference: at one time I used to like Scotch, then rye—now, I think that Bourbon would taste best to me. Wine is sweet, but like candy or anything else, I wouldn't want too much of it.*

28. "On what occasions and with whom do you usually have each kind of beverage?" *When I'm with friends at home or at their home, or at a restaurant, I might have a highball or a cocktail, to be "big time," you know, but I don't go looking for it. As for beer, if it happens to be a real warm day out—but it's so rare, I'm almost an abstainer. If I happened to be in some seafood place, beer would seem to go better with clams. I take wine when I am at a meeting, or if I didn't happen to ask for anything else—or if it was a cocktail ingredient I made up for company.* [But see question 25, above, on wine.]

29. "What are your reasons for drinking, or not drinking, each kind of beverage?" *It seems to mean good fellowship, and it's tasty, but not tasteful to the extent that you want to make a habit. I won't drink during the day because if I do my head isn't clear. I would only drink during the day if I had company or for business purposes.*

30. (a) "Do you usually have something to eat, right before, during, or right after drinking?" *Yes, there is usually some food available along with it or shortly after.*

(b) "Would you be likely to take a drink if you hadn't eaten anything recently or knew you could not get anything to eat for quite a while?" *Yes, but it depends on how hungry you are. After all, some drinks have food value.*

(c) "Can you remember any specific occasions when you had several drinks without having someting to eat, right before, during, or right afterwards?" *I can't remember, it's been so long.*

(d) "Were you uncomfortable?" *I've felt happy. I've always been conscious; it hasn't affected me to the extent that I didn't know what I was doing. I wasn't wasteful to the extent that I wouldn't eat—I'd eat first.*

31. "Do you go to bars, taverns or night clubs? About how often? With whom do you go?" *I never go to bars, taverns or night clubs now, but I used to go when I was younger.*

32. "How would you describe the person who is a drinker? A non-drinker?" *There are all kinds of drinkers. If a person takes a drink he's o.k., but if he's a nuisance —but you don't even use the term for just the occasional drinker. If he's got to have it, then you'd call him an alcoholic. I'd call an alcoholic a drinker. A non-drinker is abnormal to the other extreme in that he has very strong will power which is abnormal or else he is antisocial or has worked up a resistance to alcohol.*

"Where would you class yourself?" *I'm in between these two types.*

33. "How would you describe a person who is drunk? Tight? High?" *A drunk is a person who speaks incoherently, whose reactions are too slow or too fast—it affects people in different ways—jovial, noisy and so on. A drunk hasn't got his proper equilibrium and hasn't got the proper perception and control of his faculties; his reactions are not as controlled as they are when he is normal—his mental faculties have been affected. A person who is tight is real drunk, even more than being under the influence of alcohol—sloppy, nasty. A high person is jovial—he's had more than he should have had, but this doesn't necessarily mean that he is drunk.*

"Have you ever been drunk? High? Tight? About how often?" *I was drunk just once—when I was going to college, some fellows fooled me, but at the time I knew what I was doing. I've never been tight—I've never drunk enough not to know what I was doing. I was high about once in the last two years, but I can't remember, to tell the truth, since I haven't been out much—on special occasions, I imagine. I've always known that I've had too much, if I'd had too much. Some people can't tell you where they've been, what they've said, et cetera, after drinking.*

34. "For yourself, where would you set the limit of what is the proper amount to drink? Where for others?" *For me—two drinks. When you've had a couple of drinks you've had enough. If you quit with two then you know you're safe—after more than two you're not safe.—For others, it all depends under what circumstances—like driving a car. In that case I think they're taking chances. But I look at it from my own point of view. I don't know how other people feel—I know how I feel.*

35. "How would you describe a problem drinker?" *There are people who drink when problems present themselves and use it as an escape or to bolster up their courage.*

"Do you know any personally?" *Yes, two men.*

"Are these persons Jewish?" *No, one is either a Pole or Lithuanian and the other is an Irish Catholic.*

"Married?" *Yes, both of them are married, but both are separated.*

"Religious?" *The Pole isn't, but I don't know about the Irish fellow.*

"What is their age?" *The Pole is 40 years old and the Irish fellow is 52.*

"Their occupation?" *The Pole is a paint-sprayer for a railroad and the other works for a newspaper.*

36. "When you have a drink, do you expect to experience any sensations other than those of the taste? What are the effects that you do anticipate? How many drinks do you need to achieve these effects? Are they dependent on anything other than the amount you drink?" *In the beginning it's the taste, purely and simply—in company it seems to make them enjoy you a little better and you, yourself, have a better time—it has an exhilarating effect—I think it's mainly the taste.*

37. "Have you ever seen persons who had so much to drink that they lost control in ordinary physical activities and were unable to respond to the reactions of others —overstepping the social expectancies? Of course this doesn't mean the proverbial bum in the street." *In my younger days I had an Irish friend who used to get so bad he'd fall down.—And at a wedding my wife's nephew who was just a little kid had two or three and it put him to sleep.*

"Have you ever been in this condition? About how often? What were the occasions?" *Once, I was driving after I had been drinking, but my conscience bothered me so I drove to a gas station and had somebody else drive the car.—I never lose my head.*

38. "Have you ever had any drinking experiences which were outside the general picture that you have been describing? (I'm thinking of such things as having some drinks before breakfast, or drinking medicinally?)" *I would go out when I was younger to a night club and have six or seven drinks—of course, I'd be eating.*

39. "Have you ever been criticised for your drinking? *Yes.*

"For drinking too much?" *No.*

"For not drinking enough?" *Yes.*

"By whom?" *Some of my non-Jewish friends in my younger days would urge me to drink more by such remarks as "have a little more," and so on.*

40. "Do you ever feel critical toward any of your friends or relatives because of their drinking habits?" *No, not in my family!*

41. "Do you ever worry about your own drinking habits?" *No.*

42. "Do your parents, or would they if they were still living, approve of your present drinking habits, assuming that they knew all about them?" [No answer recorded.]

43. "Do you think, generally speaking, that the Jews of your acquaintance drink more or less than the non-Jews?" *Jews drink less.* "Do you think, as a rule, Jews should drink less than Gentiles?" [No answer.]

44. "Can you recall who gave you your first taste of an alcoholic beverage?" *It was probably my father.*

"What was the occasion?" *Seder.*

"How old were you?" *Perhaps 5 to 7 years old. I had something to drink just on holy days, but it wasn't around the house that I can remember.*

"Have your own children ever gotten any alcoholic beverage to taste? To drink in any quantity?" *They've tasted it.*

45. "Can you remember any other occasions on which you had tastes or drinks of alcoholic beverages before you reached your fourteenth birthday?" *I can't remember—people had to work too hard in those days.*

46. "Were you given any special instructions about drinking alcoholic beverages when you were a child?" *No.*

"Did you get the idea that you shouldn't ever drink any? That drinking too much is bad or unhealthy?" *Anyone could observe drunks, et cetera, you always have ideals—you don't want to be a bum and Jewish parents will let you know.*

47. "As a child, did you have the idea that drunkenness is a non-Jewish characteristic?" *Yes.*

"Were you familiar with stories, songs or poems which suggested that sobriety is a Jewish virtue? Drunkenness a Gentile vice?" *Yes, as an expression.*

48. "Leaving your childhood behind now, let's turn to the time when you were between 14 and about 21. In what ways did your drinking habits change during this period from those you have been describing for your childhood?" *Between 17 and 21 my drinking habits changed when I got into college—the kids drank in the fraternities—but not mine. One of my friends, a non-Jewish Yankee, drank, but my other friends didn't go for drinking. I wouldn't drink much, but I'd carry a flask to be a wise guy.—I'd probably have it to give to the girls as a part of my evil design. You'd think of the girls at the same time.*

49. "Did you receive any advice or instructions regarding drinking alcoholic beverages that were new?" *No.*

50. "Would you say that your habits with regard to drinking alcoholic beverages have changed much since these adolescent days?" *Little. I drink less now. I didn't drink much then, either. I'd have it for the girls to drink—that was my main purpose.*

51. "Speaking of the present now: On occasions when you drink only up to the point you consider proper, how do you know when to stop?" *I know when I can feel it. You feel your stomach a little warm, for one thing.—You feel yourself getting a little tired, a little glib.—You feel the alcohol registering in your system and you get filled up.*

52. "How do your present drinking habits compare with those of your father when he was about your age?" *I wouldn't know. My father didn't drink much; when he got older, he'd take more than he did when he was my age.—An occasional drink, that's all. I think his attitude toward drinking was about the same as mine. He did have a package store and sold liquor for a while.*

"How do your wife's drinking habits compare with your mother's when she was about your wife's present age?" *My mother would never drink. I've never known my mother to be a drinker. My wife? She'll take one drink.*

53. "If, for some reason like prohibition, you were suddenly told to stop drinking alcoholic beverages, what would be your reaction?" *I could stop. It's just voluntary.*

54. "What is your opinion of the man who abstains rigidly as a matter of principle?" *I disapprove of him.—He's nearly as bad as the man that's a drunkard.*

"What is your opinion of the person who tries to make others abstain?" *I dis-*

approve of him, too. He has strong prejudices. He's had bitter experiences or seen bitter things and has become bitter himself.

55. "Do you think that the man who occasionally gets drunk is to be considered otherwise responsible?" *I don't think a man's an outcast just because he occasionally gets drunk.*

56. "How many drinks do you need to have to get drunk? Beer.—Wine.—Hard liquor?" *It's difficult for me to tell. It might take six or eight drinks to make me unsteady. I don't know, because I think that I've never been drunk—I've always possessed my faculties.*

"What are the reasons why you never got drunk?" *What's the use in making a fool of yourself?—Drunks don't know what they're doing.*

"Have you ever wanted to get drunk?" *No.*

57. "About how often, all told, have you been high? Tight? Drunk? *I have never been drunk or tight in my life, except once in college. I have been high once in the last 2 years, but several times in my younger days.—But it's rare—it's hard to remember.*

58. (a) "Have you ever pulled a blank? For example, wakened in the morning after a party with no idea where you had been or what you had done after a certain point?" *No.*

(b) "Have you found in the course of your drinking experiences that you may have sometimes started drinking with no intention of getting drunk, only to wind up cockeyed?" *No.*

(c) "Have you ever gone on benders? For example, stayed drunk for at least 2 days but not counting Saturday and Sunday, without regard for your work or your family or anything else?" *No.*

(d) "Have you ever attempted to control your drinking by drinking in a different way than usual, that is, making up certain rules of drinking for yourself? For example, deciding not to drink before a certain hour, or to drink only at home, or to drink only in the presence of friends, or only with meals, or to drink only beer, wine, and so on?" *No.*

(e) "Have you ever felt the need to protect your supply of liquor, that is, making sure that you would have liquor always handy, making sure that family or friends wouldn't find it and take it from you?" *No.*

(f) "Have you ever had feelings of fear without knowing what you were fearing, or fearing that there might be retribution because of your excessive drinking?" *No.*

59. [This question presented a set of diagrams and required the respondent to attempt to identify himself, his parents and his children within the Jewish group. It is omitted here because the response is not sufficiently relevant to warrant reproduction of the diagrams.]

60. "As a child and in your youth, did you spend most of your time living in Jewish neighborhoods?" *Mixed.*

"Were most of your friends Jewish or non-Jewish? *Non-Jewish.*

"Would you say that your closest associations with persons your own age were with friends who were in no way related to you or with your own relatives: Brothers, sisters, cousins, et cetera?" *My closest associations were mostly with friends, but childhood friends don't mean much.*

61. "When you were about 10 to 15 years old, what were the things that occupied most of your time when you weren't actually in school?" *When I wasn't in school, I played baseball, football and, in addition, I had a newspaper route and helped my father in the store occasionally.*

62. "When you were a child and a young boy, did you get into fist fights with other boys? Was this often? Do you remember trying to avoid such fights? Do you remember what your parents' reaction was to your getting into fights?" *Yes. I thought I was pretty good. I didn't run away, but I didn't seek them* [fights] *out. My*

parents discouraged these fights, but they were too busy trying to make a living—people then didn't pay attention to kids as they do today.

63. "Do you remember what kind of a person your parents and relatives wanted you to grow up to be? Did they try to impress upon you what things were most important and how you could go about achieving them? Do you feel that you were supposed to preserve a tradition by your behavior?" *They'd tell you that they'd want you to go to college and be a doctor or lawyer, but they didn't have the time to spend with you.*

64. Whether you have a son of marriageable age or not, imagine that you have one. Suppose that he finds a congenial girl having a common interest with him, whom he wishes to marry. How important is it to you that she be of Jewish origin (though not necessarily religiously observant)? Please express your own preferences, whether you would try to influence your son's choice or not. In each of the following hypothetical instances we ask you to indicate a preference: Would you rather that the girl he is interested in be of Protestant origin (though not necessarily religiously observant), or would you rather she be Jewish even if she has some background or personal characteristic which you might consider a drawback?

(a) Now, suppose either she is Jewish and 3 years older than your son; or she is Protestant and a year younger than your son. If it were up to you, which would you prefer her to be? (Check one.)

☐ I would much prefer her to be Jewish even if she is 3 years older than he.
☐ I probably would rather she be Jewish even if she is 3 years older than he.
☐ I probably would rather she be about his age than that she be Jewish.
☒ I would much prefer her to be about his age even if she is not Jewish.

(b) Now, suppose either she is Jewish and her father was in prison for embezzlement; or she is Protestant and there is no criminal record in her family. If it were up to you, which would you prefer her to be? (Check one.)

☐ I would much prefer her to be Jewish even if her father has a criminal record.
☐ I probably would rather she be Jewish even if her father has a criminal record.
☒ I probably would rather there be no record of criminality in her family even if she is not Jewish.
☐ I would much prefer there to be no criminal record in her family even if she is not Jewish.

(c) Now, suppose either she is Jewish and is three inches taller than your son; or she is Protestant and a few inches shorter than your son. If it were up to you, which would you prefer her to be? (Check one.)

☐ I would much prefer her to be Jewish even if she is taller than he.
☒ I would probably rather she be Jewish even if she is taller than he.
☐ I would probably rather she be shorter than he than that she be Jewish.
☐ I would much prefer her to be shorter than he than that she be Jewish.

(d) Now, suppose either she is Jewish and works as a waitress; or she is Protestant and works as a social worker. If it were up to you, which would you prefer her to be? (Check one.)

☐ I would much prefer that she be Jewish than that she have a profession.
☒ I probably would rather she be Jewish than that she have a profession.
☐ I probably would rather she have a profession than that she be Jewish.
☐ I would much prefer that she have a profession than that she be Jewish.

(e) Now, suppose either she is Jewish and her father is a plumber; or she is Protestant and her father is a prominent heart specialist. If it were up to you, which would you prefer her to be? (Check one.)

☒ I would much prefer her to be Jewish than that she have a prominent father.
☐ I probably would rather she have a distinguished family background than that she be Jewish.

65. "Would you comment on your general attitude toward intermarriage between Jews and non-Jews?" *When people are of the same faith, they have the same habits.*

66. "Suppose one of your children decided to join a Christian church, how would you react? Would you try to prevent this? Would you threaten punishment for it? Would you consider the child dead?" *I would disapprove. You should be what you're born to be.*

67. "Suppose one of your children openly rejected all religion. How would you react? Would you consider the child dead?" *I would disapprove. However, I've seen some decent people who belong to ethical culture societies.*

68. "Can you remember what happened to you as a child when you didn't feel like eating or didn't want to eat very much at a meal?" *My mother would coax me to eat, telling me the benefits of eating and getting strong.*

"Do you recall ever being told that you were eating too much by your mother?" *No.*

"Do you ever recall being punished by your mother for eating too much?" *No.*

69. "When guests come to visit at your house during the day or in the evening do you usually serve them something to eat?" *Yes, I always serve food.*

70. (a) "Do your family or friends ever comment or make a fuss about how you eat—either that you eat too much or too little?" *No.*

(b) "How do you feel about the eating habits of the members of your household?" *They eat well, but they don't overeat. My daughter likes sweets; she doesn't overeat—she is naturally healthy.*

(c) "Have you ever worried about your own eating habits or had problems with your weight?" *I eat what I want to and never worry about my weight. If there's candy around, I'll eat it, but I don't go looking for it. I have never been overweight or underweight.*

(d) "Do you ever feel a strong compulsion to eat beyond the usual mealtime schedules?" *No.*

(e) "Do you ever go on eating sprees?" *No.*

71. "Many people have various habits like smoking, chewing gum, nail biting, and so forth. Do you have any habits of this kind?" *Only excessive smoking.*

"Do you like to play cards? Gamble? Bet on the horses? Play the numbers? Anything like that?" *No.*

72. (a) Your wife has a very bad cold and ought to stay in bed. You have an appointment with a manufacturer of scarce materials who's willing to let you have them if you can get the contract signed that day. You've tried to reach a baby sitter to help your wife with the children but you've been unable to get anyone. Check which of the following you would do:

☐ Definitely stay home to take care of the children.
☐ Probably stay home to take care of the children.
☐ Probably not stay home to take care of the children.
☐ Definitely not stay home to take care of the children.

[No answer.]

(b) Your sister's husband has died suddenly and left no money to support her and her children. You are not wealthy yourself, but could help to support her with some sacrifice of your comforts. What right has she to expect help from you rather than turn to public charity?

☒ She has a definite right, as a sister, to expect your help.
☐ She has some right, as a sister, to expect your help.
☐ She has no right, as a sister, to expect your help.

Would you help her, in view of her need and your own financial obligations? Check one: Yes *x* No

(c) You are at the office where you have just found out that you can, by flying to Cincinnati that very day, close a deal which guarantees you a substantial raise in income. Your wife calls up to tell you that your cousin has just had a coronary thrombosis, and has been rushed to the hospital. There appears to be no hope for a recovery but he wants to see you before he passes away. To do so would mean foregoing your trip to Cincinnati. Check which you would do:

☒ Definitely go to see your cousin.
☐ Probably go to see your cousin.
☐ Probably not go to see your cousin.
☐ Definitely not go to see your cousin.

(d) Mr. MacMillan, your business partner and friend of long standing, has gotten himself into trouble betting on the fights. He is liable to get involved in a law suit in which the name of your firm may become involved. He offers you an opportunity to dissolve the partnership and thus dissociate yourself from his illegal activities. Check which you would do:

☒ Definitely dissociate yourself.
☐ Probably dissociate yourself.
☐ Probably not dissociate yourself.
☐ Definitely not dissociate yourself.

(e) You have a very good friend who needs a loan to start a new business venture. He has not been very successful in his ventures in the past, and the bank is unwilling to make the loan. What right has your friend to expect you to give him a loan?

☐ Definite right. ☐ Some right. ☐ No right. [No answer.]

Would you give your friend the loan under these conditions? Yes No [No answer.]

Are you likely to have someone as a good friend who would be in such a predicament? Yes *x* No

(f) You are a doctor for an insurance company. You examine a close friend who needs more insurance. You find that he is in pretty good shape, but you are doubtful on one or two minor points which are difficult to diagnose. What right does your friend have to expect you to shade the doubts in his favor? (Check one.)

☐ My friend would have a definite right as a friend to expect me to shade the doubts in his favor.
☐ He would have some right as a friend to expect me to shade the doubts in his favor.
☐ He would have no right as a friend to expect me to shade the doubts in his favor.

[No answer.]

Would you shade the doubts in his favor in view of your obligations to the insurance company and your obligations to your friend?

Yes No *x*

(g) You are a New York drama critic. A close friend of yours has sunk all his savings in a new Broadway play. You really think the play is no good. What right does your friend have to expect you to go easy on his play in your review?

☐ He has a definite right as a friend to expect me to go easy on his play in my review.
☒ He has some right as a friend to expect me to do this for him.
☐ He has no right as a friend to expect me to do this for him.

Would you go easy on his play in your review in view of your obligations to your readers and your obligations to your friend?

Yes No [No answer.]

(h) You have just come from a secret meeting of the board of directors of a company. You have a close friend who will be ruined unless he can get out of the market before the board's decision becomes known. You happen to be having dinner at that friend's home this same evening. What right does your friend have to expect you to tip him off?

☐ He has a definite right as a friend to expect me to tip him off.
☒ He has some right as a friend to expect me to tip him off.
☐ He has no right as a friend to expect me to tip him off.

Would you tip him off in view of your obligations to the company and your obligations to your friend?

Yes No [No answer.]

(i) Rabbi X one night, while very tight after a wedding party at which you were present, got into an argument with a traffic cop over whether or not he had violated a red light. You were along in the car and know that the cop was right in his claim. The rabbi was called into court for defying an officer of the law. He asks you to be his witness. Which would you do?

☐ Definitely give evidence on his behalf.
☐ Probably give evidence on his behalf.
☐ Probably not give evidence on his behalf.
☒ Definitely not give evidence on his behalf.

Would you think the rabbi ought to be dismissed?

Yes *x* No

(j) Mr. Van der Weyden, an old friend of yours from your bachelor days, has come into town for the first time in 15 years. He had gone to Europe and never got back here before the war. He asks you to come and spend the afternoon with him at a restaurant with some other buddies because he must go on to San Francisco at 6 o'clock. Your boss has asked you to give him a sales report for the year that afternoon. He is irascible and you are wary of calling that off. Which would you do?

☐ Definitely go to see your friend.
☐ Probably go to see your friend.
☒ Probably not go to see your friend.
☐ Definitely not go to see your friend.

Bibliography

1. BACON, S. D. Alcoholism: nature of the problem. Fed. Probation **11:** 3–7, 1947.
2. BACON, S. D. Inebriety, Social Integration and Marriage. (Memoirs of the Section on Alcohol Studies, Yale University, No. 2.) New Haven; Hillhouse Press; 1945. Also in: Quart. J. Stud. Alc. **5:** 86–125, 1944.
3. BACON, S. D. Sociology and the Problems of Alcohol: Foundations for a Sociological Study of Drinking Behavior. (Memoirs of the Section of Studies on Alcohol, Yale University, No. 1.) New Haven; Hillhouse Press; 1944. Also in: Quart. J. Stud. Alc. **4:** 399–445, 1943.
4. BACON, S. D. Studies of Drinking in Jewish Culture: *I*. General Introduction. Quart. J. Stud. Alc. **12:** 444–450, 1951.
5. BAINTON, R. H. The churches and alcohol. Quart. J. Stud. Alc. **6:** 45–58, 1945.
6. BALES, R. F. Cultural differences in rates of alcoholism. Quart. J. Stud. Alc. **6:** 480–499, 1946.
7. BALES, R. F. The "Fixation Factor" in Alcohol Addiction: An Hypothesis Derived from a Comparative study of Irish and Jewish Social Norms. Doctoral dissertation; Harvard University; 1944.
8. BARRON, M. L. The incidence of Jewish intermarriage in Europe and America. Amer. sociol. Rev. **11:** 6–13, 1946.
9. BECKER, R. Die Geisteserkrankungen bei den Juden in Polen. Allg. Z. Psychiat. **96:** 47–66, 1932.
10. BEREZIN, F. C. (Letters from Readers.) Commentary **13:** 293, 1952.
11. BERNHEIMER, C. S., ed. The Russian Jew in the United States: Studies of Social Conditions in New York, Philadelphia, and Chicago, with a Description of Rural Settlements. Philadelphia; Winston; 1905.
12. BIENENSTOCK, T. Social life and authority in the East European Jewish Community. Sthwest. J. Anthrop. **19:** 238–254, 1950.
13. BOSSARD, J. E. S. and BOLL, E. S. Ritual in Family Living: A Contemporary Study. Philadelphia; University of Pennsylvania Press; 1950.
14. BRAV, S. R. Jewish Family Solidarity: Myth or Fact? Vicksburg; Nogales Press; 1940.
15. BRUCH, H. and TOURAINE, G. Obesity in childhood. *V*. The family frame of obese children. Psychosom. Med. **2:** 141–206, 1940.
16. BUNZEL, R. The role of alcoholism in two Central American cultures. Psychiatry **3:** 361–387, 1940.
17. CHASSEL, J. Family constellation in the etiology of essential alcoholism. Psychiatry **1:** 473–503, 1938.
18. CHEINISSE, L. La race juive, jouit-elle d'une immunité à l'égard de l'alcoolisme? Sem. méd. **28:** 613–615, 1908.
19. CLARK, W. Portrait of the mythical gentile: One stereotype breeds another. Commentary **7:** 546–549, 1949.
20. DEMBITZ, L. N. Jewish Services in Synagogue and Home. Philadelphia; Jewish Publication Society of America; 1898.
21. DOLLARD, J. Caste and Class in a Southern Town. New Haven; Yale University Press; 1937.
22. DUBNOW, S. M. History of the Jews in Russia and Poland from the Earliest Times to the Present Day. Transl. by I. FRIEDLÄNDER. Philadelphia; Jewish Publication Society of America; 1916–20.
23. DURKHEIM, E. The Elementary Forms of the Religious Life: A Study in

Religious Sociology. Transl. by J. W. Swain. London; Allen & Unwin; 1915.
24. Durkheim, E. Le Suicide. Paris; Alcan; 1897.
25. Feldman, W. M. Racial aspects of alcoholism. Brit. J. Inebriety **21:** 1–15, 1923.
26. Finkelstein, L., ed. The Jews: Their History, Culture and Religion. 2 Vol. New York; Harpers; 1949.
27. Fishberg, M. The Jews: A Study of Race and Environment. New York; Scott Publishing Co.; 1911.
28. Gans, H. T. Park Forest: Birth of a Jewish Community. Commentary **11:** 330–339, 1951.
29. Ganzfried, S. Code of Jewish Law (Kitzur Schulchan Aruch): A Compilation of Jewish Laws and Customs. Transl. by H. E. Goldin. New York; Hebrew Publishing Co.; 1927.
30. Gerth, H. H. and Mills, C. W. From Max Weber: Essays in Sociology. New York; Oxford University Press; 1946.
31. Glad, D. D. Attitudes and experiences of American-Jewish and American-Irish male youth as related to differences in adult rates of inebriety. Quart. J. Stud. Alc. **8:** 406–472, 1947.
32. Glazer, N. Why Jews stay sober: Social scientists examine Jewish abstemiousness. Commentary **13:** 181–186, 1952.
33. Glover, A. K. Jewish Law and Customs. Wells, Minn.; Hammond; 1900.
34. Goldschmidt, W. Social class in America: A critical review. Amer. Anthrop. **52:** 483–497, 1950.
35. Gordon, A. I. Jews in Transition. Minneapolis; University of Minnesota Press; 1949.
36. Graeber, I. and Britt, S., eds. Jews in a Gentile World: The Problem of Anti-Semitism. New York; Macmillan; 1942.
37. Guttman, E. Beitrag zur Rassenpsychiatrie. Doctoral dissertation; Freiburg University; 1909.
38. Haggard, H. W. and Jellinek, E. M. Alcohol Explored. New York; Doubleday; 1942.
39. Hall, D. Section meeting on culture and personality (1938). Amer. J. Orthopsychiat. **8:** 619–622, 1938.
40. Herskovits, M. When is a Jew a Jew? Mod. Quart. **4:** 114–121, 1927.
41. Hollingshead, A. B. Elmtown's Youth: The Impact of Social Classes on Adolescents. New York; Wiley; 1949.
42. Hollingshead, A. B. Trends in Social Stratification: A Case Study. Amer. sociol. Rev. **17:** 679–686, 1952.
43. Horton, D. The functions of alcohol in primitive societies: a cross-cultural study. Quart. J. Stud. Alc. **4:** 199–320, 1943.
44. Hughes, E. C. Social change and status protest. An essay on the marginal man. Phylon **10:** 58–65, 1949.
45. Infield, H. G. The concept of Jewish culture and the State of Israel. Amer. sociol. Rev. **16:** 506–513, 1951.
46. Jellinek, E. M., ed. Alcohol Addiction and Chronic Alcoholism. (Effects of Alcohol on the Individual: A Critical Exposition of Present Knowledge. Vol. I.) New Haven; Yale University Press; 1942.
47. Jellinek, E. M. A document of the Reformation period on inebriety: Sebastian Franck's "On the Horrible Vice of Drunkenness," etc. (Classics of the Alcohol Literature.) Quart. J. Stud. Alc. **2:** 391–395, 1941.
48. Jellinek, E. M. Immanuel Kant on Drinking. Quart. J. Stud. Alc. **1:** 777–778, 1941.

49. JELLINEK, E. M. Phases of alcohol addiction. Quart. J. Stud. Alc. **13:** 673–687, 1952.
50. JELLINEK, E. M. Phases in the Drinking History of Alcoholics. Analysis of a Survey Conducted by the *Grapevine*, Official Organ of Alcoholics Anonymous. (Memoirs of the Section of Studies on Alcohol, Yale University, No. 5.) New Haven; Hillhouse Press; 1946. Also in: Quart. J. Stud. Alc. **7:** 1–88, 1946.
51. JELLINEK, E. M. Recent Trends in Alcoholism and in Alcohol Consumption. New Haven; Hillhouse Press; 1947. Also in: Quart. J. Stud. Alc. **8:** 1–42, 1947.
52. JELLINEK, E. M. and KELLER, M. Rates of alcoholism in the United States of America, 1940–1948. Quart. J. Stud. Alc. **13:** 49–59, 1952.
53. JOHNSON, C. S. Shadow of the Plantation. Chicago; University of Chicago Press; 1934.
54. KENNEDY, R. J. R. Single or triple melting pot? Intermarriage trends in New Haven, 1870–1940. Amer. J. Sociol. **49:** 331–339, 1944.
55. KLUCKHOHN, F. Dominant and substitute profiles of cultural orientations: their significance for the analysis of social stratification. Social Forces **28:** 376–393, 1950.
56. KOENIG, S. Ethnic factors in the economic life of urban Connecticut. Amer. sociol. Rev. **8:** 193–197, 1943.
57. LA BARRE, W. The Aymara of the Lake Titicaca Plateau, Bolivia. (Memoirs of the American Anthropological Association, No. 68.) Amer. Anthrop. **5** (No. 1, pt. 2): 1–250, 1948.
58. LANDMAN, R. H. Studies of drinking in Jewish culture. *III*. Drinking patterns of children and adolescents attending religious schools. Quart. J. Stud. Alc. **13:** 87–94, 1952.
59. LESLAU, W. Falasha Anthology. New Haven; Yale University Press; 1951.
60. LOLLI, G., SERIANNI, E., BANISSONI, F., GOLDER, G., MARIANI, A., McCARTHY, R. G. and TONER, M. The use of wine and other alcoholic beverages by a group of Italians and Americans of Italian extraction. Quart. J. Stud. Alc. **13:** 27–48, 1952.
61. McCARTHY, R. G. and DOUGLASS, E. M. Alcohol and Social Responsibility—A New Educational Approach. New York; Crowell; 1949.
62. McKINLAY, A. P. Ancient experience with intoxicating drinks: Non-classical peoples. Quart. J. Stud. Alc. **9:** 388–414, 1948.
63. McKINLAY, A. P. Ancient experience with intoxicating drinks: non-Attic Greek states. Quart. J. Stud. Alc. **10:** 289–315, 1949.
64. McKINLAY, A. P. Attic temperance. Quart. J. Stud. Alc. **12:** 61–102, 1951.
65. MACRORY, B. E. The tavern and the community. Quart. J. Stud. Alc. **13:** 609–637, 1952.
66. MALZBERG, B. Social and Biological Aspects of Mental Disease. Utica; State Hospitals Press; 1940.
67. MANGIN, W. P. The Cultural Significance of the Fiesta Complex in an Indian Hacienda in Peru. Doctoral dissertation; Yale University; 1954.
68. MOORE, G. F. Judaism in the First Three Centuries of the Christian Era: The Age of the Tannaim. 3 Vols. Cambridge, Mass.; Harvard University Press; 1927–30.
69. MYERS, J. K. The Differential Time Factor in Assimilation: A Study of Aspects and Processes of Assimilation among the Italians of New Haven. Doctoral dissertation; Yale University; 1949.
70. MYERSON, A. Alcohol: a study of social ambivalence. Quart. J. Stud. Alc. **1:** 13–20, 1940.

71. MYERSON, A. The social psychology of alcoholism. Dis. nerv. System **1:** 1–14, 1940.
72. PARSONS, T. The Social System. Glencoe; Free Press; 1951.
73. PARSONS, T. Essays on Sociological Theory, Pure and Applied. Glencoe; Free Press; 1949.
74. PFAUTZ, H. F. The current literature on social stratification: critique and bibliography. Amer. J. Sociol. **58:** 391–418, 1953.
75. PHILIPS, A. TH., transl. Daily Prayers. New York; Hebrew Publishing Co.; n.d.
76. POHLISCH. La prophylaxie de l'abus des stupéfiants. Ann. Méd.-psychol. **96**[2]**:** 633–638, 1938.
77. REISMAN, D. A philosophy for 'minority' living. Commentary **6:** 413–422, 1948.
78. RILEY, J. W., JR. and MARDEN, C. F. The social pattern of alcoholic drinking. Quart. J. Stud. Alc. **8:** 265–273, 1947.
79. ROBERTS, B. H. and MYERS, J. K. Religion, national origin, immigration and mental illness. Amer. J. Psychiat. **110:** 759–764, 1954.
80. ROSENAU, W. Jewish Ceremonial Institutions and Customs. Baltimore; Fredenwald Company; 1903.
81. RÜDEN, E. Der Alkohol in Lebensprozess der Rasse. Int. Mschr. Erforsch. Alkoh. **13:** 374–379, 1903.
82. SAMUEL, M. The World of Sholom Aleichem. New York; Knopf; 1947.
83. SARTRE, J.-P. Portrait of the inauthentic Jew. Commentary **5:** 389–397, 1948.
84. SCHOTTKY, J., ed. Rasse und Krankheit. München; Lehmann; 1937.
85. SCHWEISHEIMER, W. Maimonides' medical opinions in the light of modern medicine. Med. Leaves **5:** 75–81, 1943.
86. SHILS, E. A. The study of the primary group. In: LERNER, D., and LASSWELL, H. D., eds. The Policy Sciences: Recent Developments in Scope and Method. Stanford; Stanford University Press; 1951.
87. SHOLOM ALEICHEM. Inside Kasrilevke. Transl. by I. GOLDSTICK. New York; Schocken; 1948.
88. SICHEL, M. Die Geistesstörungen bei den Juden. Neurol. Zbl. **27:** 351–367, 1908.
89. SKOLNICK, J. H. A study of the relation of ethnic background to arrests for inebriety. Quart. J. Stud. Alc. **15:** 622–630, 1954.
90. SNYDER, C. R. Culture and Sobriety. A Study of Drinking Patterns and Sociocultural Factors Related to Sobriety among Jews. Doctoral dissertation; Yale University; 1954.
91. SNYDER, C. R. and LANDMAN, R. H. Studies of drinking in Jewish culture. *II.* Prospectus for sociological research on Jewish drinking patterns. Quart. J. Stud. Alc. **12:** 451–474, 1951.
92. STEINBERG, M. A Partisan Guide to the Jewish Problem. Indianapolis; Bobbs-Merrill; 1945.
93. STONE, G. P. and FORM, W. H. Instabilities in status. The problem of hierarchy in the community study of status arrangements. Amer. sociol. Rev. **18:** 151–163, 1953.
94. STRAUS, R. A note on the religion of male alcoholism clinic patients. Quart. J. Stud. Alc. **12:** 560–561, 1951.
95. STRAUS, R. and BACON, S. D. Alcoholism and Social Stability. A Study of Occupational Integration in 2,023 Male Clinic Patients. New Haven; Hillhouse Press; 1951. Also in: Quart. J. Stud. Alc. **12:** 231–260, 1951.

96. Straus, R. and Bacon, S. D. Drinking in College. New Haven; Yale University Press; 1953.
97. Straus, R. and McCarthy, R. G. Nonaddictive pathological drinking patterns of homeless men. Quart. J. Stud. Alc. **12:** 601–611, 1951.
98. Sumner, W. G. Folkways: A Study of the Sociological Importance of Usages, Manners, Customs, Mores and Morals. 2d Ed. Boston; Ginn; 1940.
99. Sutherland, E. H., Schroeder, H. G. and Tordella, C. L. Personality traits and the alcoholic. A critique of existing studies. Quart. J. Stud. Alc. **11:** 547–561, 1950.
100. Thomas, W. I. and Thomas, D. S. The Child in America: Behavior Problems and Programs. New York; Knopf; 1928.
101. Thorner, I. Ascetic Protestantism and alcoholism. Psychiatry **16:** 167–176, 1953.
102. Ullman, A. D. The first drinking experience of addictive and of "normal" drinkers. Quart. J. Stud. Alc. **14:** 181–191, 1953.
103. Ullman, A. D. The psychological mechanism of alcohol addiction. Quart. J. Stud. Alc. **13:** 602–608, 1952.
104. Warner, W. L. and Lunt, P. S. The Social Life of a Modern Community. (Yankee City Series, Vol. I.) New Haven; Yale University Press; 1941.
105. Warner, W. L. and Srole, L. The Social Systems of American Ethnic Groups. (Yankee City Series, Vol. III.) New Haven; Yale University Press; 1945.
106. Wexberg, L. E. Alcoholism as a sickness. Quart. J. Stud. Alc. **12:** 217–230, 1951.
107. Wikler, A. A psychodynamic study of a patient during experimental self-regulated re-addiction to morphine. Psychiat. Quart. **26:** 270–293, 1952.
108. Wirth, L. The Ghetto. Chicago; University of Chicago Press; 1928.
109. Zborowski, M. The place of book learning in traditional Jewish culture. Harv. educ. Rev. **19:** 87–109, 1949.
110. Zborowski, M. and Herzog, E. Life Is With People: The Jewish Little-Town of Eastern Europe. New York; International Universities Press; 1952.
111. The Jewish Encyclopaedia. New York; Funk & Wagnalls; 1905.
112. The Greater New Haven Directory. New Haven; Price & Lee; 1951.
113. Alcohol, Science and Society. Twenty-nine Lectures with Discussions as Given at the Yale Summer School of Alcohol Studies. New Haven; Quarterly Journal of Studies on Alcohol; 1945.

Index